the smallest giant

the smallest giant

AN ACTOR'S LIFE

MICHAEL CRAIG

ALLEN&UNWIN

First published in 2005

Allen & Unwin
83 Alexander Street
Crows Nest NSW 2065
Australia
Phone: (61 2) 8425 0100
Fax: (61 2) 9906 2218
Email: info@allenandunwin.com
Web: www.allenandunwin.com

National Library of Australia
Cataloguing-in-Publication entry:

Craig, Michael 1929- .
    The smallest giant : an actor's life.

    Includes index.
    ISBN 1 74114 565 1.

    1. Craig, Michael, 1929– . 2. Circus performers -
    Biography. 3. Motion picture actors and actresses -
    Biography. 4. Television actors and actresses - Australia -
    Biography. 5. Actors - Great Britain - Biography. 6.
    Actors - Australia - Biography. I. Title.

Set in 11/14.7 pt Sabon by Bookhouse, Sydney
Printed by Griffin Press, South Australia

10 9 8 7 6 5 4 3 2 1

Preface

I was happy enough in the circus, appearing as the tallest midget in captivity, but when my employer decided that I should also appear as the smallest giant in captivity, I decided it was time to move on and seek my fortune in a different sphere.

•

I dreamed that sentence some years ago and woke up laughing; and, although it may not be the equal of Coleridge's 'In Xanadu did Kubla Khan a stately pleasure dome decree', it has a certain resonance. It seemed to me to be up there with, 'It was the best of times, it was the worst of times', or even 'Call me Ishmael'. Unfortunately, unlike Coleridge, Dickens or Melville, I didn't, or couldn't, continue. My great opening line for a great prize-winning novel remained just that—a great opening line, but no novel. Then it occurred to me that, as a jobbing actor who has spent more than fifty years in the hurly-burly of all forms of show business, I had in fact been the tallest midget and the smallest giant in captivity, and various other sideshow freaks as well. My life was my novel.

I had no compelling urge to write my autobiography—it seemed to me that there were more than enough actor's autobiographies already—until one cold grey January day in 1999 when I was persuaded to think again.

•

I was standing in a street in Berwick Market in London, outside my nephew's restaurant, having a smoke. It was my seventieth birthday and inside the restaurant my wife, and my brother and his wife and children, and my children and one grandchild, and a lot of friends were eating and drinking and doing their best to celebrate the event. Actually it was a very jolly occasion. It was only when I stood by myself in the chilly twilight, lighting my pipe and watching the punters nervously or boldly going into the knocking shop next door, that I realised I wasn't having as good a time as I should have been having.

My daughter Jess, who had to catch a train back to Cambridge, came outside to tell me to come in as it was time to cut the cake. I must have looked less than enthusiastic because she told me to 'get a grip' in that bossy maternal way that daughters of twenty have with their fathers, and then asked what was bugging me.

'I'm old, Jesso,' I said. 'I'm three-score fucking years and ten. I'm bloody seventy.' She looked at me with barely disguised scorn.

'That's just a number Dad, no big deal. Yesterday you were sixty-nine; today you're seventy. So what?' I tried to explain.

'When you hear of some bloke snuffing it at sixty-nine, you think, "Poor bugger was only in his sixties". But if he was seventy, you think, "Ah well, he *was* in his seventies". And that's the difference.'

'Well,' she said, 'in that case you'd better get on with it, hadn't you.'

'Get on with what?' I asked.

'You know . . .' she said. '*Lies My Father Told Me* or *Where Did It All Go Right?* or whatever you decide to call it . . . *your* story, Dad. At least it should give me and Stephen and MJ [my sons by my first marriage] a bit of a laugh.'

•

Well that was nearly four years ago and, since nothing else much is occupying my time and I don't want another bollocking from Jess, I thought I'd give it a go.

ONE

Small time

I never meant to become an actor, and there has been more than one smart-arse critic who has written that I never did become one. Still, if you believe critics, you'll believe anything.

One New York critic, writing about Harold Pinter's *The Homecoming*, in which I was appearing for the Royal Shakespeare Company at the Music Box Theatre in New York in 1967, wrote that one of the high points of the production had been the brilliant sound effect in one of the pauses in Act 2. Being a Pinter play, there had been a lot of pauses, but the critic went on to identify the particular effect more exactly: 'A deep, almost subsonic rumbling note which so exactly matched the underlying tensions of the play.' Or words to that effect. What he had actually heard was the *Queen Elizabeth II* blowing her hooter to signify her imminent departure from the Cunard berth on the Hudson River just down the road. Needless to say it never happened again in the six months I stayed with the production, but it did reinforce my feeling that a lot of theatrical criticism should be treated with a large amount of scepticism. Perhaps I should qualify that: Bad notices should be treated with scepticism; good notices should be taken more seriously. However, all that was a long way down the track and I promised Jess and the boys that I'd begin at the beginning.

•

I was born on 27 January 1929 in Poona, or Puna as it is now called, in India. My birth name was Michael Francis Gregson and my father, Donald Gregson, was a Captain in the 3rd Indian Cavalry. Nine years later he transferred to the 5th Royal Inniskilling Dragoon Guards which, as the name suggests, was an Irish cavalry regiment with the dubious distinction of having green trousers as part of its uniform. Quite what he was doing in India I'm not sure—maintaining the British Raj I suppose, and having a hell of a good time. Pa wasn't a great military man but he was a wonderful horseman and played polo for the British Army in India.

My mother had been sent to India to get over an unfortunate marriage which had recently been annulled. She was part of the 'fishing fleet' of younger daughters sent to meet a mate; one more suitable than the man she had just left. Such were the mores of the times. It's hard to believe now that Ma could have unknowingly married, and lived with, a well-known and more than somewhat flaring homosexual, who, far from hiding in the closet, had a succession of charming and handsome young men staying with them in their house in Switzerland. She was clearly not only innocent but also ignorant. Although she was vaguely aware that something was missing from the marriage, it wasn't until she spent a few days in London with a newly married friend that she found out what it was. Her first marriage was never consummated; poor Ma was still 'untouched'.

Much to my grandmother's annoyance, Ma decided to have the marriage annulled rather than go through a divorce. It involved a complicated legal and medical procedure designed to provoke the maximum of embarrassment for my mother and grandmother, and to provide the maximum of amusement to their friends.

Granny was a formidable beauty—the daughter of a Lord Mayor of London and the widow of a Sheriff of London, who would have been Lord Mayor too if he hadn't been carried off by a ruptured appendix when he was in his mid-forties. She had been left very comfortably off thanks to her husband's family business, Hansons of Eastcheap. It was 'trade', of course, a grocer's business of a sort, but it had the merit of having an historical connection with the East India Company, which gave it some sort of cachet. Her family, the Winters, went back to the Norman Conquest, according to her—my daughter Jess has a sort of family tree which traces the family back to 1066 and includes two Winters who were executed with Guy Fawkes for taking part in the Gunpowder Plot in 1604. Later, Granny claimed to be related to the Byrons of the poetic notoriety and at one point thought I might have inherited the Lord title through some extremely complicated lack of primogeniture in a distant cousin.

Comfortably off and beautiful Granny might have been, but she was unlucky with her children. As well as my mother's misadventure in marriage, her son Charles (Uncle Charlie), Ma's handsome and popular elder brother, came to a mysterious end in the River Thames somewhere between Monkey Island and Teddington Weir. He had foolishly married a woman called Violet, whom my grandmother considered to be 'no better than she should be'. She was a few years older than Uncle Charlie and also had an incumbent boyfriend. One weekend Uncle Charlie unwisely but innocently invited the boyfriend to stay with him and Violet at their place on Monkey Island in the Thames near Marlow. At some point during the evening—so the coroner was told—Charlie and the boyfriend rowed across to the nearest pub on the mainland to buy some more whisky. According to the boyfriend and other witnesses in the pub, Charlie had already had more than his fair share and somehow, while rowing back to the Island, had clumsily and sadly fallen into the river. Try as he might, the boyfriend had been unable to save him. A day or two later, Charlie's body with a slightly damaged head fetched up at Teddington Weir.

The coroner decided on a verdict of accidental death and, after the usual warnings about 'the demon drink', offered his condolences to the family. Charlie had died intestate—he was only in his late-twenties—so Violet, his widow, inherited his quite considerable fortune. My grandmother was furious, and sad I suppose, and was convinced until the day she died at eighty-four in 1963, that the foulest of play had occurred. However, even with the aid of private detectives she was unable to prove anything and had to sit back in impotent fury when, a discreet time after Charlie's death, Violet and the boyfriend moved to Paris where they married and, as far as I know, lived happily ever after.

As soon as my mother's annulment came through, my grandmother decided it would be in everyone's best interests if Ma were removed from the limelight. Granny could have borne the shame of divorce, especially if Ma had been the innocent party, but there was something inherently ridiculous about an annulment on the grounds of non-consummation—especially when the non-consummation had been overlooked for more than two years. This argued a lack of sophistication—to put it in the most charitable way—in my mother, and redounded unfavourably on my grandmother. So Ma was despatched to India—out of sight, out of mind; and best of all, out of London. Granny could then pursue her life without the embarrassment of 'that silly girl'.

The 'silly girl' was trolled around with the rest of the Indian 'fishing fleet' to meet and hopefully marry some eligible bachelor. It was Ma's good or bad luck, depending on your point of view, that the eligible bachelor she met was Pa. He was a few months younger than her and was no doubt intrigued by her good looks, scandalous first marriage and comfortably-off connections. 'Podge', as he was known to his friends, had no money of his own, nor any expectations, but he had immense charm, reasonable looks and, of course, the luck of the Irish. They married and Ma's ignorance of the facts of life was speedily corrected as she had four children in the next five years: my two elder sisters, Bridget—known to us as Betty—and Hilary, then me and fifteen months later my brother Richard.

Something my parents might have had in common, if they had ever discussed it, was the mutual loss of a sibling. My father's sister, Aunt Peggy, like Uncle Charlie, predeceased my birth by several years. She had been on her honeymoon in Italy—

in Florence, I think—and had apparently sleepwalked off her bedroom balcony, which unluckily for her was on the fourth or fifth floor. Another 'accidental death', which left me and my siblings without aunts or uncles but with two bereaved and angry grandmothers.

I have no memory of my life in India. We all returned to England in 1931 when I was only two and a half, but I've been told that I dearly loved my ayah and my father's bearer, and could speak Hindi before I could speak English. Still, I am indubitably an Indian national, and this has been a bit of a problem for me all my life. Not, I hasten to add, because of any anti-Indian feeling, but because, when filling in the countless forms that are so much a part of life, one inevitably has to state one's place and date of birth. The unqualified writing of 'Poona, India, 27/1/29' without any explanation, has provoked some searching looks and the occasional muttered comment at many an immigration desk and check-in counter, and once almost caused me to go to war.

In the late sixties I was asked to travel to India to play a maharajah—unlikely as it seems now—in some film for a company whose name escapes me. I wasn't doing anything else at the time and rather fancied a trip to the Punjab, so I said yes. I'd had my costumes made by a London costumier (at the film company's expense of course), completed my briefings and vaccinations and was all ready to go. At the last moment someone looked at my passport and saw the incriminating facts—'Born: Poona, India' etc. I received more than a searching look and muttered comment this time. I was informed that, as an Indian national and a fit male person in his thirties, I would be liable to conscription if I returned to the country of my birth. The first war with Pakistan had just started and India and Indians, including me, were at battle stations.

I didn't fancy being a sepoy in some Rajput regiment and going off to fight the Pakistanis, whom I'd seen playing a rather aggressive style of cricket and hockey. So I reluctantly returned my costumes to the wardrobe department and withdrew from the film. Since then I've flown over India many times, and landed once to change planes at Bombay Airport on a flight from Australia to England, but I have never been back.

•

I vaguely remember the boat trip to England in my infancy, or I think I do. It's hard to know if it is a real memory or just pieced together from hearing people talk about it over the years since then. I think I enjoyed the voyage very much, apart from dropping my golliwog into the swimming pool. I subsequently gave my heart to my father's Indian batman, who plunged in and rescued it, losing his turban in the process. The first memories that I am sure about are of a large country house in Sussex called Robin Post. In those days it was quite common to rent a country property rather than buy it, and there were any number of 'Manors', 'Granges', 'Old Rectories' and 'Halls' for rent to the right applicant.

While we lived there my father was on some sort of reserve status with his regiment. He had chronic malaria and was pursuing a lacklustre career in The City working for my mother's family company, Hansons of Eastcheap. They produced and marketed, amongst other things, a product line called Red White and Blue Tea and Coffee. I don't think Pa's heart was in it, but it got him out of the house. Each morning he took the train to London and returned every evening to Robin Post, where he would arrive red in the face and smelling of whisky. We children would be presented to him on his return and he would spend a few minutes reviewing the day's events with us. This could be a tricky time for my brother and me, as the nanny or governess would have briefed him with a list of the more serious crimes we might have committed during his absence before we were presented. We never quite knew whether we'd be getting a humbug to suck and a big hug and a kiss, or a quick bending over his knee and a fair-to-middling slippering. Apart from this daily ritual we saw very little of him. We didn't see a lot of Ma either. A brief audience every morning, and a kiss goodnight before being sent off to bed.

We lived our lives in the nursery or schoolroom, where we were looked after by a nursemaid and nanny, then later by a governess who was responsible for our behaviour and basic education. I don't think any of us minded this regime. We didn't know any other kind of life and what you don't know, you don't miss. In any case we were well fed and comfortable enough, apart from the occasional slipperings, and there were dogs and cats and each other to play with in the house, and ferrets and ponies and horses to play with in the stables and garden. My parents weren't rich, they were reasonably well-off middle class people, but they were able to afford a cook, a parlourmaid (both of whom stayed with my mother until well after the war), a nursemaid, a governess, a gardener-cum-chauffeur, a gardener's boy and a groom who lived above the stables.

Both my parents were very into horses and everything connected with them. Pa kept a polo pony (retired), two hunters (one for him and one for Ma) and a couple of ponies for us children. My parents hunted every winter, my mother riding side-saddle, and, as soon as we were old enough, my sisters and then me and my brother followed them into the field. My mother finally had to stop after a bad fall while tally-hoing across the downs. She broke her hip and for some reason it didn't heal properly, leaving her with one leg shorter than the other. At the time she reacted to the accident with typical British phlegm—insisting on paying May, the groom, the sixpenny fine we all had to pay if we fell off, before being taken away to the hospital.

I viewed horses and riding and all things equine with some indifference. I could take it or leave it, an attitude that I've kept all my life when required to ride in films and television shows. Unfortunately, as a child I wasn't allowed to leave it, and had to grin and bear it under May's and my father's steely eye when we rode our ponies up and down a jumping lane which had been built in the paddock. We hopped over hay bales and logs and low hurdles—head and heart high, heels and hands low, according to one of Pa's favourite adages—until even I could manage it without too much difficulty. Of course, as always, the bar was raised. Then we had to go over the jumps without stirrups, without reins and finally without either. I don't think I ever achieved this ultimate test of skill, and my pocket money was greatly diminished by the sixpenny fines I had to keep giving May for falling off. However, my sisters and brother were really pretty good, and were forever winning rosettes and cups at the local gymkhanas and pony clubs.

I'm afraid I was a bit of a disappointment to my father. I was, after all, his son and heir, born after two daughters, but unlike him I preferred a more sedentary life and spent as much time as I could reading. I read anything and everything. According to Pa, my head was never out of a book and he expressed his view of this in a piece of doggerel he wrote about each member of the household. My verse was: 'M is for Michael, he's called Mickey Mouse/He does nothing in the garden, and less in the house.'

We didn't stay very long at Robin Post. After a couple of years we moved to Fairseat Manor in the village of Fairseat near Sevenoaks in Kent. It was a big house with servants' quarters, a large garden, an orchard, stabling for five horses and a three-acre paddock where the hellish jumping lane was re-established. My parents' lives seemed to be the same—Red White and Blue Tea and Coffee for Pa, and a bit of lady-like gardening and house-hold supervision for Ma—but for us children, life became a lot more serious. My two sisters went away to a boarding school in their tweed skirts and pudding-bowl hats, and for my brother and me, Nanny was replaced by Miss Collins, the governess. 'Coll' began the task of turning Richard and me into English gentlemen with an unswerving devotion to King, Country and Kipling. Then in 1936, when I was seven and a half, it was decided that I was old enough and big enough to go off to prep school.

Stone House was the chosen school. I don't know why this particular one, there were almost more prep schools than school-boys in those days. But for me it was a very happy choice. It was a large Victorian building with playing fields, a primitive swimming pool, a chapel and a small wood nearby in which we did our Boy Scouting or, in my case, Wolf Cubbing. It was within easy walking distance of the cliffs and sea at Broadstairs in Kent. For some reason, that whole area of north-east Kent was considered to be healthy, even though, in the winter, it was one of the coldest places in the British Isles and so there was an abundance of prep schools, nursing homes and retirement establishments in the vicinity.

I did pretty well in the classroom and won the odd prize—books with their faded inscriptions on the fly leaves mostly, some of which I still have. I was also quite good at games and won the Junior Victor Ludorum (best junior all-round athlete) at the school sports day. Each Sunday we would write our weekly letter home:

> Dear Mummy and Daddy,
> Lewis Minor sprained his ankle playing squash . . . we beat St Peter's Court at Soccer 3 to 1 . . . and could I please have a two-shilling postal order to get a new kind of fountain pen I saw advertised in the *Boy's Own Paper*. I am well and Mr Winser says my arithmetic is getting better. Love to you both and to all the dogs and horses . . . How are the ducks?
> Michael

At the end of my second year the family moved from Kent to an old farmhouse called Limbury, a few miles from Bridport in Dorset. Pa left his City job and tried his luck as a gentleman farmer. I loved it. Stone House in term time and Limbury in the hols—it was a good and secure existence but, of course, it didn't last. Neville Chamberlain came back from Munich, waved his document and said there would be peace in our time. But others knew better. My father was recalled from reserve status and rejoined the 'Skins' in Bovington, where the regiment was being mechanised. But there would be no more horses and polo and pigsticking and tent-pegging; now it was tanks and armoured cars and Bren gun carriers, and Pa hated it. He was thirty-eight and still only a Captain—if he had to go to war, he didn't want to go in a steel box and a boiler suit.

There was more and more talk of war. The adults looked increasingly worried and then, at eleven o'clock on Sunday morning on 3 September 1939, we all gathered round the wireless in the drawing room to listen to Neville Chamberlain announce that we were at war with Germany. It was a surprisingly untraumatic moment for me. Nothing happened. I expected bugles to blow, sirens to howl, bombs to drop and German tanks to come thundering down the lane. Not at all. British phlegm ruled supreme. My mother and father, and Esther the parlourmaid and Kitty the cook and my two sisters and my brother Richard and I, who had all been listening to the prime minister, smiled shyly at each other and then dispersed to carry on doing whatever we'd been doing before this Declaration.

A few days later my father went back to Bovington to learn more about his loathed tanks, my two sisters went back to Sherborne School to learn more about whatever they were learning about, and Richard and I went off to our prep school, where I was to learn the first principles and theories of fornication and the four-letter words commonly used to describe them.

By this time Stone House had moved to Yorkshire as Broadstairs was considered to be in the frontline of possible hostilities. Marsh Court, near Winchester, was where we now found ourselves. I loathed the place and degenerated from a bright enthusiastic scholar and athlete into a slug. I was determined to run away to sea to serve my King and country, as soon as I figured out how one did this.

One night the war came quite close. A German bomber on its way back across the Channel dropped a couple of bombs on the nine-hole golf course that was part of the school grounds. They must have been small bombs because I slept through the whole event, but the next day we visited the site and climbed excitedly in and out of the bomb craters. They were no bigger than some of the bunkers on the course, but there were bomb fragments to be collected. They looked like pieces of broken flowerpots, only heavier. For a couple of days there was an excited buzz in the school but it didn't last. Life soon subsided into the dreary monotony of an English winter.

To my great delight my father and his regiment were sent to France with the British Expeditionary Force. This filled me with pride—my father fighting the Hun. It didn't occur to me that he could be killed or captured or wounded. Pa would sort the buggers out, and anyway the Maginot line was impregnable; Herr Hitler and those other nasties would get what they deserved. We'd hang out the washing on the Siegfried line and the war would be over by Christmas.

Christmas was a grave disappointment. The war wasn't over and an early form of rationing had begun. Not that we did without, but it just wasn't the same. Pa was in France, Ma was worried and muttering about doing some sort of war work, Hollobone the gardener-cum-chauffeur-cum-everything else had been called up, and I didn't want to go back to Marsh Court. Then suddenly there was talk of evacuation. My sisters' school was off to Canada, lock stock and barrel, to join forces with some school in Toronto, and my sisters were going with it. April soon passed, and by May even I was aware that the end, or something very much like it, was nigh. It was obvious that France was about to surrender and then it could only be a matter of weeks before Hitler and his loathsome lot would be marching down Whitehall and moving into Buckingham Palace.

My father, with what was left of his regiment and the British Expeditionary Force, had retreated to the Channel coast and was waiting to be rescued from the beaches in that extraordinary and lucky operation known forever after as 'Dunkirk'. He got back to England with a percentage of his regiment and the clothes he was wearing and nothing else. I only saw him a few more times before I too was on the move, but I remember how tired he looked. Tired, defeated and old.

My parents, for what I'm sure were the best of reasons, decided to send me and my brother to the safer shores of Canada as well, to a boarding school in Toronto so we could be near our sisters. The irony of that decision became apparent within a year—during the five years I spent in Toronto I hardly ever saw the girls and never for more than a day or so. However, the decision was made and in late June of 1940, in spite of the fact that shipping in the Atlantic was being torpedoed more or less routinely, Richard and I were on our way. We took the train to Liverpool, spent one night in the Midland Hotel, kissed our mother, shook hands with our father, boarded the *Duchess of Atholl* with hundreds of other children and sailed away to the west. I was eleven and a half, and Richard was just ten.

All I knew about Canada was what I'd read in RM Ballantyne's and Grey Owl's novels. Wolves and grizzly bears, Mounties and redskins, beavers and moose and trap lines. None of this stood me in much stead when in mid July we arrived at the St Lawrence River, sailed up past Quebec City and the heights of Abraham, and finally came into Montreal. We had reached the New World— and a very new and different world it proved to be.

TWO

Mark time

Canada, as presented by Montreal, was as alien to me as Planet X. I knew nothing of modern North American culture. Even the films I'd seen, including the Hollywood variety, had been of the historical kind based on books: *Elizabeth and Essex, Lives of a Bengal Lancer, King Solomon's Mines* and even *Snow White*—the sort of films my father or, more importantly, Miss Collins might approve. The cars in this new land seemed like monsters dreamed up by Jules Verne—chromium-covered snarling giants—and, of course, they were driving on the wrong side of the road. The only icon of Canadian culture I recognised was a member of the Royal Canadian Mounted Police, resplendent in his scarlet tunic and boy scout hat, but even he was astride a motorbike instead of a horse.

My brother and I disembarked from the *Duchess of Atholl* and waited with dozens of other children to be met and taken . . . God knew where. Finally a middle-aged couple approached us, asked if we were Michael and Richard Gregson and introduced themselves. I can't remember their names, or even what they looked like, but they seemed to know us. So with the blind trust and obedience of the totally naive, we collected our Revelation suitcases, shuffled through customs and climbed into their monstrous glittering car. We drove through the impressively alien streets of Montreal—tall buildings, rattling streetcars and blazing neon signs wherever one looked—and made desultory and dutiful conversation on our way to the station and our final destination, Toronto.

We were enrolled at the Upper Canada College Prep School and the first year passed while events in faraway Europe went from bad to worse as the German army achieved victory after victory. We received occasional letters from my mother and wrote dutiful replies. My father and his regiment were now part of the Eighth Army and were in North Africa doing battle with Rommel. Pa had been promoted to Major, which wasn't before time as he was now forty-one. He never rose above Major, though, due to his somewhat cavalier attitude to the chastity of his Colonel's wife, and an even more cavalier attitude to 'King's Regulations'.

Some time in late 1942, during the summer term of my first year in the Upper School, I was told by my housemaster, Jimmy Biggar, a balding Scot with the hairiest nose I have ever seen, that my two sisters had come to see me and my brother. Richard was duly produced and Bridget and Hilary in their school uniforms and pudding-bowl hats met us on the First XI cricket ground and gave us the bad news: Pa and Ma were getting divorced. By the time we got this news, they might have already been divorced given the time the mail took to get from England to Canada, if it arrived at all. We looked at each other in solemn wonder. It didn't seem very important to me—I hadn't seen either of them for over two years and had no idea if and when I'd see either of them again—but the girls were clearly upset. Bridget, I think, because she was more aware of the difference it would make and also because of her adopted Canadian conservative stance towards that sort of thing. Hilary had a wonderfully straightforward view of life and couldn't imagine that Mummy and Daddy could do such a thing. What Richard thought I don't know, but we all looked suitably solemn and adult then went our separate ways—and our separate lives.

During that summer holidays I was asked by a boy at school if I'd like to work with him on his father's farm in Quebec province. Since I had no other plans or expectations I accepted without really thinking about it. My first daily task was to muck out the pigs in the barn, seventy or eighty of the dirty little buggers who did nothing but eat and defecate as they went from birth to two hundred pounds in weight in ten weeks before taking their final ride to the abattoir. In time I became a dab hand with them, even assisting in the slaughter of one for the family table. I grew physically stronger on the farm and, apart from a vile spell working inside one of the silos when we were filling it with cut clover mixed with molasses and water, I enjoyed myself thoroughly.

On 6 June 1944, the Allies invaded the coast of Normandy and it looked as if the war might finally be coming to an end. I had written to my mother several times to ask if I might come back to England too, but the answer had been no. I don't really know why she decided to keep me in Canada. I suspect there were a number of motives, some possibly selfish—I had heard she had met a new man—but no matter, I was stuck where I was for the foreseeable future. Lacking the resource and, I must admit, courage to run away to sea, I had to make the best of it. This I did by getting a job on the Great Lakes when the next summer holidays began with a friend of mine called Sam Toy.

Sam and I were employed as 'bellhops' on the SS *Kingston* which carried about two hundred passengers. Our duties included carrying the passengers' baggage from the gangway to their cabins and catering to all their other whims and desires. These were quite often of a bizarre and personal nature as the *Kingston* was widely used as an illicit trysting place. On one memorable occasion a pair of 'trystees' became literally locked into their passion and had to be off-loaded on a stretcher, one atop the other, to be uncoupled later in the hospital in Rochester. Our hours seemed endless as we travelled and arrived and departed night and day. Life consisted of almost non-stop announcements, accompanied by a little tune on a xylophone, that we were about to arrive or depart somewhere or other. Then followed the lugging of suitcases and the procuring of food and drink and various prophylactic articles. The pay was terrible but the tips were good and at the end of two weeks and seven round trips I walked off the ship with nearly a hundred dollars in small change tied up in a woollen sock. We then signed on as deck-hands on the lake freighter SS *Fernie*, and spent the rest of the summer travelling the length and breadth of the Great Lakes, from the far west to Montreal in the east.

I returned to school with even more self-confidence than I'd gained from my stint on the farm. In fact, I must have been a real pain in the arse to the teaching staff and most of my fellow students. I loathed being at school and couldn't wait for my sixteenth birthday, when it would be possible for me to leave. I'd also become so addicted to tobacco by this time that I was nicknamed 'Weedy'.

Soon enough I did turn sixteen, in January 1945, and was ready to leave and take my long-delayed place in the fight against the Nazi hordes. But I was too late. In May the Germans surrendered and the war in Europe was over. True, the war against Japan was still going on, but it was hardly the same thing.

After I failed my Junior Matriculation in the June, my mother agreed I could take my place in the adult world. I took the train to Montreal, where I signed on as a supernumerary aboard the cargo ship MV *Defoe* and sailed for Liverpool. I had been away for five years and had grown from a little boy of eleven to a strapping teenager of sixteen. I now faced the re-acquaintance with my mother and father with a certain amount of trepidation.

•

I'm not sure what I expected on my return to England—a little bit of fatted calf killing perhaps, a modicum of celebration—but it was not to be. When I arrived at my mother's flat in London, I was greeted by Esther, the parlour maid, who told me that Ma and 'Major Adams' (I detected a slightly shifty expression at the mention of this name) were in Dorset, where Ma had bought a little house called Old Chimney Cottage. They would be back in London in a day or two. When my sister Hilary returned from St George's Hospital, where she was working as a probationary nurse, she got me up to speed. Ma was being courted by, and 'sort of living with', Major Adams . . . Roland. Very nice but not of course as nice as Daddy, who was still abroad with the army in Florence and living with, or married to, a lady called Catherine.

When Ma arrived with Major Adams, we went through the ritual greeting ceremony as performed by most of the middle class families of that era: nothing emotional or spontaneous, a kiss and a handshake and leave it at that. Major Adams, who insisted that I call him Roland, was extremely charming and to my great surprise treated me like an adult. He listened to what I had to say about what I wanted to do and promised to do what he could to help. Ma seemed to think my going away to sea was a good idea—no doubt better than having me hanging about at home— so that was the first hurdle safely cleared. Roland in his peacetime life was a barrister in the Admiralty's Divorce and Probate Division and had a lot of contacts in the shipping world. He organised for me to become a cadet with the Eagle Oil and Shipping Company, which was an oil tanker company registered in London that had about twenty-five ships, all named 'San' something or other. I sailed in the *San Vulfrano*, my first ship, then in the *San Wenceslao*, and finally in the *San Veronico*.

While researching for this book I came across my old Discharge Book. It was issued to me in 1945, when I first went to sea, and it contains a record of the ships I sailed in, the dates I signed on and off them, and the master's comments under two headings: Ability and General Conduct. These were always stamped VG for Very Good. It didn't mean much but was better than DC, which was a real condemnation as it stood for Declines to Comment. It also contains a photograph of my sixteen-year-old face staring sulkily at the camera above a number chalked on a piece of board—R 337829. I could have been any Borstal boy or dead-end kid on his way to life imprisonment or the gallows.

All in all, I spent four-and-a-bit years with Eagle Oil. During that time Ma and Roland bought a house called Gubbions Hall, which was set in a hundred acres of farmland and woods. It was a fairly ordinary seventeenth-century manor house—a bit dark and not terribly comfortable, in spite of some ill-judged modernisation which previous owners had carried out—but its really unique feature was that it had a moat around it. Roland saw himself as a gentleman farmer and the plan was for Richard to graduate from Agricultural College so he could take over the running of the farm. But I don't think Richard's heart was ever really in it and his life and career eventually took a very different turn. Ma and Roland were now married and were converting to Roman Catholicism. A complicated business as they had both been divorced, but they managed to get some sort of special dispensation from the Vatican and had been allowed to marry on the condition that there was to be no sexual intercourse between them. I assume this was agreed to by both parties. They were only forty-nine when they married and they lived together for the next thirtysomething years in mutual celibacy.

I left the *San Veronico*, having completed my apprenticeship, and was all set to go to Nautical College and sit for my second mate's ticket. It became obvious that I couldn't live at Gubbions Hall while studying in London. My mother's bank manager was a wizened little man who suggested I board with his nephew, Patrick, who was about ten years older than me; a cheerful and charming young doctor. He was married to another doctor, Margaret, and lived in a flat in Cheyne Walk in Chelsea, which was then still quite down-market. These arrangements were made by Ma, who told me in faintly disapproving terms that Patrick and Margaret were getting divorced. Apparently Margaret had left Patrick for another man and gone back to Birmingham. What Ma didn't tell me was *why* Margaret might have gone off with someone else.

THREE

Starting time

Life at 128 Cheyne Walk was very pleasant. I lived in the back room, which had no outlook, but I did have access to the front living room that overlooked the river and its houseboats. At one magical time one of these was occupied by Dorothy Tutin, for whom I nurtured a deep, but unexpressed, passion. At Nautical College in London's East End, I would spend my days lost in the complexities of the kind of signals a fishing boat in the South China Seas would exhibit while hauling in its nets; in the evenings I'd indulge in a moderate pub crawl in Chelsea with friends, or occasionally Patrick would give a dinner party. He was a good and inventive cook and was the first person I met who followed Elizabeth David's recipes—not an easy thing to do in the austerity of 1949. He'd invite lots of painters and actors and musicians and writers to these dinners, but hardly ever any girls. The guests would look at me in a discrete knowing way as they sipped their coffees and listened to Patrick's records.

A couple of months passed in this pleasant way and then, a few days before Christmas I had to take my eyesight test for the Board of Trade. In those days deck officers had to have 20/20 vision—glasses were unacceptable and not many ships had the benefit of radar to assist the visually challenged. I failed. It was a question of colour blindness. The tiny red, green and white lights that flashed on and off in the pitch dark of the examination room were indistinguishable to me. I could see they were lights, but what colour they were was a matter of guesswork. I was allowed three goes but it was no use. The Merchant Navy wouldn't take on someone who couldn't tell the difference between a green starboard light and a red port light, especially as failure to do so could lead to a collision and worse. Captain Thompson, my marine superintendent, was sympathetic and kind—so was everyone else—but the plain fact was that if I couldn't pass my eyesight test, I couldn't get my second mate's ticket and without that a career at Eagle Oil, or any other shipping company, was impossible.

I'd learnt a lot during my time at sea: how to splice wire ropes; how to deal with drunken and recalcitrant shipmates; how to sew and iron and starch collars (taught to me by a wonderfully gay and funny second steward called George Higgs); how to navigate using a sextant and spherical trigonometry; and, especially the thing that all young men think important—the best knocking shops in the ports in the West Indies and South America, and even some in Texas. However, none of this knowledge was going to do me much good in a non-seagoing career. I was coming up to my twenty-first birthday and I had to think of something else to do.

I didn't know what I was going to do with my life, but I knew it wasn't going to involve any further education or training of a formal sort. I was discussing this with Patrick one night, after a good dinner and a lot of wine, and suddenly he said, apropos of nothing, 'I'm queer you know'. I suppose I must have looked a bit startled. It hadn't occurred to me that a doctor could be gay. I mean George at Eagle Oil had definitely played on that team, but Patrick was a serious GP. I couldn't imagine him in a silk blouse and high heels serving drinks to hairy-arsed stokers in the crew bar on board some P&O liner on its way to the Far East. He went on.

'I didn't know I was until after I married Margaret. I hated what it did to her, but I'm used to it now.' I nodded wisely and asked him if he wanted me to move out, but he said I was welcome to stay if I still wanted to. I suppose in hindsight he was advising me that my reputation—not that I had one—might be compromised by living with him, but I was too callow to understand or care. Besides I had nowhere else to go at that moment so we let the matter drop.

I discussed my possible future with anyone who might have a clue but all the advice pointed to going back to some kind of school and getting some kind of degree. That wasn't on. I hadn't even finished high school, and I couldn't face being a student again after four years at sea. While trying to figure out what to do next I amused myself in the Soho pubs and clubs, which were full of artists and painters and film-makers and poets, some of whom I'd met at Patrick's dinner parties and they probably thought I was looking for a bit on the side. I wasn't and I told them so. What I was looking for was a girlfriend. Finally, in the old Oxford Street Jazz Club, I found her—Wendy Abbott, who later became the celebrated and notorious Henrietta Moraes.

Henrietta, who had a half-page obituary in the *Times* when she died a couple of years ago. Henrietta, who was celebrated for being celebrated, who had been married several times, once notably to the Indian poet Dom Moraes, whose name she kept. Henrietta, who had been left a studio in Apollo Place in Chelsea by the artist John Minton when he died in the mid-fifties. Henrietta, who had been painted in the nude by the great Lucien Freud and had been the unofficial queen of the demi-monde in Soho and Piddletrenthide and somewhere in Ireland. I don't know what it was that Wendy had, but she had it in spades and it was much more than I could cope with. She broke my heart, necessary for anyone at age twenty-two, but she also taught me a little bit about women and sex and the grown-up world and I'm grateful to her for that.

The old Jazz Club was in a large basement at 100 Oxford Street. I first went there with friends of mine, the Robinsons, who were knowledgeable and enthusiastic fans of the music. They had a huge collection of records and could name each and every musician and his instrument in even the most obscure ensembles. I wasn't in their league but I too enjoyed the music. After a bit I could distinguish between Louis Armstrong and Cootie Williams or Pearl Bailey and Ella Fitzgerald. Humphrey Lyttleton, an ex-Etonian and Guards Officer and latter day BBC pundit and wit, was the leader of my favourite group at the Jazz Club. He played a great trumpet and was accompanied by Wally Fawkes, who played clarinet and had created the cartoon character 'Flook' in the *Daily Mail*. There was also the extraordinary and flamboyant George Melly camping around and belting out the 'blues' in his personal and idiosyncratic way.

I was there one night, half-full of Worthington draught and jitterbugging in my clumsy way with anyone who would join me, when I came across Wendy. She was eighteen and had the most beautiful face I'd ever seen. Wide eyes, cheek bones to die for, short brown hair and a gorgeous mouth and smile. I couldn't see what her body was like—she was wearing jeans and a loose sweater—but she moved like a thoroughbred. To my surprise she came towards me. We danced and smoked and drank and then, wonder of wonders, went home together. I was completely smitten. I'd never had a girlfriend, never spent the whole night with someone, never been in love before.

Wendy shared a flat in South Kensington with two other girls but spent most of her nights in Cheyne Walk with me. At the time she either had a kind of secretarial job, or was training for one, I can't remember which. But she was obviously destined for more than the typewriter and filing cabinet. Her background was somewhat obscure—she'd been to the Dragon School in Oxford and had some kind of guardian or relative there. I romantically assumed that she was the bastard daughter of a duke or a minor royalty but I never really knew. Patrick seemed to approve of our relationship. He liked Wendy and introduced her to Norman Parkinson, who was the top fashion photographer of the day. He thought she had real potential as a model but needed to lose a few pounds. Wendy couldn't be bothered, she could never be bothered to do anything she didn't want to do, so the chance went begging.

The subject of my career inevitably surfaced and Wendy decided that I should become an actor. I was stunned. I knew nothing about the theatre or acting, it was something that weird and exotic people did, and I was neither. I'd only been to the theatre a couple of times—to see *Peter Pan* and another pantomime when I was a child—I'd never seen a serious play. Wendy was unmoved—I was a good-looking young bloke, I should be in the movies. I thought about it, and the more I thought about it the more it appealed to me. I rather fancied myself in a blazing gun battle in Dodge City, outdrawing the guy in the black hat and riding off into the sunset with a gorgeous girl at my side. Yeah . . . why not? I would be a movie star, make loads of money, marry Wendy and live happily ever after! The only problem was that I hadn't the faintest idea how to go about it. Patrick, of course, came to the rescue.

Patrick knew John Gielgud and some lesser lights in the world of show business, and he told me he would find out from them what I should do. A lot of young men who had been in the services during the war were being de-mobbed and, rather than go back to their pre-ordained lives as clerks or mechanics or postmen, were using their service grants to enrol at drama schools or art schools or anywhere rather than return to where they came from. Things were changing in the theatre—ordinary people were getting involved—so why couldn't I?

I discounted the idea of going to RADA or any other drama school—I didn't have the time or the money. I needed a job right away. In 1950, which was when I was making this great decision, there were film studios at Pinewood, Denham, Ealing, Elstree, Shepperton, Twickenham, Teddington, Hammersmith, Walton on Thames and Boreham Wood. There may have been others but those were enough for me to start with. However, I was advised by Patrick's contacts that, before I aimed at a film career, stardom and Hollywood, I should at least find out for myself whether I was suited to the work and, even more importantly, whether I had any talent. Start small was the advice, get a job in 'rep' and see how you go.

There was very little television back then—only one channel run by the BBC, producing the occasional drama, but no commercial television. There was, however, an abundance of regional theatre. This ranged from the grand companies of Liverpool, Bristol and Birmingham, whose productions ran for five or six weeks with rehearsal time to match, and the less grand companies, such as one in York which had a fortnightly turnaround, to the companies found in most small towns—dozens and dozens of them—repertory companies which were known as 'weekly reps'. There was even a subdivision of this last type which was almost too dreadful to mention—the *twice*-nightly weekly rep'— at the very bottom of the barrel, which I finally scraped two years later.

I bought a copy of *Spotlight's Contact,* a small booklet containing the names and addresses of all the managements and theatres in the country. I had my photograph taken and sent it out with a letter I had composed to fifty companies:

Dear Mr So and So,
I am twenty-two years old, six-foot tall blah . . . blah . . . blah . . . I have had no real experience but am anxious and willing to learn. I would be happy to accept any position you might offer. I am enclosing my photograph and a stamped self-addressed envelope and look forward, very much, to hearing from you . . .

Optimistically, I started with the best companies. I got the occasional reply but no offers, so I worked my way down the list. I had to get more photographs, envelopes and stamps but I kept at it, sustained by the love of a 'bad' woman and the fact that I had nothing else to do.

In the meantime, Wendy and I were happy together, or so I thought. We went to the pubs and clubs in Soho—The French Pub, The Gargoyle, The Mandrake, The Colony—and wherever we went Wendy was the star attraction and I the source of much envy. I even took her to Gubbions Hall one weekend, where she seemed to charm my mother and Roland. Since we were allocated separate bedrooms at Gubbions, we were forced to sneak off to the barn for our dalliances. I had an inkling that there might be a worm in the apple when we were travelling on a bus one evening and she started to give me hell. No reason, nothing I'd said or done, just a grade 1 bollocking out of the blue. I was hurt and appalled and finally she relented. She kissed me and smiled and said she'd thought it was time we had a fight and, as there was nothing to fight about, she'd made it all up. I relaxed and hoped I'd be as good an actor as she was, but the writing was on the wall, if only I'd had the wit to read it.

Finally the letter I was waiting for arrived:

Dear Mr Gregson,
We have a vacancy for an assistant stage manager: Equity minimum, play small parts if and when required, one-month probationary engagement, start next Monday. Suggest you arrive Sunday to arrange digs etc. Please let me know soonest if this is acceptable

. . . or words to that effect. It was signed, Peter Gordon, Castle Theatre, Farnham. I replied in the affirmative, sooner than soonest, and Wendy and Patrick and I celebrated the start of my new career. I met my mother and Roland at Claridges and gave them the news over dinner. They were mutedly supportive and wished me well.

Farnham is, or was, a prosperous little town about forty miles south-west of London. It was stockbroker–commuter–dormitory territory, near Aldershot and not far from the Hampshire border. I arrived there on a Sunday afternoon and was met by the stage manager, a very tall saturnine chap called John Temple. He escorted me to my digs—a smallish bedroom in a house which he also inhabited—introduced me to my landlady and took me to the theatre.

I don't know what I was expecting—something like the Haymarket perhaps—but the Castle Theatre, named for the real castle in the centre of town, was a bit of a disappointment. It was tucked into the corner of some sort of municipal building just off the main square and, if you didn't know it was there, you'd miss it. The stage and the auditorium, which seated a maximum of one hundred and fifty, were on the ground floor and above them was a large room which we used for rehearsals and office work. Above that was a flat in which lived Peter Gordon the director/producer/manager of the Company and his wife who was also the leading lady.

Mr Temple (he insisted on formality—we always called the members of the company 'mister' or 'miss' in the theatre and at work, no matter what we called them in the pub) showed me around backstage and outlined my duties. The stage was small and only a couple of feet higher than the floor of the auditorium. People sitting in the front row could prop their feet on it and sometimes did. There was no 'flying space' (room to hang backdrops or scenery above the stage, out of sight of the audience, ready to descend or ascend as scene changes demand) and the wings were extremely cramped, especially on the prompt side, where there was the prompt desk with its cue lights and prop table and 'Bessie', a coke-burning stove. Bessie was the only form of heating in the theatre and one of my duties was to keep her lit and nourished; I was in big trouble if I allowed her to fall below a certain temperature.

My other duties included finding and collecting props and furniture as required from various friendly shops in the town and returning them to their owners after the week's run of the show. A push barrow was supplied to me to transport the larger items. I nodded enthusiastically—this, at least, I could do. Mr Temple regarded me sadly, 'You haven't a clue have you?' I admitted I was pretty clueless, but a willing and quick learner. He grunted, 'We'll see' and took me to the pub, where I was allowed to call him John. Over a pint he continued to outline what was expected of me:

You will arrive at the theatre at 9.30 a.m. and arrange props and furniture in the rehearsal room. Rehearsals start promptly at ten. There are no excuses for being late. You will sit on the 'book', marking pauses and noting anything which the director asks for which is not in the script.

We always used the French's Acting Editions of play books, which were a comprehensive and exact description of the play and its West End production. Every move, every piece of stage business, every prop, every piece of furniture, every pause was meticulously noted and adhered to by most directors, who had no time to be original or inventive. I sipped my beer and nodded as he continued: 'You will prompt the actors if and when required, so *never* lose your place in the script and, whatever you do, DO NOT PROMPT UNNECESSARILY.' I ventured to ask how I would know if it was necessary and he smiled bitterly:

> You won't. Actors are both arrogant and insecure and will do almost anything to maintain their myth of infallibility. If at rehearsal they stop in the middle of a scene, stare vacantly into the middle distance and sigh, do not immediately leap in with the next line. They are likely to look at you with loathing and say, 'I know the line, dear boy. I was considering a pause there, or perhaps a slightly different move, what do you think, Peter?' as they turn to the director. A brief discussion will then take place; it will be agreed that it might be best to leave things as they were plotted and the actor, 'face' preserved, will turn to you with a patronising smile and say, 'Right, just where were we, dear boy?' You will then give him the line which he had previously forgotten; rehearsals will proceed and his honour and *amour propre* will have been preserved. Always remember an ASM [assistant stage manager] is the lowest of the low; you are there to do all the shitty things that no one else will do, to be abused and exploited and, above all, to keep the fucking actors happy.

I must have looked a little shocked because he smiled his bitter smile again.

'You'll learn old chap, or . . . or . . . you'll have to get a proper job.' I offered to buy him another drink but he shook his head.

'Tomorrow is a bugger of a day, Michael—dress rehearsal, notes, and then the first performance. You're going to be as much use as a fart in a colander, so I'm going to get my head down.' There was no answer to that, so we drained our glasses and plodded back to our digs.

A lot of what Mr Temple told me at that first meeting was pretty accurate. On the whole the company was affable and easy-going and I soon fitted in but Peter Gordon was something else. He was a bearded choleric man with what seemed to be a permanent boil on the back of his neck. He ran rehearsals like the schoolmaster he had been before he'd been called up into the army during the war. He was a terrible actor but, fortunately, he seldom cast himself as he had too many other things to do. Still, he had the lease of the theatre and was the boss, so we had to make the best of it. A couple of the cast members became good friends of mine and I've worked with them on and off over the years in other theatres, and in television and films. I don't know how many of them are still alive today but I owe all of them my enduring gratitude for making my first few weeks in the 'business' as easy and pleasant as it was.

The weeks hurtled by, with a new play every week. We did *The Lady's Not For Burning*, *The Giaconda Smile* (in which I had a non-speaking part as a warder in the death cell), *French Without Tears, Murder at the Vicarage, Mountain Air* . . . I can't even remember all the titles. I got into the routine easily enough:

Monday—dress the new set and assemble props in time for the dress rehearsal at 2 p.m. Complete dress rehearsal, notes and first performance at 7.30 p.m. Go to pub, get pissed and congratulate or commiserate depending on how the show had gone.

Tuesday morning—full company read the play for the following week and block it.

Tuesday afternoon—ASM tracks down and borrows furniture and props for new play.

Tuesday evening—do second performance of this week's play.

Wednesday morning—rehearse Act 1 of new play, the actors having learned it the night before.

Wednesday afternoon—2.30 matinee.

Wednesday evening—fourth performance of current play (in good shape by now), possibly a drink in the pub after the show.

Thursday morning—rehearse Act 2 of new play, without books.

Thursday afternoon—carry on rehearsing, including Act 1.

Thursday night—fifth performance and pay day.

Friday morning—rehearse Act 3 of new play. (Nearly all plays were in three acts then; if they were more than that, they were squeezed into three to accommodate the bars and the tearooms.)

Friday afternoon—carry on rehearsing, possibly to sort out any persisting problems.

Friday night—sixth performance of current play.

Saturday morning—rehearse all three acts of new play, short break for tantrums and lunch, and then run the play again.

Saturday afternoon—five o'clock matinee, followed by final evening performance of that week's play.

After the Saturday night show the stage staff—that is, Mr Temple, the designer and myself—would strike the set in preparation for the 'set up' on Sunday morning of the new play. On Sunday morning we'd erect the new set—usually painted canvas flats with standard door, fireplace and window pieces—and with any luck we'd be finished by midday. I would then catch the train to London and spend the night with Wendy who, after a week's absence, would be very glad to see me. Early Monday morning I'd be back in Farnham, back on schedule returning the previous production's props and furniture and collecting any pieces we still needed for the week's production.

My worst nightmare would be if an armchair or table I'd been promised had been sold before I could get it as I'd then have to frantically try to find a substitute. It didn't happen often, but when it did I was in deep shit. But I survived my probationary period and was employed on a permanent basis. I was learning all the time but none of it was very difficult and, in spite of the horrendous workload, no one complained. It was like my time working on the lake boats—you knew what you were taking on when you started and, if you didn't want to or couldn't take it, you did something else. When I've mentioned what it was like to young actors these days, most of them can't believe it. The ones who can and do believe it are the ones who are working in, or have worked in, television soaps. So what else is new?

Business was pretty good and in April 1950 Peter Gordon decided to celebrate Shakespeare's birthday (23 April) with a production of *The Merchant of Venice*. This was a major undertaking as there were no French's Acting Editions of Shakespeare—he'd have to work it out for himself. As well as that, he needed extra actors. Our company consisted of the standard weekly rep contingent—leading lady, leading man, juvenile lead male, juvenile lead female, character actor elderly, character actress ditto and a character 'juve', who did all the other bits and pieces. *The Merchant Of Venice* has a *dramatis personae* of twenty named characters as well as 'Magnificoes of Venice, Officers of the Court, a Justice, Gaoler, Servants and other Attendants' as prescribed by WS. Even allowing for some cutting and doubling, and going light on the Magnificoes etc., I could see we were seriously under-manned and would need a few extra bodies to help out. Mr Gordon hired two extra bodies, cast himself as the Duke of Venice and Tubal, and conscripted Mr Temple and myself to make up the numbers. My moment had arrived—my first real acting role, and in Shakespeare. I was elated, and so was Wendy, who promised to come and watch me 'break my duck' (make my debut).

Mr Temple was a dreadful actor, worse than Peter Gordon, and hated having to do it. However, he was an imposing figure with an extensive range of disguises (wigs, nose putty, beards and moustaches) and he could be depended on to 'rhubarb' (ad lib in mock Elizabethan chat, 'gadzooks, by my troth' etc.) away reliably as a Magnifico or Gaoler or whatever else was asked of him. I, on the other hand, thought it great fun and not in the least difficult or demanding except when being directed to play Balthazar, Servant to Portia, as camp. I didn't do very good camp—I had a strange accent, a mixture of standard English, Canadian, Liverpudlian, Geordie, and any other kind that I'd heard at sea, and it didn't go well with a prissy hiss. However, I thought of George, the second steward, and did my best. I also made up the numbers as Solanio, Salarino, or Salerio (known as 'the Salads') when necessary.

My real *pièce de résistance* was Balthazar. He had entrances and, even more importantly, an exit which traditionally was designed to bring the house down. I didn't know that of course and, when in Act 3 I was told by Portia to speed away to Padua on an errand of utmost importance, I pouted my line, 'Madam, I go with all convenient speed', flapped a limp wrist, and was off like a shot. Mr Gordon was outraged.

'No, no, no, you bloody fool. You bow, you kiss her hand and then you exit *very, very* slowly. Best laugh in the show.' My head wasn't in it. I've always been a literal-minded bloke and to me 'speed' meant celerity, expedition, haste, velocity and all the other synonyms in the thesaurus. Still I wasn't prepared to argue the toss with the choleric Mr Gordon, so I did as I was told.

On the first night, to my great surprise and greater delight, the line and the exit got a big laugh and a small round of applause. It taught me a lesson that I've remembered all my life— directors aren't *always* wrong. As they're there, you might as well listen to what they have to say even when you don't agree with it. Wendy told me I'd stolen the show and I basked in the warmth of her praise and later her smooth lithe body. My exit as Balthazar grew more and more protracted as the week wore on until Mr Gordon had to tell me to pull my bloody finger out or we wouldn't get to the pub before closing time. Another lesson learnt—*more* is not necessarily *better*. Still, I was launched. Pinewood, Hollywood, any bloody wood you could name—here I come!

FOUR

Marching time

Lightning struck. I received my call-up papers. I was to report to some dismal army depot in Colchester where I would be given a physical examination and, subject to passing that, I would then report to Buller Barracks in Aldershot, where I would do twelve weeks' basic training in the Royal Army Service Corps (RASC). After that, I would be assigned to further duties to serve out the eighteen months of my National Service. Hollywood would have to wait.

I tried everything I could think of to avoid my fate—everything short of eating soap, which a shipmate some years earlier had told me he had done to avoid conscription. Apparently it had a short-term effect on the heart beat, but I wasn't game to try. I said goodbye to the Company and to my career at the Castle Theatre. Wendy attempted to cheer me up—there would be weekend leave; Aldershot was closer to London than Farnham; I'd be taught to drive in the RASC; I'd look great in uniform; and she loved me. As it turned out, the only element of truth in her remarks was that Aldershot was closer to London than Farnham.

I arrived at Buller Barracks with a couple of hundred other recruits on a Monday morning in May 1950. After ten weeks of basic training I was informed I'd been selected to attend the

WOSB (War Office Selection Board), where I would be assessed as potential officer material. I duly reported to the WOSB at East Grinstead, where the tasks we were set were similar to the problems we had to solve in the Cubs—how to get a mythical cannon over a mythical river using two pen nibs and a ball of string . . . well, that sort of thing.

On the third day I was called before the examining board, told that I had satisfied the criteria set by the War Office and asked if I had any preference about what I'd like to be. I replied that if it was all the same to them I'd like to be a civilian, and waited for lightning to strike again. To my surprise the reaction was quite jolly.

> Ha ha, yah, dashed amusing! I like to see a chap with a sense of humour . . . I see your father was in the Skins? Right, Gregson, providing you don't make a balls-up between now and your passing out parade, we're recommending you for officer training at Mons Barracks. And good luck.

Life at Mons Barracks was more of the same except that we now wore white discs behind our cap badges, white flashes on our battledress jackets and were called 'Sir'. This title was nominal in the extreme—a senior NCO (noncommissioned officer) would scream his usual bollocking, à la, 'You, you horrible little man, get those shoulders back, get your horrible bloody arms swinging and double round the square . . . Sir!' I was becoming more and more depressed by the futility of it all and the fact that Wendy was clearly going off the boil. As she had said, Aldershot was closer to London than Farnham, but things were changing. 'My boyfriend, the National Service "squaddie"' didn't have the same cachet as 'my boyfriend, the actor'.

At the time there was a war in Korea. It was not going well and I didn't fancy facing the Chinese hordes on the Imjin River under the command of the kind of officers who were in charge of our training. Something had to be done, if only I could figure out what it was. In the end three things happened more or less simultaneously to convince me that I had to make a move.

The first and most persuasive event was the increase of National Service from eighteen months to two years. If the powers-that-be could increase National Service to two years without any consultation with me, there was nothing to stop them increasing it to three years or five years or life, for Jesus' sake.

The second event was my passing the first six weeks of training and being transferred from the RASC to the Royal Artillery to complete the twelve-week course. I had absolutely nothing against the 'Gunners', in fact the Royal Artillery would be considered by some to be a definite step up from the Royal Army Service Corps, but once again I hadn't been consulted. Some unseen, unknown power was running my life and I didn't like it.

The third and final straw that broke my back was Wendy. I was given a forty-eight-hour pass to celebrate my passing the initial six weeks and my transfer to the Gunners. When I got to the flat in South Kensington on Friday evening, Wendy wasn't there. There was a note to say that she was going away for the weekend with an actor called Maxwell Reed, who was at that time a quite popular if minor film star. He had a boat moored at the Chelsea embankment and they would be travelling to France in it, '. . . so see you when we get back. Love Wendy.'

Even though I'd been sort of expecting it, or something like it, I was shattered. I got the bus down to Chelsea and tracked down Mr Reed's boat, which was called the *Black Swan* or something equally fanciful, considering its total lack of distinction. There were lights in the cabin and the sounds of a party, but I had not been invited. I sat on a bench and watched the boat for about an hour and then went to the pub and got plastered. By the time chucking-out time arrived, the boat had gone. So had Wendy, the only cheery thing in my life. The next morning I returned to the pub and cured my hangover with more of the same and decided I'd had enough.

I arrived at Mons Barracks at about six o'clock on the Saturday evening and cleaned out my locker, arranging every item of army issue in the prescribed fashion on my bed. Then I went in search of someone in charge, finally tracking down a Duty

NCO in the guardroom, who regarded me with surprise and animosity as he asked, 'What the fuck do you want . . . Sir?'

I handed him my pay book (it contained my identification number and all pertinent military details) and told him in a patient and reasonable way that I'd decided to leave the army as I'd had enough of it. I just wanted to let someone know of my decision as I didn't want to be considered a deserter, or a thief. I had left everything that had been given to me at my enlistment on my bed in the barrack room. He looked at me with growing disbelief and then, as is usual in the Army when in doubt, he passed the buck.

A succession of increasingly senior and irritated officers appeared and appealed to my sense of duty and patriotism; but I stuck to my guns (no pun intended) and each of them went away shaking his head in baffled disgust. I had no idea what might happen, but so far, so good. At least I hadn't been clapped in irons, or shot. Finally two large medical orderlies arrived and deprived me of my tie, belt and shoelaces. They took me to Cambridge Hospital, where I ended up in the 'psycho/neurotic ward'. Later I was transferred to the Royal Military Hospital at Netley, on Southampton Water, where I was stripped and body-searched and locked in a padded cell. After a month had passed, I was finally directed to take the pentothal test.

Pentothal was known as the 'truth drug' and the theory was that, while rendered unconscious by its effects, you would answer any and all questions without being able to lie or prevaricate. I was a bit worried I'd give myself away as a completely rational bloke trying to work his ticket, but perhaps I was nuttier than I thought. A couple of days later I was summoned before a board of senior medical and regimental officers and told that the board had decided I was a hopeless case and of no further use to the army. I was to be discharged on medical grounds as, 'PN [psycho-logically neurotic] Grade 5'. I suppose I must have shown my relief and gratification at this decision because the senior board member pulled me up smartly with these words:

It's nothing to be pleased about, Gregson, it's a very serious matter. PN Grade 5 will be on your record for the rest of your life. You realise there are a number of professions you will be unable to pursue. For example, you will never be able to be a policeman.

I adopted a suitably sober expression and, after a final admonition to try to get my act together and grow up, I was sent back to Mons Barracks to sign off my military career, collect the rest of my personal belongings and then get lost.

It was a pretty muted return of the prodigal. My mother behaved as if I'd just recovered from some socially unacceptable disease, like rickets or a hernia operation, and refused to let my reappearance disturb the even tenor of her life. She never asked me what had happened or why it had happened. She never referred to it at all. Roland went along with her, although he did offer assistance if and when I decided what I was going to do next.

I got a job in nearby Dunmow, loading and unloading railway wagons and lorries. It was hard and boring work humping sacks of grain all day, but it suited my mood at the time and did me good. I stayed there for about three months, but by Christmas I'd had enough and decided to have another crack at show business. I think I believed that a renewal of my actor's status might win Wendy back, but I was wrong.

I tracked her down through her South Kensington flatmates and met her in London one Saturday night. She had moved on from Maxwell Reed and was living in Soho with a film director called Michael Luke. Anyway, she wasn't interested in me and, when I pressed my suit overvigorously in the Mandrake Club, she stuck a fork into my hand. I would see her on and off over the next few years as she established her position as one of the icons of the Soho arty set, but we never got together again.

FIVE

High time

I came to realise that if I was to succeed in the acting business I had to do something about my accent. Back then one had to speak with the right sort of BBC tones, and mine were anything but that. It would be another ten years or so before the regional accents of *Saturday Night and Sunday Morning* or *Alfie* and *Billy Liar* became fashionable, allowing leading men a bit of latitude. Even Michael Caine spoke 'proper' the first time I saw him on the stage in the West End in 1951. Only comics and character actors were allowed to sound like real people.

Somehow or other I managed to get a place at the Central School of Speech and Drama, which was housed at that time in the Albert Hall. So, in January 1951, I reported there and was enrolled. I'd missed the first term of the academic year, but it didn't seem to matter. I was introduced to the mysteries of 'rib reserve' (a way of controlling the diaphragm, so that you don't run out of breath in the middle of a long speech), enunciation, breathing, mime, movement and, occasionally, if I was very lucky, allowed to do a bit of acting. The Royal Academy of Dramatic Art was the number one *drama* school in the world, or so it thought, but Central fancied itself pretty strongly too. The school prided itself on its speech training. Cicely Berry, who was there in my time, is still at it and occasionally gives classes in Sydney. Some of my fellow students went on to have successful careers as actors—Kenneth Haigh (the original Jimmy Porter in *Look Back in Anger*), Barry Foster (alas, now departed) and a few others. But the real star to emerge from that year made his name as a writer, a name that has been absorbed into the language like 'Dickensian' or 'Byronic' or 'Shavian'. His name was, and is, Harold Pinter and Pinteresque has become a term describing his particular and fascinating writing characteristics.

In those days his writing was a bit too deep for me. I remember a poem of his, in which he used the phrase, 'the sea is boxes of fishes'; I told him that, speaking as an ex-sailor, the sea was no such thing. We rubbed along together well enough, and he and Barry and Kenneth and I formed a bit of a gang for the brief time I was there.

I began working as a film extra, which paid two guineas a day plus a free lunch. It was a pretty attractive deal as I was nearly always broke and hungry. I also had the naive hope that, as I stood there with the other thirty or forty 'peasants' or 'soldiers' or 'passersby', my innate talent and looks would so impress a director that I'd be hailed from the crowd and given a starring role. Needless to say, this didn't happen but at least I was paid and fed and learned a little about how films got made.

My problem was that no professional work was allowed to be undertaken by students at the Central without permission of the staff. There was no way they were going to allow me to miss 'voice and movement' in order to ponce around as a wounded soldier in Anna Neagle's triumphant movie, *Florence Nightingale*. Finally push came to shove and I was told that if I persisted in missing classes for whatever reason, I would have to leave. No contest—I'd come to realise that most of what went on in drama school was a wank. Acting was easy—a child could do it, and frequently did. There were a few tricks of the trade one needed to pick up, but I'd already learnt them in a matter of weeks, as well as how to speak with a passable accent. So I agreed to stop my extra activities for the rest of the term and leave when the Easter holidays began.

In between dodging voice classes and working as a film extra I had contrived some vague sort of social life. Somewhere along the line—I don't remember how—I met an Australian actor called Claude Watson. Claude was in his early thirties, camp as a row of tents and a truly lovely chap. He was working with a repertory company in Reading near Oxford and asked me if I'd like a job there as a juvenile lead. I didn't need a second invitation so, as soon as the Easter holidays arrived and I had checked out of the Central School, I caught the train to Reading and joined the Pendragon Players.

It was a professional company, but only just. I was to be paid five pounds a week and members of the Company did everything, including setting up the seats in the auditorium, which was the Pendragon school hall by day and our theatre by night. The Company was led by a true eccentric called Kevin Barry (his real name was Barry Laffan, but Kevin Barry, the Irish Patriot, had a more romantic ring to it he thought). Kevin directed most of the productions and played leads when he felt like it. Claude was the official leading man and hated it when Kevin usurped a role which he felt should rightfully go to him. The leading lady was Mary Yeomans, a beautiful blonde. Bob was the character man and he also painted the scenery. There was a juvenile girl whose name I can't remember and a part-time stage carpenter, who was a middle-aged man with a broad Berkshire accent.

I arrived in Reading on a Sunday afternoon and found that Claude had kindly arranged digs for me in the house where he was staying. In fact they were in the same *room* where he was staying, he told me with a twinkle in his eye. I told him to lose the twinkle as I wasn't that sort of 'girl' and, to give him credit, in the six months that we shared this accommodation we never had a cross word or an awkward moment. He wasn't a very good actor and had a bit of an Australian accent, which was a drawback then, but he had an encyclopaedic knowledge of, and an abiding love for, all forms of the entertainment business. He stopped being an actor in the late fifties and became an assistant film director. In 1958 I had the pleasure of working with him on a film called *The Silent Enemy*, which was shot mainly in Gibraltar.

My first production with the Pendragon Players, in the summer of 1951, was *Pygmalion*, in which Claude was to play Colonel Pickering, Kevin was Higgins, Mary was Eliza, Bob was Doolittle, Keith Campbell, an Australian friend of Claude's, was several other characters and the girl whose name I can't remember was several other female characters. I was to play Freddy Eynsford Hill, the soppiest of soppy juves. On the Friday after one week of rehearsals, Kevin was forced to go into hospital for an operation on his piles, which had exploded. It was decided that I should give up the part of Freddy to the stage carpenter (middle-aged man with Berkshire accent) and take over the role of Henry Higgins. The argument in favour of this arrangement was that Freddy was the smallest part and not all that important, and that it would cause the least disruption all round if I took over Higgins. It didn't seem to matter that I was at least fifteen years too young for the role and would only have a maximum of two and a half days to learn and rehearse one of the most famous and technically demanding parts in the English theatrical canon.

Instead of being terrified and reluctant, as I would be now because I understood the enormous task I was undertaking, I was absolutely thrilled. I learned the part in a few hours. On the Monday night, my face covered in lake liner and with touches of grey at my temples, I sailed through *Pygmalion* from 'There! There! There! There! Who's hurting you, you silly girl?' all the way to 'Pickering! Nonsense: She's going to marry Freddy. Ha ha! Freddy! Freddy!! Ha ha ha ha ha!!!!!' Curtain and ringing applause. What the performance was like I have no idea—terrible, probably—but the achievement was considerable on my part and my position in the company was secure for the rest of the season. What the audience made of a forty-five-year-old balding 'Freddy' bashfully muttering his lines with a Berkshire burr is probably better left unknown.

All in all I had a wonderful time with the Players. I played Stanley Kowalski in *A Streetcar Named Desire*, Charley in

Charley's Aunt, various suspects in various Agatha Christie plays, and Jack Favell in Daphne Du Maurier's old warhorse *Rebecca*. This last production sticks in my mind because Claude, who was playing Maxim de Winter, knocked me out and broke one of my front teeth. In the course of the action of the play Maxim and Jack have a confrontation, which culminates in Maxim's punching the caddish Jack, who then 'exits stage left vowing vengeance' or something like that. We had rehearsed the punch, and all should have been well, but on the opening night, assailed by nerves and with sweat pouring out of every orifice, Claude lost the plot. I could see it coming, however, there was nothing I could do about it except stand there and wait for him to hit me, which he duly did. I couldn't have been 'out' for more than a second or two and I woke up to the taste of blood in my mouth and the sight of a repentant Claude trying to get me to my feet. I managed to shuffle off stage left, lisping rather than vowing vengeance, and the performance continued. Poor Claude was deeply upset and guilt-stricken and probably realised then that a career as an assistant film director was a better option for him than one as a leading man.

So began a period of my life that followed a fairly predictable routine. Seasons of weekly rep were interspersed with a few weeks in London attending general auditions for The Old Vic, or HM Tennant, or Henry Sherek, or anyone else who was casting. I had no agent but, like most of my peers I bought a copy of *The Stage* each week to check the 'situations vacant' ads on the back page.

'Character Juvenile required Bexhill-on-Sea summer season. Must have good wardrobe and be prepared to ASM' Nah, no more ay-ess-emming for me.

'Fit up tour in Ireland for Anew McMaster, play as cast.' (Anew McMaster was a very tatty touring manager doing one- or two-night stands of Shakespearean plays all over southern Ireland, and 'play as cast' meant that you could be called upon to play any and every part in the production.) This was not an attractive proposition for an ambitious young 'juvenile' like me so no, thank you. Although, in a way, I wish I had given it a go—Harold

Pinter (under his acting name of David Barron) and Barry Foster did a season with the great McMaster and apparently had a wonderful time. But it wasn't for me, and nor was anything else in *The Stage* at the time, so each week I'd go off to Denton and Warner's theatrical agency in Cambridge Circus to see what the dreaded old Miriam Warner and Smithy, with his trademark fag in mouth, might have to offer. Well, not much—the Robert Marshall Players, twice nightly, of course. What the hell, the money was okay—eight quid a week, which was better than most, and St Helens sounded okay. I needed a job, any job, so I got my rail ticket and set off.

In my ignorance I'd thought that St Helens was on the Isle of Wight and was pretty discouraged to discover it was actually halfway between Manchester and Liverpool. When I got off the train it was like stepping back in time. Clinkers were falling out of the sky, which was battleship grey with greenish streaks, and there was a reek of chemicals unlike anything I'd smelled since the oil refinery in Maracaibo, Venezuela. St Helens was the home town of Sir Thomas Beecham, whose family business produced, amongst other things, Beecham's Pills. St Helens was also a glass-producing centre, which accounted for the smell and the cinder-filled atmosphere. The redbrick buildings were black with grime and the few people on the streets were straight out of a Lowry painting.

The theatre was vast and I suppose had once been imposing. It was one of the many Theatre Royals in England and had been one of the last theatres Sir Henry Irving played on one of his many farewell tours—or so I was proudly informed by the manager as he showed me around its crumbling grandeur. Performances were at 6.15 p.m. and another at 8.30 so the plays were short, or severely cut. The theatre seated fifteen hundred in stalls, dress circle, upper circle and gallery. At the early performance we might have a hundred people huddled in the vast darkness but the second show was usually respectable, especially if we were doing a North Country play such as *Hindle Wakes, A Cure For Love, Up in Mabel's Room* or some weird concoction called *A Yank in Lancashire*. This had been specially written for the Northern circuit and referred to the vast American airbase at Burtonwood, just up the road from St Helens. I played the Yank, and that's all that can be said about it.

Life for me consisted of rehearsals, performances, learning lines, eating, drinking and sleeping, so there was no time to worry about the smell or the clinkers or anything else. After a few weeks I was transferred from St Helens to Robert Marshall's number one company at the Royal Court Theatre in Warrington. This was a step in the right direction—a newer, smaller theatre in a much more prosperous town between St Helens and Manchester and, best of all, digs with an indoor loo. No more chamber pots or midnight treks to the two-holer in the backyard. This was living!

Bob Marshall and his wife and leading lady, another Wendy, ran a very successful operation. The Royal Court seated seven hundred. At an average ticket price of five shillings, takings would be a hundred and eighty pounds a show. With twelve shows a week, even though we weren't playing to capacity, there could be a weekly take of well over a thousand pounds. After the theatre split, cast wages (eight of us at eight pounds each) and royalties to the playwright were paid, I calculated Bob and Wendy were making about two or three hundred pounds a week. This was at a time when the average working man was earning less than fifteen. Not bad.

Carmen Silvera, who went on and on and on as a very successful actress (she was the dreadful bar owner in *'Allo 'Allo!* on television), was in the company and became a very good friend of mine. So good in fact, I was named as a co-respondent in her divorce from her first and, as far as I know, only husband, a Mr Cunliffe. A few years later we bought a house together in Baron's Court in London—a purely business arrangement by then—and she lived there for more than fifty years until she died in 2003 at the age of eighty-two. Five decades in the same house must be something of a record in these peripatetic days. We kept in touch all those years, and she was kind enough to appear on the *This Is Your Life* episode that British Television did on me in 1995.

The season wore on. I played the usual parts, in the usual plays—a few Agatha Christies, *Rebecca* again—and some weird ones such as *Dracula,* in which I unsuitably played Professor Van Helsing, and *Uncle Tom's Cabin,* in which, even more unsuitably, I played Uncle Tom. In the latter, the curtain rose to the sound of Paul Robeson singing *Water Boy* while Topsy escaped from Simon Legree in a mime skit before I entered. My face and hands were black, my hair was covered by a grizzled woolly wig and, doing my best to sound like Paul Robeson, I sang *My Old Kentucky Home* in my deepest baritone. I don't think anyone was fooled by my get-up or singing ability.

There was a fair bit of singing in this particular production. We used the local choir, all properly blacked up à la black and white minstrels, but sadly they were unable to lose their local accents. I did refuse to blacken my feet and play it barefoot because there was no bath in my digs. Foot washing to that extent was a real problem. So I wore black socks and sandals and left the rest to my acting abilities. These were tested to the extreme during my death scene, as I choked out my final speech, 'Don't you call me poor Tom . . . I'se half way through the gates going into glory . . .' while the choir sang in their broadest Lancashire accents, 'Swinggg loow, sweet chah-rye-oh-ohtt . . . coominggg for to carry me 'ome'. I passed away as peacefully as I could, stifling my sniggers and grateful when the chariot swung low for the last time and they segued into 'Goinggg 'ome, goingg 'ome, Ah'm a goinnggg 'ome'.

The audiences loved it though and were wonderfully loyal. It was before anyone had television and the local rep was an integral part of the social scene, like the public baths and the library. The same people came every week, sat in the same seats and tended to take a proprietorial interest in members of the Company. They loved to see you do something different and Uncle Tom was certainly that. In a play called *Jupiter Laughs*, an adaptation of an AJ Cronin novel, my character gave up the woman he loved and went off to become a missionary in China carrying his worldly possessions in a small suitcase. It was the climax to the third and final act and my exit usually got a round of applause, which the actress whom I was leaving in tears gratefully shared. On one occasion, as I made my heroic, selfless farewell, a lady in the stalls remarked to her friend: 'Eee, poor lad, not tekkin mooch to China is he?' It slightly broke the mood and I was extremely annoyed until I realised that it was a great compliment. The lady was so carried away by my performance that she couldn't distinguish fact from fiction. Well, that's my story and I'm sticking to it.

When we had to finish in December, to make way for the seasonal pantomime and variety shows, Mr Marshall took some of us to the Eden Theatre in Bishop Auckland for a six-week rep season of (oh joy, oh rapture!) only *one* nightly performance. I'd got so brainwashed with work in Warrington and the unremitting routine that in our last week there, with no new play to learn and rehearse, I found I'd learned the first page of a detective story I was reading in bed before I realised what I was doing. Bishop Auckland really was the back of beyond and I was glad to return to London afterwards for a few weeks or more, at least while my savings lasted.

In London I had a place to live, courtesy of the gay network, in a huge house in one of the squares behind Harrods. The room belonged to a man called Duncan Melvin, who was a ballet photographer of some fame. Through him I met a number of ballet dancers, including the great Svetlana Beriosova, whom I worshipped from afar. I did have an affair with one of the ballerinas from the Royal Ballet, but it was an humiliating experience. Once she was out of her leotard and tutu and into my bed she was as thin and sinewy as a mooring rope, and quite a lot stronger than me. I did my best, but I'm pretty sure it wasn't good enough. We didn't pursue the relationship.

The owner of the house was a famously eccentric heiress called Jean Baird. She was in her fifties and she lived with her girlfriend, who was equally famous for her eccentricity and other qualities. Her name was Brenda Dean Paul and she had apparently been one of the great swingers of the twenties and thirties. According to Duncan she'd had affairs with everyone from Greta Garbo to Adolf Hitler and had finally settled on old Jean, who had enough money to keep her housed and supplied with gin and heroin. I never saw her without the fullest of full makeup, a blonde wig and sunglasses. She loathed daylight and would scurry away from a sunbeam like Dracula's mother. She littered the kitchen and bathroom, which we all shared, with her syringes and would peer blearily at me over a gin while I made my morning coffee and toast. You couldn't say life wasn't interesting.

I went to quite a few auditions. One was for a replacement in the chorus of *South Pacific*. I tried to sing *Younger than Springtime*, cracked on all the high notes and didn't get the job. Another was for a play called *Stalag 22,* which was an American import that was later made into a film starring William Holden. There were about a dozen parts up for grabs as the action took place in the barrack room of the eponymous stalag, in which a group of American prisoners of war were held captive. A sort of early version of *Hogan's Heroes*. The part I tried out for was a very minor one, just making up the numbers really, but it would have been my West End debut and I was very keen to do it. I read my bits three times and was told that I'd got the part and should turn up for rehearsal the following day. I was even given a script. The next day, when we all sat down to read through the play, I became aware that something was wrong. Two of us were reading Gus, or Jake, or whoever it was. During the lunchbreak I was told that a mistake had been made. The other bastard had the part and, 'sorry I'd been bothered'.

I also auditioned for the Old Vic. This was a long and laborious business as it started off as a general cattle call with perhaps two hundred hopefuls trying out for eight positions as walk-ons and understudies. A week went by and I was told to come back with two different pieces of Shakespeare to do a second audition. Things were looking up—the hopefuls had now been culled to about fifty—so I went through my paces again. Ten days later another call, two more new pieces to learn and, hopefully, third time lucky. The fifteen of us who turned up for the

third time were old enemies by now and eyed each other bale-
fully as we waited in the wings for our moment of death or glory.
At least seven of us would be told 'Thanks, but no thanks'. I
was determined I wasn't going to be one of them. I did my best—
Romeo's final speech (I wonder how many times my judges had
sat through that one) and, as a contrast to show off my versa-
tility, a couple of the Clown's speeches from *Measure for Measure*
Act 2. I based this character on the Freddy-playing Berkshire
carpenter from my Pendragon days—a lot of *arrrh, arrrh* and
dropped consonants—and felt I'd done really well. They thanked
me kindly and I went home to await my fate.

I'd been hanging about for over a month while all this was
going on and funds were running very low. Finally I got the call
and was offered the job. Walk on and understudy, Equity
minimum: six pounds ten shillings a week. I was shocked and
enraged—I'd been getting eight pounds a week from Bob Marshall
and couldn't possibly work for less. I couldn't afford to work
for less and live in *London*, it was out of the question. Couldn't
they pay a bit more? The short answer was no they couldn't. If
I didn't like it, I should stop wasting their time. I didn't like it.
I really regret never working at the Old Vic, but that's the way
it was.

I hung about in the Salisbury pub in St Martin's Lane, where
jobs were sometimes to be found, and landed a couple of 'special
weeks' with the Harry Hanson Players in Tonbridge Wells. I played
Jack Favell in *Rebecca* yet again, and one of the murderers in
Rope. Harry Hanson ran a number of companies in the south
of England. He was a slightly less tatty equivalent of Frank
Fortescue, who ran companies in the North. Harry was a funny
little chap whose mood could be judged by the colour of the
toupee he was wearing. If it was the blonde one, he was in a
good mood and all would be fun and frolic; but if it was the
dark one or, God forbid, the grey one, look out.

In between these random engagements I eked out a precar-
ious existence sponging (if that's the right word) off homosexual
admirers. The London theatre scene was predominantly gay in

those days. You didn't actually have to be gay to get work in the West End, but it certainly didn't do your chances any harm if you were. The film business wasn't quite as blatant in its predilections as the theatre, but I did have the hard word put on me by one director, who told me that if I was really serious about my career, there was nothing I wouldn't do to get on. I looked at his pendulous gut and double chins and decided I wasn't *that* serious.

The gay men I knew, most of whom were business or professional men, weren't interested in me physically. They all seemed to like 'rough trade' and they would go to a pub called the Bag of Nails near Buckingham Palace to pick up guardsmen, or cruise the public lavatories and other venues when they wanted sex, which they were happy to pay for. What they wanted with me and with other young men like my brother, as he later told me, was to be seen out and about with good-looking young things so they could impress and irritate their friends. Looking back on it now, I can see that my behaviour was pretty unforgivable, but at the time it seemed perfectly okay. I never had to do anything I didn't want to do; they knew I was completely heterosexual and left it at that. I wonder why, but I still do feel a bit guilty.

In the early spring of 1952 I lobbed up at Cleethorpes on the Lincolnshire coast just south of Grimsby—a pretty desolate location out of season. Its Empire Theatre was situated on the pier, which shifted slightly and groaned when high tide surged round its pilings. Harold G Roberts ran the company there. He had a fearsome reputation, which was well deserved. He was in his fifties, was stocky and purple-nosed, and had a filthy temper. His wife, a faded-blonde lady in her late forties, was his leading lady, in spite of the fact that she wasn't very good. She was frequently miscast and was obliged to play parts she was fifteen or twenty years too old for. Still that was par for the course in those days. I remember seeing the great Sir Donald Wolfit just about get away with a middle-aged Hamlet, while his wife, the not-so-great Rosalind Iden, was painfully miscast as a middle-aged Ophelia. The third member of the Roberts family was the son, Carl. He was in his twenties, tall, dark and ugly, with a vocal impediment caused by an only partially corrected cleft palate. The Roberts family trio played all the leading parts and the rest of the Company made up the numbers. Harold G also directed the productions and his directorial technique was brutal and obscene.

After a less than scintillating first performance of a dreary farce called *Worm's Eye View,* he assembled the Company on the Tuesday morning and delivered his verdict.

'Good Christ on a bicycle, you were terrible, fucking terrible. Might I remind you that *Worm's Eye View* is supposed to be funny, and you lot were about as funny as a rubber crutch. It's a comedy, for fuck's sake—a comedy, not Opeedius fucking Rex.'

'Opeedius fucking Rex!' I tried to stifle a snigger but Harold G turned on me like a maddened bull.

'Nothing to laugh at, you hopeless cunt—you were the worst of the lot. You're sacked! You get your fucking cards at the end of the week.' He turned away, then turned back resignedly: 'No, forget that. I fucking need you for the next fucking production.' You had to be tough—and not just because of the language.

And so it went.

There was an Australian girl in the company called Shirley Cameron and we had a brief liaison until a minor film star called Derek Bond turned up to do a 'Special Week' of a play called *Who Goes There.* The Special Week was a phenomenon of the time. An actor or actress with a bit of a name would tour the provinces in a certain role, usually the lead they'd had in a recent West End success, and the local rep company would mount a production around his or her performance. Derek was charming and generous and a good actor, and, alas for me, his glamour outweighed mine and Shirley shifted her affections to him. I didn't blame her, we were all ships just passing in the night.

Special Weeks could be a bit disconcerting sometimes, as one never quite knew what the visiting star might have in mind. When I was at the Theatre Royal in Chatham some time later we did a production of a farce called *Ten to One.* It was a horseracing story and the lead character was a bookie who, for some reason, was on the run from some kind of racecourse gang. The bookie was played in our case by a well-known and popular comic called Lupino Lane. He'd filled the Victoria Palace during the war years and after with his production of *Me and My Gal*, which included the hit number, *Doing the Lambeth Walk, Oi!* I can't imagine why he wanted to do a week in Chatham with *Ten to One*, but do it he did, in his own individual way.

Mr Lane attended the read-through, but he couldn't get to the rehearsals later in the week. As it happened we didn't see him again until the dress rehearsal. He arrived with his own costume and a suitcase full of props and gadgets. We shot through the dress rehearsal, not bothering to do his scenes, which he said didn't need rehearsing, and waited with some anxiety to see what would happen when the curtain rose on our first performance.

Mr Lane did his comedy business—juggling, funny hats, conjuring tricks, a little tap dancing, topical gags and a song or two—while the rest of us stood about waiting for him to finish each particular turn. When he did finish, one of us would speak the next line and the play would lurch forward to the next opportunity for Mr Lane to demonstrate his skills. The audience loved it but it was a nerve-racking for us. We had to judge the right moment to speak the next line and get on with the play. Mr Lane didn't like having his moments cut short and was quite likely to ignore his cue the first time it was offered while he produced yet another bouquet of flowers from his sleeve and then look at you as if you'd farted in church. It was quite an education.

●

When I got back to London, I managed to get a real agent for the first time—Jimmy Fraser of Fraser and Dunlop. Jimmy was a wonderfully funny Scottish 'queen' who became one of the industry's major players. When I first met him, he was fairly low level (or else, I suppose, he wouldn't have taken me on). He got me little bits of film work. A day here and a day there—for example, as a focus puller on a David Niven film called *The Love*

Lottery, which was shot at Ealing Studios. This involved measuring the distance between David's nose and the lens and saying to him, 'Can I have the clinch position please, Mr Allerton' (David was playing a film star called Allerton, about to kiss Peggy Cummins). After this I would retreat to my position next to the camera. I managed it okay, but I was so green that, when I was told to look through the viewfinder, I looked through the wrong end. Jimmy also got me a role as a young naval officer in a film called *The Malta Story*, with a line or two up on the bridge with Jack Hawkins. It was after this performance that the aforementioned director put the hard word on me. I was also a survivor in *The Cruel Sea*, floundering in the freezing tank at Ealing studios, trying to look as if I was drowning with the water not much more than knee deep.

These jobs didn't pay very much, five or six pounds a day, but it was better than nothing. I'd moved in with a girl who lived in Maida Vale. She illustrated books and magazines for a living and was very talented, but so neurotic she found it almost impossible to finish a drawing and deliver it on time. She was terribly in love with the painter John Minton, who had been one of her art teachers. Sadly for her, he was homosexual. She didn't like me very much and I didn't like her very much either, but we were both a bit lonely at the time and I helped to pay her rent. Our affair turned out to be quite disasterous. We went to Paris together, my first time ever, and when we returned she told me she was pregnant. I agreed to pay for the abortion as it was my responsibility to do so, but nonetheless I felt pretty miffed as I'd assumed she was looking after that side of things. After she'd had the operation, she blamed me for depriving her of the baby she'd never had. It was all a bit ugly so we went our separate ways. Looking back on it, it wasn't one of my finest hours.

In amongst all this turmoil I had the misfortune to appear in a production of *A Tale of Two Cities* as Charles Darnay. The man playing Sydney Carton looked nothing like me and this rather spoilt the illusion of his saving my life by taking my place in the Bastille and finally at the guillotine ('Tis a far, far better thing I do' etc.) without anyone noticing the difference. It was during this production that one of the more embarrassing moments of my brief career up to this point occurred. I was slumped in my prison cell in the Bastille awaiting the chop. The 'cell' was made from two canvas flats, hinged in the middle to open up like a book, and painted to look like stonework. On this occasion they had been set too far down stage so when the curtain rose at the start of Act 3 to reveal me in my misery, it struck the top of the flats, all eighteen-foot of them, and they fell forward enclosing me in a sort of canvas tent. As I was slumped over a small desk, pretending to be asleep, I couldn't figure out what was happening. Eventually I emerged from this 'tent' and, not knowing what else to do, managed to re-erect the flats, which rocked slightly but remained upright. This got a small round of applause from the audience and, again not knowing what to do, I resumed my position at the desk. This got a few titters but nothing like the huge laugh which greeted Sydney Carton's first line, when he entered to chloroform me and take my place. With the utter inevitability of Sod's Law, his line referred to the absolute impregnability of my cell and the Bastille in general, and how impossible it would be to escape from it. The audience roared with laughter as the canvas flats gently swayed in the glow of the footlights and my shoulders shook with suppressed hysteria while manfully trying to remind myself that 'the show must go on'. I tried to explain to the Sydney Carton actor that it hadn't been my fault and I hadn't known what else to do, but he never forgave me and only ever spoke to me afterwards in the line of duty.

•

Finally I got a real break. I was hired for a season at the Theatre Royal in York. This was run by Geoffrey Staines and it had a very good reputation. Even better, it was *fortnightly* rep. The luxury— a fortnight to rehearse and a fortnight of performances—it was like coming into money. The fortnightly turnaround was achieved by having two separate companies in two different venues, the Theatre Royal in York and the Opera House in Scarborough, forty miles away on the Yorkshire coast. One of the companies would open and play a week in York while the other one was in Scarborough, and then we'd swap over and play the second week of the production in the other theatre followed by the first week of the next production. It meant having to shift our digs every two weeks but we'd swap with the other actors and it all worked out very well.

York was, and still is, a beautiful city and I thoroughly enjoyed the nine months I was there. I discovered for the first time that a stage performance could be more than just a feat of memory and audibility. In weekly rep there wasn't and couldn't be time to create a real performance until it was time to finish, but with two weeks' rehearsal and then sixteen performances it *was* possible to make a character your own creation, and not just something copied from a French's Acting Edition.

The Company was a very pleasant bunch and I got on well with them. Lester Barrett, the character lead, was in his sixties and he had enjoyed a successful career as an actor without ever playing London or Stratford, or anywhere south of The Wash. He was a legend in the north and could play any of the usual repertory roles without having to think. They were filed away in his brain and emerged intact whenever called upon. He drank a great deal of beer and his hygiene was questionable, but it was good fun to watch him work and I learnt a lot from doing so.

While I was there there was a sixteen-year-old art student who came in to help the designer paint sets or whatever else needed doing. Her family came from York—they were Quakers—and her elder brother Geoffrey was in the other Company. She was, and still is, Judi Dench—Dame Judi now—and she became a very good friend of mine. I didn't work with her at York, I don't think she'd started her acting career the season I was there; but ten years later we worked together at the Nottingham Playhouse in its heyday under John Neville. We had a great deal of fun together, both on and off stage. The last time we met was in 2001 in New York, where she was starring in *Amy's View*. We had lunch together and laughed a lot, had a lovely nostalgic wallow, and went our separate ways. Such is the life of a jobbing actor—forever saying goodbye and then (with luck) saying hello again.

Someone else who became a good friend was an Australian actor from Sydney called Ronny Fraser. He was tall and lean with a comical expression and was genuinely funny in the campest of camp ways. He had managed to crack the Binky Beaumont/HM Tennant circle in London's West End, more through his personality than his ability, and had been hired to understudy the great Bernard Lee in a play called *Seagulls Over Sorrento*. Binky, whose real name was Hugh, ran the HM Tennant organisation, which at that time was the most powerful and influential theatrical management in the West End. He was an immensely elegant man, devotedly homosexual, ruthless and charming, and he could make or break an actor's career. When I came to Australia in 1971, one of the first people I met in Sydney was Ronny. He'd returned to his home base and carved out a fairly successful career in cabaret. A couple of years later my wife Sue worked with him in one of the last revues at the old Chevron Hotel in Kings Cross. He was good fun and great company. He sadly died in his late forties from a heart attack.

While I was at York I got a new agent. A variety agency called Lew and Leslie Grade (later to become the Grade Organisation— masters of all they surveyed in British television) decided to start a branch of their agency handling straight actors rather than variety performers. A man called Monty Lyon was put in charge of this department. He was a lovely chap, middle-aged with a huge nose and a pipe everlastingly clamped between his teeth. He had been on a reconnaissance of provincial theatres looking for potential talent and had seen me in York in a play called *Ring Round the Moon*. I had a very showy part playing identical twins, a part in which Paul Schofield had had a huge success within London. It was a Christopher Fry translation of a Jean Anhouilh play. He asked me to come and see him in London when the season finished, with a view to signing an exclusive agency agreement. I knew Jimmy Fraser wouldn't mind if I moved—I had no exclusive deal with him—and I was flattered and touched by Monty's interest. He was very bullish about my chances of success, especially in the film world, so I told Jimmy I was off. He wished me luck, and that was that. I stayed with Monty for eighteen years, until he was approaching eighty and starting to lose the plot.

In the winter of 1953/54 Monty and the agency were very up-and-coming. I was introduced to the great Lew Grade, later Lord Grade, who stared at me for a moment, removed his cigar from his mouth briefly and remarked elliptically, 'You're not as big as you look'. I looked at Monty for enlightenment but he hurried me out and introduced me to Lew's younger brother, Leslie. He was less elliptical and pleasant enough. He wished me well and sent me on my way to meet the third brother, Bernard Delfont.

Monty was as good as his word about the film business. He got me a leading part in a B movie called *The Embezzler*, which still comes back to haunt me on late late late-night television a couple of times a year. It was made by a company called Tempean, which offered me a contract at £750 a year but, on Monty's advice, I knocked it back in the hope of something better. Another film I did was *Svengali*, which was an adaptation of the Daphne Du Maurier novel, *Trilby*. I had a small part as one of the friends of Terence Morgan (the hero) and I spent a few larky days down at the old studios at Walton-on-Thames. The great and eccentric Robert Newton was playing Svengali but, after the first few days of his being incapable due to drinking at lunchtime, he was replaced by Donald Wolfit. The scenes which I'd already shot with Newton had to be re-shot but, alas, I was unavailable for the re-shoot so my appearances in the film are few and far between.

I also did some small films for television. I remember one in which I played a young French resistance fighter in a piece called *A Summer In Normandy*, and another called *A Call on the Widow*, which was a sort of thriller. The widow was played by Jean Kent, who was on the wane after a successful career as a film star. She didn't like slumming it in television at all and was very grand and one scary lady.

This new idea of doing television plays on film made the actor's task a lot easier. In the earlier days all television drama was done live and, in the case of the BBC Play of the Week, it was done live twice—once on the Sunday evening, and then again on Thursday evening. In a play called *George and the Dragon*, which I did in 1951, we had a completely different camera crew for the Thursday night performance, so the usual glitches of cameras or microphones in shot were even more in evidence. The audiences never seemed to mind when an actor was briefly obliterated by a passing camera or had some strange cylindrical object dangling in front of his face. The directors did mind, but they were a hardy lot and able to cope with anything. One friend of mine was in a live production when one of the leading actors died on screen while the play was being transmitted. The action took place in a coalmine and dealt with a group of miners who had been trapped by some disaster, so there was no way of cutting away to something else. The cast didn't know the poor chap had died—as far as they knew he had simply passed out—so they struggled on as best they could, speaking his lines where and when necessary. The director, Ted Kotcheff, who became an international film director and now lives and works in Hollywood, was told that the man was dead when they stopped transmitting for the 'interval', which was part of television production in those days. He decided it would be better not to tell the cast about this until the show was over. So the technical staff removed the body and the play went on with Ted improvising his shots and the cast sharing the corpse's dialogue.

It was about this time I got a big break. I went to the Oxford Playhouse to do a play called, *Man About the House*. The Oxford Playhouse was run by a young man called Peter Hall, recently down from Cambridge. He'd made a bit of a name in London by doing shows at the Arts Theatre and was making more of a name at Oxford. The Company was made up of some very fine actors, including the young, wonderfully skilful Ronnie

Barker, an Australian actor called Trader Faulkner, who subsequently gave up acting and became a virtuoso flamenco dancer, and an eighteen-year-old student ASM called Maggie Smith—Dame Maggie now. I had a very showy part as an Italian sort of gigolo—curly hair and lots of brown skin—who marries a rich English lady for her money, then gets up to all kinds of naughtiness with a young and sexy village girl. It was adapted from a book of the same name but it wasn't much of a play to be honest. However in 1954, the Rank Organisation was trying to invent itself as a sort of Hollywood in the home counties.

Rank decided one of the ways to do this was to sign up a 'stable' of male and female actors. The theory was that one or two of them might turn out to be box office successes, capable of turning Pinewood Studios into a rival to MGM or Twentieth Century Fox or Warner Brothers. A lady called Olive Dodds was sent out into the country to find potential stars and she saw me at the Oxford Playhouse and I was offered a seven-year contract. The money wasn't great—£20 a week for the first year, £30 a week for the second year and then the big jump to £80 a week in the third year, and up and up after that.

There was, of course, an option clause on their side, which allowed them to fire you at the end of any year, but with the misplaced confidence of youth I didn't think that would happen to me. It didn't as a matter of fact but it might have done, and it certainly happened to most of my colleagues. In September that year I signed my contract with Rank. There were forty-three men and women under contract. They varied from the well-known such as Peter Finch, Jack Hawkins, Dirk Bogarde and Anthony Steel to unknowns such as Patrick McGoohan and me, and a slew of pretty blonde girls—June Laverick, Belinda Lee and Diana Dors among them. When my contract finished in 1961 there were only two of us left still contracted to Rank—Dirk Bogarde, who had a very different kind of deal to mine, and me.

Rank never became a major production house in the international film business. Pinewood never became a real rival to MGM or Fox Studios. I never became a box office star. Still we weren't to know that then and a guarantee of £20 a week for a whole year was too good to miss.

In between all this, I managed to have quite a jolly personal life. I played a lot of poker with a group of actors who were working in London shows or hoping to. One of them was Leslie Phillips, who I later worked with in films and nominally shared a greyhound at Wembley Stadium. Another was Bobby Desmond, who got out of acting and into property and mini-cabs. Carmen Silvera from my Warrington days was another player, as was a young South African actor who spent a lot of his spare time at the greyhound tracks and could tell you the form of every dog running in London. He had a lot of spare time then, but things changed for the better after we lost touch because Nigel Hawthorne ended up being knighted and winning all kinds of awards.

At one of these poker sessions Bobby Desmond, who was host, had a girlfriend helping out with tea and sandwiches. I didn't pay much attention at the time—after all she was Bobby's girl—but later on they broke up and she and I got together. Her name was Babette Collier—Babs—and in time she was to become my wife.

SIX

Screen time

My personal and private life now became a lot more settled. When I turned twenty-five I inherited the £5000 Granny Winter had left in trust for me. I used half of it to buy the house in Barons Court with Carmen Silvera, as mentioned earlier. I moved into the top flat with my new girlfriend, Babs. I didn't see much of my family—Betty was happily married and a mother of two in Toronto, Hilary was married and living in South Africa, and Richard had gone into the tea business and, after a spell in Sri Lanka, had been posted to Java, which was still part of the Dutch East Indies.

The Rank Organisation, my new employer, was nominally run by J Arthur Rank, an avuncular Yorkshire businessman whose family fortune derived from flour milling and distribution. 'Uncle Arthur', as he was generally known, though not to his face by me, was a staunch Methodist and had got into the film business by making short religious films. I never saw one but I was told they were decently made and as boring as a wet Sunday in Leeds, which was where they were made. Uncle Arthur would attend the premieres of Rank films, and make modest introductory speeches in a Yorkshire accent before handing over to the real head honcho, the dreaded John Davis.

JD, as he was known, was originally an accountant and he became the managing director of the Rank Organisation in the late forties. He made it his mission to restore the company's fortunes, which had been going down the tubes in a massive way for a number of years. He was omnipresent and tried to put the fear of God into everyone he worked with. He had an obsession about shoes and insisted that all the staff should wear highly polished black Oxfords. Suede shoes were anathema to him and could provoke him into a real rage.

JD and I loathed each other and had more than one serious falling out during my time at Rank. During our rows Olive Dodds, who was in charge of contract artists, as we were known, would sit trembling in the corner and beg me later to apologise. She was a pleasant little woman in her early middle age, had a missing or malformed hand, which she covered with a glove, horn-rimmed glasses and the demeanour of a spinster schoolmistress. I liked her a lot and she always treated me well in spite of the fact that I must have been quite a trial to her. But how she got to be what she was, or where she came from, I never really knew.

JD and I had major rows over what he chose to call discipline, and what I called unwarrantable interference. I refused to work out in the gym at Pinewood, run by an elderly ex-stuntman. I was extremely fit and very strong, in my twenties, but I was also quite skinny so I was told I had to build up my physique. I went along with this until one day I found myself in the gym with a fellow, but senior, contract artist called John Gregson. We were both exercising away in a moody and resentful fashion until Johnny asked me what I was trying to achieve. I told him I was supposed to be bulking up and he started to laugh. 'I'm supposed to be bulking down,' he said. 'And we're both doing the same fucking exercises. Bollocks to this, I'm off to the bar.' I joined him and neither of us ever returned to the gym.

It was because of Johnny that I had to change my name. There couldn't be two Gregsons under contract so, as Johnny already had quite a name and reputation—*Genevieve* was one of his most famous films—I was ordered to find an alias. At about that time, there was an infamous murder case which involved a man called Bentley and a youth called Craig. The two of them had been involved in a robbery during which a police sergeant was shot and killed. Both of them were convicted and sentenced to hang. Bentley, who was mentally not the full quid but was over eighteen, was executed. Craig, who had actually committed the murder but was only sixteen, had his sentence commuted to life imprisonment and was released after about fifteen years, still a relatively young man. The case caused a terrific furore and made an enormous impression on me. When Olive Dodds and Monty asked me what name I'd like to use instead of my own, it must have been very much on my mind. 'Craig,' I said. 'Michael Craig . . . sounds all right doesn't it?' They agreed and I've been Michael Craig ever since. I suppose I might just as well have said 'Bentley', but I think there was another actor called Bentley working in films about then and, apart from one occasion when I appeared in a play with Wendy Craig, my adopted name hasn't been a problem. Actually, on reflection, Michael Bentley does sound quite good, but perhaps a touch too actorish.

I duly got a memo from Olive Dodds, signed by JD, censuring me for my lack of commitment to the Rank Organisation as shown by my dropping out of the gym. Other censorious memos were provoked by my wearing suede desert boots, by my choice of drink in the bar at Pinewood—Guinness rather than some more up-market concoction—and by my car, which for the first two years of my contract, was an old and unreliable Ford Prefect. It was a 1948 model and it looked like it had been built in the thirties—it even had a running board. I realised it wasn't the kind of car JD wished his up-and-comings to be associated with, but it was the best I could afford at the time. I replied to his memo along those lines, hinting that a raise in salary could easily solve the problem. But he ignored the hint and we both had to suffer the indignity of my Ford Prefect until they picked up my option at the end of year two and I received the magnificent sum of eighty quid a week—less Monty's ten per cent commission and National Health Service deductions, of course.

Passage Home, my first film for Rank, was a very strange experience for me. Most of the action took place aboard a tramp steamer sailing from some South American port back to England. However, in the interests of economy, we never went near the sea but spent the entire shoot in Studio E at Pinewood, filming against the dreaded blue backing used for a process called travelling matte. It's what, in a much more sophisticated form, they now use to shoot films like *Star Wars* and *The Matrix*—the actors perform on a bare set and the background is inserted later in the labs.

The Captain of the steamer was Peter Finch, the Second Mate was Anthony Steel and the Love Interest was Diane Cilento, cast as a passenger and the only woman in the all-male environment. The crew was made up of the usual suspects of the day—Sam Kidd as your Lovable Cockney, Geoffrey Kean as the resolute Bo'sun, killed by my character in an unfortunate accident, Cyril Cusack as the Chief Steward, Bohannan. Typically, Cyril, who was as Irish as the pigs in Docherty, chose to use a South London accent, which confused everyone including the director, who was a charming chap called Roy Baker. Some of the younger actors were Bryan Forbes, who became a highly successful film writer, director and tycoon in the sixties; Gordon Jackson, who'd already had a lot of success at Ealing Studios and at Denham; and Patrick McGoohan, who was a Rank 'starling' like myself.

I was very much the baby of the group in age and experience but, apart from Tony Steel, who treated everyone with casual arrogance, the cast and crew accepted me and my inexperience with friendly support. Our set was half of a full-sized tramp steamer, built and mounted on rockers taking up the entire sound stage. I was very impressed—every rivet, every piece of equipment, including the anchor windlass, was exactly as I knew it should be from my days at sea. It all looked exactly like rusty steel and peeling paint and I couldn't believe it was in fact made of wood and plaster. The art department, if no one else, had done us proud.

It was a fairly long schedule, over three months, and included attempted rape, drunken rage, manslaughter, a love story and of course the obligatory Force 10 storm. We spent days on the rocking deck, dressed in oilskins being deluged by great skips of water, which were tipped down chutes to simulate the waves breaking over our foundering vessel. Tony, with British grit and understatement, rescued Diane Cilento from a watery grave and we finally made it into port and some sort of happy ending.

I only had one really uncomfortable moment, when I had to have a fight with Geoffrey Kean, the Bo'sun. I was obliged to punch him in the stomach, a blow which apparently ruptured his spleen and caused his death (the Bo'sun that is, not Geoffrey). I duly rehearsed the action with the stuntman and felt confident I could do it without hurting Geoffrey or myself. However, when we came to shoot the scene I was so tense that, as I delivered the punch, I farted with such sound and fury that we had to do another take for the soundman. I was mortally embarrassed but the crew were delighted, giving me a round of applause.

At the end of each day's shoot most of us would go to the bar and have a few—in my case a Guinness or two, much to JD's annoyance. Peter Finch, who was reputed to be a bit of a boozer, would get stuck into the wine. Finchy's boozing was rather a myth—a couple of glasses and he'd be well away. He never seemed to get any more drunk as the bottle went down, but he'd be off and running before the rest of us felt the first faint buzz. He was a carefree spirit in his cups—one night he relieved himself into the fire in the Pinewood Bar because he felt the room was overheated.

We finished filming by Christmas in 1954 and I went home to await my next assignment. Babs was working for an agency that provided good-looking young ladies to demonstrate new products at trade fairs and in the big department stores such as Harrods. She was kept quite busy. We spent Christmas at Gubbions Hall with my mother and Roland but it was not much fun. My mother always disliked Babs, and in the early days the dislike was more than mutual and expressed with icy politeness. I couldn't wait to get back to London.

When we did get back, Babs had a surprise for me. She was pregnant. I'm ashamed to say, I was shattered—for the first time in my life I had a little money to spend, a little bit of success and security, and the chance to meet new and exciting people, which in my case meant a lot of wild and fairly willing girls. However, Babs and I had been living together and had got along pretty well for seven or eight months so there didn't seem to be any reason why we shouldn't legitimise the arrangement and the baby she was carrying. I guess that's how a lot of marriages start out. So, to my mother's great annoyance, we got married at Kensington Registry Office on 9 April 1955. Relations with Ma remained strained for some time and weren't helped by my insistence on visiting my father in Scotland, where, retired from the army, he now lived with his new wife and step-daughter.

The first half of that year I had no work to do apart from the occasional film premiere and publicity event I was obliged to attend. I would be picked up in a chauffeur-driven limousine from my unfashionable address in Barons Court and taken to an equally unfashionable address somewhere else, where we would pick up one of Uncle Arthur's young ladies, quite possibly someone I'd never met. The two of us would be driven to the Empire in Leicester Square, Rank's number one cinema in London, where their latest film would be opening. We would smile charmingly at the assembled fans, who had no idea who we were, while the Rank publicity team would try to persuade the bored and cynical press snappers to take our photographs. These might or might not appear later in *Picturegoer* or *Photoplay*, accompanied by some banal story about the up-and-coming film star, handsome, talented Michael Craig, seen at the opening of *XYZ* (starring Dirk Bogarde and Joan Collins perhaps) with his latest love, the equally talented and up-and-coming Miss ABC, soon to be seen in *Doctor Up a Gumtree* or whatever. I found the whole process boring and embarrassing in equal measure. The fact that I was married and Miss ABC was living in sin with a

Captain of Industry was never mentioned and the entire exercise was one of fantasy and fatuity.

On one occasion I was co-opted to attend an event called the Black and White Ball, which was some sort of publicity event dreamed up to advance the Rank Organisation's cause in Belgium. The Rank stable of actor heavyweights, including Tony Steel, John Gregson, Dirk Bogarde, James Robertson Justice, Belinda Lee, Diana Dors and the young Donald Sinden, were to be flown to Brussels and Antwerp, where, in the company of JD, Uncle Arthur and whoever else could spare the time, they would try to persuade stolid Flems and Walloons that films like *An Alligator Named Daisy* or *Doctor in Love* were the answer to their cinema-going needs. This two-day junket would culminate in the aforesaid Black and White Ball. The wardrobe department provided fabulous creations for the ladies to wear—black and white, of course—and the gentlemen were provided with white tie and tails.

I had not been included in this trip but at the last moment, for some reason, Donald Sinden couldn't go. This caused panic stations in the publicity department. Advance fliers had been issued all over Belgium and photographs of the attending 'stars' had been sent to all the venues to be signed for the adoring fans, but now the tall dark one with the wonderfully far-back accent wasn't going to be there. The easy solution was to send me in Donald's place, which is what they did. White tie and tails were hastily provided, found in the wardrobe department, and I was on my way. I don't know if it was ever mentioned that I *wasn't* in fact Donald Sinden—probably not, because I spent two days happily signing 'Best wishes, Donald Sinden' on his photographs while bewildered fans compared my face with the one in the picture and marvelled at the cunning of the photographer's art.

Back in Manchester, I took part in one enjoyable publicity jaunt with Peter Finch and Diane Cilento to open the latest Rank Odeon Cinema with a screening of *Passage Home*. We left Euston in the company of a publicity man called Harold Shampan at about 9.30 in the morning. Almost before the train had cleared the station, Finchy was ordering champagne. I don't know what Mr Shampan's budget was, but I'm pretty sure it didn't include champagne for breakfast. However Finchy was a star and had to be accommodated, so champagne was ordered. Indeed, more and more champagne—so much champagne that, by the time we reached Manchester, we were well away and Mr Shampan was looking extremely worried. His worries were fully justified because Finchy insisted on inviting every actor and actress in Manchester to this special screening and to the reception at the Midland Hotel that followed it. About three hundred showed up and, with Finchy leading the festivities, we raged on into the night.

It was a subdued group that travelled back to London the next day. Finchy and Diane and I were pale green and hungover, and Mr Shampan was dark green with terror. The bill for the night's party was over £3000, a sum that he would have had great difficulty in justifying to the accountants at head office. I suspect he probably never did because soon after he left Rank and went into the music business.

Finally, in the early summer of 1955, I was given another film to do. I was cast as a Bedouin sheik called Faris in a film called *The Black Tent*. The stars of this production included Tony Steel and Donald Sinden, while Donald Pleasence was in a key support role. My only lines were in Arabic and I met an early death for betraying Tony Steel to the Germans. The director of this epic was the man who had previously told me that, if I was sincere in my ambitions, there was nothing I wouldn't do to attain them. I didn't mention our former meeting and neither did he—perhaps he'd used the line so often he'd forgotten he'd used it on me— and we maintained a pleasant enough relationship during the three or four weeks I spent on the picture.

It was my first foreign location and I enjoyed it immensely. Libya was then more Italian than Arab, at least in Tripoli, which was where we were based, and it was quite a swinging town. I learned my few words of Arabic, rode my stallion (whose balls were contained in a hairnet, to prevent him mounting anything that moved), died at the hands of the goodies and went home.

It was good fun and I became very friendly with Donald Pleasence, who coined the phrase 'Rank Starling' when referring to me and my ilk. I don't think Sheik Faris advanced my career very much—a friend of mine saw the film recently and asked me which one was me—but it was another credit for the résumé, and I achieved a nice tan in the desert.

Soon after I got back from Tripoli, to everyone's surprise and alarm, Stephen was born. It was a nightmare time as he was ten weeks early and nothing was ready, including me. It was touch-and-go whether he would survive. He spent the first five weeks of his life in an incubator with tubes attached to most of his orifices, but Babs coped very well, and even my mother rallied around a bit and provided a few of the more necessary pieces of equipment, such as a cot and a bath from Selfridges.

I had very mixed feelings about Stephen's birth. I was immensely proud to be the father of a son, and I loved him dearly. I especially loved the way he had coped with the physical problems his premature birth had caused, and still remained a good-tempered, loving and lovable baby. But—and it was a sizeable but—I was only twenty-six and neither prepared for, nor eager to accept, fatherhood. Babs seemed happy enough, but I couldn't help resenting—just a little—the restraints my new status inevitably imposed on my life. Then of course I'd feel guilty, and guilt can be the most useless and destructive emotion.

My next assignment was a very boring part in a film called *Eyewitness*, another one which crops up in the small hours to help the insomniacs sleep. Donald Sinden was again the star, with the up-and-coming and very beautiful Belinda Lee and a lady called Muriel Pavlow, to whom I was married in the story. I think I was a young doctor—a part I was to play so often that I should have my own practice by now. The only memorable thing about the whole enterprise was the eccentricities of the director, Muriel Box. She was the wife of the powerful and respected producer, Sydney Box, whose sister was Betty Box, another legendary producer. Muriel was very different. I think she'd been Sydney's secretary, or something in the art department, and her skills as a director were confined to the ability to say 'Action!' and 'Cut!' She was a very nice lady, a bit like a deputy headmistress, but her main concern while filming seemed to be how the set was dressed. She would prowl about, peering at the pictures on the walls, the curtains and the furniture, while the cast and crew sat about waiting for her to decide all was well, or whether that fox-hunting print over the fireplace should be replaced by *The Death of Nelson*. I suppose it was some sort of stratagem on her part, to delay the awful moment when she'd have to make a real decision; but at the time it was irritating in the extreme.

Still it did me no harm and, to my delight, the option for my continuing services was exercised on the due date with the contracted increase in salary, and my future was assured for at least another year. This was a great relief as I had a wife and child to support now and it made it possible to do a bit of entertaining and have the occasional meal in a restaurant or go to the theatre. I still played a lot of poker, usually winning, and though we didn't play for high stakes my winnings provided a few extra luxuries which, as I think about it now, usually ended up being an extra bottle of Scotch.

For my next job I was loaned out to Associated British Pictures to do a film called *Yield to the Night*, starring Diana Dors. This was a thinly fictionalised version of the Ruth Ellis murder case, which resulted in her being the last woman to be hanged in England. The writer always maintained that she'd written the film before the Ruth Ellis case happened, but if she did she must have been remarkably prescient as the similarities were obvious. Ruth Ellis shot her lover, who was a second division racing car driver, because he was unfaithful. An absolutely classic *crime passionel*. She pleaded guilty—there was no defence except her emotional distress—and she was sentenced to death and hanged at Pentonville.

Diana played the Ruth Ellis part, which was a big departure and risk for her, and for the director and producer. She was well-known for her sexy blonde image—the 'English Marilyn Monroe', the tabloids called her—and had never played a serious dramatic lead in a film. I was cast as the faithless lover and eventual victim but, instead of being a racing car driver, my character was a piano player in a West End cocktail bar. I had a slight problem with this as I don't and can't play the piano. In fact I am so right-handed that I can't make my left hand operate independently of my right hand if my right hand is already doing something else—a definite drawback for a pianist. I was told that my hands would never be seen on the keys, so, with a bit of coaching from a piano-playing friend and my fingers well hidden from the camera, I performed with confidence. During my scene at the piano, in which I seduced Diana Dors. I was playing *A Nightingale Sang in Berkley Square.* When they dubbed in the music, to save on paying the copyright, on screen I was playing something composed by the musical director. Needless to say, my hands weren't in sync with this new piece but nobody seemed to care.

The director was J Lee Thompson, a small, very intense man with a violent temper, which could be provoked by practically anything or nothing. He had a nervous habit of tearing sheets of paper into long thin strips. One of the assistant directors was detailed to keep him supplied with reams of foolscap, which he absentmindedly demolished throughout the day, leaving a paper trail behind him as he scurried around the set.

Diana was terrific—hardly any makeup, hair scraped back, dressed in a shapeless prison dress—as she went through the emotional hoops of this young woman, driven by jealousy to murder, and then having to suffer the trial and horrific experience of day after day in the condemned cell waiting for death. Babs knew Diana and the three of us once had a memorable lunch with Diana's then husband, Dennis Hamilton Gittins, at their country house on the river near Marlow in the Thames Valley. Dennis had a bit of a reputation as a spiv and a conman, and he died young, worn out by his excessive lifestyle. Diana married again—more than once I think—but sadly she too has passed on now. Although we lost touch over the years, I remember her with great affection and respect as one of the most free-spirited and professional actresses I worked with.

I finished on *Yield to the Night* in the winter of 1955/56. At about this time, to my great surprise and delight, Richard came home from Java, just managing to get out unscathed when Soekarno took over and the Dutch East Indies became Indonesia. He used his legacy from Granny Winter to buy a little house near mine in West London and, shaking the tea business from his shoes forever, he embarked on a long and successful career, which culminated in his becoming a literary agent, film producer and writer. It was a remarkable journey as Richard's only previous contact with the literary world had been in a job selling religious books for the Faith Press in Westminster. For the first time since we'd been small children, we started to see a lot of each other, and became the great friends we are today.

My next assignment after *Yield to the Night* was the lead role in a sort of forerunner to the James Bond type of movie. It was a huge part involving fights and shootings and love scenes and derring-do of all kinds, including the 'with one bound Jack was free' sort of escape from a plane by parachute, leaving the baddies to crash and burn while I lived happily ever after. The film was called *House of Secrets*, shot in colour on lots of foreign and local locations. In spite of all our best efforts it ended up being fairly boring. It was directed by a man called Guy Green, with whom I later became good friends. Guy was a great cameraman—he'd worked with David Lean and had won an Oscar for *Great Expectations*—but was not a very experienced director.

Even though I played the lead in *House of Secrets*, I was still only being paid thirty quid a week. I remember buying a drink for the crew after our last day's shoot in Paris, when the bill for that one round was more than my week's salary. This was soon to change because at the end of August 1956 my option was again picked up and I was now on £4000 a year. I sold my share of the house in Barons Court to Carmen and Babs found a house for us to buy near Wimbledon Common, overlooking the tennis club. Five bedrooms, three reception rooms, garden back and front, garage—and all for £7500. We could now have either nannies or au pair girls to help out; not that Babs was overburdened with work, but that was the way it was back then and I went along with it.

We were getting along well enough; Stephen was a lovely and endearing baby, we had an amusing social life, a reasonable income and, in my case, enough work and success to keep me satisfied. My only niggle was that Babs wouldn't, or couldn't, do anything that didn't involve me. She seemed to have no life outside the family circle, and was pretty and bright enough to have had her own career at *something*. But she never did, and as the years went by I found it more and more irritating that she lived vicariously through me and the boys. I didn't want the responsibility of someone else's life and happiness and in the end I ran away from it.

I was kept pretty busy workwise. My next movie, *High Tide at Noon*, was a love story set in Nova Scotia amongst lobster fishermen. It was shot in black and white for reasons of economy, or so I always thought. There was also this theory at the time that only musicals and comedies should be shot in colour; black and white was for *real* drama. I played a lobster fisherman in trouble because the lobsters had disappeared from the fishing grounds. My mother was played by Dame Flora Robson, my father by an eminent Canadian actor called Alexander Knox, and my rival for the hand of the local beauty, played by Betta St John, was Patrick McGoohan. We had the usual troubles associated with filming boats at sea—directors never seem to realise that you can't stop a boat on a mark like you can stop a car or that the camera boat always drifts at a different speed to the object boat. It will also always rain, the sun will always be in the wrong position, and everyone will always lose their temper. At the end of the film I got the girl and the lobsters came back so it was a happy ending, but one has to question the talent of the scriptwriter who gave me the last line: 'The bugs are running, the bugs are running,' as I clutched Betta to my chest. 'Bug' was local argot for lobster, but I always felt I might have had a less ambiguous and happier line to bring down the curtain.

While we were filming *Hide Tide at Noon*, I started to play golf on the local links at Salcombe in west Devonshire. It became an addiction which has stayed with me for the rest of my life. Meanwhile, life in Wimbledon was reasonably pleasant. Pa, who continued to live the life of a country squire in the Scottish borders on practically no income, occasionally came south, staying at the Cavalry Club, commonly known as the 'In and Out'. He loved the fact that I was now making films and was forever namedropping to his neighbours, who weren't the least bit interested. The first time he saw me on screen, in *Passage Home* at a quiet matinee at the Empire in Leicester Square, he nearly fell off his chair at my first appearance. 'My God,' he boomed through the quiet stalls, 'My God, Meesh, it's you.' I shushed him as best I could but he went on muttering at my every appearance, looking at me in the seat next to him, and then at my image up on the screen, and chortling in delighted disbelief. He was fifty-five going on about six.

Early in 1957 I was assigned to play a supporting lead in a film called *Campbell's Kingdom*, an adaptation of a Hammond Innes adventure story. We spent six weeks on location at Cortina d'Ampezzo in the Italian Dolomites. Dirk Bogarde was the action hero, an unlikely choice since he was small and slender and not overly athletic, but he was the top box office attraction at Rank and had had a lot of success playing neurotic and romantic young men. I think he wanted to change his image into something more robust, but the sight of him threatening to knock the block off some burly oil driller in a Canadian bar was more ludicrous than robust.

I had an odd sort of relationship with Dirk. He was ten or twelve years older than me and an established star in the British film industry before I signed with Rank. I think he saw me as a threat to his position. I was a similar type, dark, conventionally good-looking, and had the potential to become a romantic lead. He was always polite and pleasant enough but we both knew that I was a rival, even though I'd have been more than pleased to break my so-called image and do something different. He lived in great style with his long-time companion Tony Forwood (Tote) in the country not far from Pinewood. They occasionally entertained with lavish good taste. Dirk was amazingly discreet. In all the years I knew him there were never any stories in the media that he was anything but the charming, romantic hetero-sexual chap he portrayed on the screen.

While we were in Cortina d'Ampezzo an American film company arrived to shoot parts of Hemingway's *A Farewell to Arms*. This was a huge production, starring Rock Hudson and Jennifer Jones and directed by Charles Vidor. They made our efforts look very small, and the staff in the hotel in which we were all staying relegated us to the second division. I remember one morning in the dining room the maître d'hôtel being reduced to tears by some assistant director on *Farewell* screaming abuse because there was 'no jelly jam' for Miss Jones's breakfast.

For some reason the great American director John Huston turned up at the hotel. He was a noted gambler and one evening asked if he might join our usual evening poker game. I was very nervous; Huston's reputation as a poker player was daunting and he was probably earning more in a week than I was earning in a year. However I had good hands and was well ahead, betting only a little more than I could afford. Towards the end of the session Huston and I were the only two left in a hand of seven-card stud. There was a lot of money in the pot and Huston was leading the betting, showing three aces on the table. I had two pairs showing on the table, kings and tens, but what Huston didn't and couldn't know was that I had two more kings in the hole and the fourth ace. The bet got up to £1200 and I started to sweat. I knew I had him beaten; he couldn't have four aces and neither could he have a running flush with the cards he was showing. There was no way that I didn't have the winning hand. But I was still nervous. I wanted to raise the bet but I didn't have any more money so I had to see him. Sure enough he had a full house, aces high, not quite good enough against four kings. I raked in the pot with shaking hands and he gave me a friendly grin. 'Nice going, kid. See you tomorrow night.' I smiled weakly and shuffled off to bed. We were leaving the next day and I was extremely relieved that the great John Huston wasn't going to have a chance to get his own and my money back.

My next assignment was supposed to be a piece of Regency rubbish called *The Gypsy and the Gentleman*, directed by the famed ex-pat Hollywood director Joseph Losey and starring, for some weird reason, the Greek actress Melina Mercouri. She had just had a huge international hit with *Never on Sunday* and, I can only assume, wanted to do an English language film no matter what. It had the creakiest of plots—gypsy girl snares English aristocrat and marries him against all the odds—and I was summoned to meet Joe Losey at his Knightsbridge house. He had a great reputation both as a director and, more importantly to me, as a man of integrity. Rather than give evidence to the McCarthy investigations into Hollywood communists, he had given up his life and career in Los Angeles and come to Europe to find work. In his defence, I suppose he needed the job. Perhaps, if he had been honest with me, I'd have gone along with it. But he treated me like an idiot and tried to tell me it was a fine script which would make a fine movie and I was lucky to be given the chance of being in it. And, I inferred, lucky to be working with him. I dug my toes in and refused.

I had no contractual right to decline this film, so I was hauled up before JD and the rest of the brass to face a bollocking and the strictest of orders to do what I was told. I wouldn't budge and was suspended with dire threats. But luck was on my side. Jimmy Woolf of Romulus Films offered me a part in *The Silent Enemy*, starring Laurence Harvey. Rank were paid my year's salary for loaning me out; my suspension was revoked and Keith Michell played the part I was supposed to do in *The Gypsy and the Gentleman*.

The Silent Enemy was another war film. It was based on the exploits of a Commander Crabbe, who formed a group of underwater frogmen from naval volunteers and waged a successful war against the Italian Navy in the Mediterranean in World War II. We spent six weeks in Gibraltar doing location shooting for the film. For the first time Babs and Stephen were able to come with me on a foreign location and we all had a good time. Babs adored being on foreign locations. She had everything she wanted—room service, a beach, sunshine, a nanny for Stephen, the dubious pleasure of my company at the end of each day's work, and the knowledge that I wasn't out and about and up to no good with some other lady. Stephen knocked himself out cold by running into a closed glass door which he didn't see in the Rock Hotel, but, apart from that we all had a good time.

In the film, I was playing a real character called Leading Seaman Sidney Knowles. My fellow band of heroes consisted of Sid James, Alec McCowan, Nigel Stock and Ian Whittaker, all under the inspiring leadership of Larry Harvey. Larry was always in trouble with the British press, which regarded him as a pretentious upstart, deploring his somewhat over-the-top lifestyle. Larry didn't give a shit. He fostered his playboy image with malicious good humour. He always wore the most elegant suits, complete with cufflinks from Aspreys, shirts from Turnbull and Asher, and hand-made shoes from Lobb. He chain-smoked through a long holder and lit his cigarettes with a solid gold lighter. He lived in Albany and drove a Rolls Royce which had his initials as part of its number plate, long before anyone else had thought to do so in England. He'd come a long way from the South African/Lithuanian called Lawrence Skikne, who'd arrived in London ten years earlier to make his way as an actor. Larry's kind of style and charm didn't always get across on screen but it worked very well for him in his private life. He was good company, generous to his friends and, in spite of his reputation as a user, I liked him a lot.

While we were filming in Gibraltar he was planning to marry the beautiful Margaret Leighton, an actress a few years older than he was. This decision raised a number of eyebrows as Larry wasn't thought to be the marrying kind. I don't think he quite knew what he was doing, but he did it anyway. The wedding was to take place on a barge in Gibraltar harbour at the end of a day's shoot. A few hours before he was due to exchange his vows, he and I were dressed in our frogman gear and poised to leap into the water to do some shot or other. He was looking very depressed, so I asked him if he was okay. He grinned sadly and said, 'You know what I wish, Michael? I wish that when I go underwater to do this shot, I never come up again.' Well he did come up again, married Miss Leighton, subsequently divorced her, married someone else and went on to do a lot of successful films, including *Room at the Top* and *The Manchurian Candidate,* to name two of his best. I worked with him again eight years later in *Life at the Top* and found him as funny and charming as ever. The poor fellow got cancer of the bowel while still in his forties, bore it with immense courage and died far, far too young at fifty.

My next film, *Nor the Moon by Night,* took five disaster-ridden months to shoot in South Africa. The director was Ken Annakin—Panickin' Annakin as he was, not very lovingly, known by the crew. Briefly, it concerned a young nurse, played by Belinda Lee, who arrives in Africa to marry a game warden, played by Patrick McGoohan, whom she has never met. The game warden is unable to meet her on her arrival so his brother—another game warden called Rusty (yuck), played by me—turns up in his place. Needless to say, Belinda falls for Rusty and vice versa. After many adventures of a most predictable kind, we end up in each other's arms, and Patrick finds solace with his child-hood playmate, whom he discovers he has really loved all the time. The cast of exotic fauna included, of all things, a friendly porcupine called Percy, or Peter, or some such alliterative name. Imagine, if you can, the scriptwriter who devised the following scene and actually got it into his bloody script:

Sc. 57. Exterior. Day. Campsite.
Rusty emerges from his tent and notices that Belinda is still in bed. With a mischievous smile on his lips he softly calls Peter/Percy the porcupine, who trots into sight and, responding to Rusty's

signal, enters Belinda's tent. Belinda emerges in her short nightie panicked by Peter/Percy's attempts to be friendly and hurls herself into the safety of Rusty's manly arms. Rusty laughs gleefully. When Belinda discovers that the porcupine is Rusty's pet she is furious and slaps his face.

How long did that take to write? The writer plainly had no knowledge of the ways of the porcupine. There is probably no stupider animal in all of Africa than the porcupine, and it is untrainable and untameable. The most you can hope for is that it will move more or less the way you direct it, lured by food, and spurred on by fear. We spent several hours trying to get the animal to do anything. Each time it baulked at its task, lost its temper, lashed its tail and shed some more quills until, after seven or eight aborted takes, it looked like the last turkey for sale on Christmas Eve. Finally the wrangler and Annakin decided to tie a long fishing line to the beast's front paw and drag it into Belinda's tent, making sure that the fishing line wasn't visible in the shot. And there it is in the final cut—this furious bald animal being towed jerkily across the ground, digging its little toes in and making porcupine noises of outrage while Rusty smiles encouragingly, mischievously pointing the way to Belinda's tent.

Filming was slow and frustrating, but we seemed to be getting there as we broke for Christmas. Belinda, who was in love with and having an affair with an Italian Prince, flew off to Rome after promising faithfully to be back in five days to resume shooting. Babs came out to join me for Christmas, leaving Stephen behind in the care of a nanny. Our time together was quite enjoyable, but I was full of guilt because I had fallen for a local South African girl, Shirley, who helped out on the movie. Then we heard the bad news. None of the footage we had shot was useable and the lighting cameraman was to be replaced. We had to start again. It wasn't the best of Christmases. But it got worse. The new cameraman arrived but Belinda didn't. Apparently her romance had come unglued and she'd taken an overdose.

She was lying comatose at death's door in an Italian hospital. She would not be back for a couple of weeks, if ever.

Finally Belinda did return, pale and chastened, and we soldiered on. Babs returned to England and I fell deeply in love with Shirley. It was the first time I'd strayed since I'd married Babs and it hit me really hard. When we finally finished filming and I flew back to London I was an emotional mess. We'd been away for five months, spent a lot of Rank Organisation's money, and made a really crappy film which hardly anyone wanted to see. My marriage was pretty well destroyed by this initial infidelity, even though Babs wasn't aware of it at first. Babs and I muddled on for another fourteen years one way or another, but my affair with Shirley was really the beginning of the end. Shirley and I agreed we had no future together—I was married and a father. Best to make a clean break: no phone calls, no letters, no contact. Less painful in the long run, that way. We said our miserable goodbyes at Durban airport and I flew back to London where I almost immediately broke my promise about writing letters, with the inevitable result.

Around this time I, with several others, was detailed to attend the Royal Premiere of a film called *Les Girls*. Prior to the showing of the film, each of us had to appear on stage and present some facet of the film industry. When we had finally saluted everyone, from the Pinewood tea ladies to the plasterers and carpenters at Shepperton, we all lined up and took a bow. I was standing between Sophia Loren and Jayne Mansfield in the line up. They were both wearing dresses of such a revealing nature and tightness that they were unable to bow or curtsey without my support. I was nearly pulled to the floor by their combined weight as they struggled to rise from their deep obeisances to the Queen.

For some reason of protocol, we weren't allowed to sit in the cinema after Her Majesty had been seated and were made to wait in the basement until just before the film's end. Then we were taken up to the foyer and lined up prior to being presented to the royal party. It was actually quite jolly down in the basement.

There was a well-stocked bar and generous bartenders so that, by the time we were summoned, most of the chaps, myself included, were well away. We stood there in the foyer, swaying gently in our rented white tie and tails as the royal party sauntered down the line.

I'd never realised how small the Queen was, or how truly amazing the jewellery she wore was. She seemed to literally blaze with the blue and white fire emanating from her diamonds and amethysts, and, I have to say, from her dazzling smile. I managed to get the bow, the 'Your Majesty' and then 'Ma'am' out all right as she paused briefly to do her duty by me and I sighed with relief, only to be faced by Phil the Greek. I could *not* remember what I was supposed to call him. We had been briefed that we should initially address him as 'Your Royal Highness' and subsequently as 'Sir', but my mind went blank. I bowed and winged it hoping for the best. 'Your Royal Sirness' was how it emerged and, even in my inebriated state, I knew that wasn't quite right. A faint spasm crossed his face—whether of distaste or amusement I know not—but he stayed for a minute or two and we chatted about the Commander Crabbe of *The Silent Enemy* and about Leading Seaman Sidney Knowles, who was the real-life character I had played.

In the spring of 1958 I had lunch with my friend Guy Green to discuss a film he was going to direct for Bob Baker and Monty Berman of Tempean Productions. They were about to make their first feature, *Sea of Sand*, starring Richard Attenborough, John Gregson and me, if I accepted. It was a war film set in the North African desert and was a fictionalised version of an exploit by the Long Range Desert Group. It was quite a good story—lots of action and a good part—but I was reluctant. As it would be a loan-out from Rank, I didn't have to do it contractually and I couldn't be suspended for knocking it back; but of course it would earn Rank my year's salary, which was now £5000 a year. This was quite a plus as there was a chance I could do another loan-out that year, actually earning some overage. There was also the inducement of ten weeks' location—in Libya once again. The way my marriage was going, a spell away from Wimbledon was very attractive. Babs had found out about my affair with Shirley from South Africa. She had found a letter which left no doubt about what our relationship had been, and was justifiably hurt and angry.

So why was I so reluctant? Well, as I told Guy, it was now 1958, thirteen years after the war had finished, and we were still making war movies. Surely there must be some kind of contemporary, dramatic stories we could tell. Stories that reflected the society in which we lived. 'Such as?' Guy asked. I thought for a moment and told him of a man I'd known in York who'd committed suicide.

In those days York was very much a company town. You worked for Rowntrees or Frys, the old chocolate-making Quaker families, or you worked for the railways. The railway yards in York were where, amongst other things, the engines were maintained and repaired for the whole country. It was a highly skilled and highly unionised enterprise. For some reason an unofficial wildcat strike had been called, against union instructions, and this particular man refused to join it. He had a family to support, he didn't agree with the strike and it hadn't been sanctioned by his union. He braved the picket lines and the abuse of his fellow workers and continued to turn up for work. Finally the strike was settled and everyone went back at work, but the workers felt it necessary to punish this man for being a scab. He was sent to Coventry—no one would speak to him, no one did speak to him. His family was ostracised, his children were bullied at school and he was treated like a leper. He stood it for over a year and then he gassed himself. He'd done nothing wrong, he'd acted within his legal and union rights, but he and his family were made to pay a very heavy price for going against the mob.

'That's the sort of story we should be telling,' I told Guy.

Guy's eyes lit up. Dicky Attenborough had just started a production company called Beaver Films with our mutual friend Bryan Forbes and they were looking for subjects.

'Do you have a script?' I fibbed and told him I had an outline.

'Well,' he said, 'Ten weeks in Libya would give you a chance to get to know Dicky and chat about your strike story, and quite possibly get it set up as Beaver's first production.' And that's what happened. I went to Libya, made *Sea of Sand*, and during that time Dicky Attenborough and Bryan Forbes became increasingly enthusiastic about my project.

Sea of Sand was a tough shoot, not made easier by the broken-down old trucks our producer, Monty Berman, had provided as our action vehicles. They were the real thing—the Long Range Desert Group had used them back in 1943—but they had been sitting in a dump since the end of the war. In spite of being refurbished, they were a great trial and sometimes quite dangerous. Monty had bought them for bugger-all, I imagine— he was, like most producers, tight when it came to paying for anything. He was a constant pain in the neck with his economies. At the end of the shoot we gave Guy a silver tray inscribed, 'To Guy, from those of us who fought with Monty in the desert.'

It was an all-male cast, about ten of us, and we managed to enjoy ourselves in our different ways. I struck up a friendship with Vincent Ball, which has lasted to this day. Whisky cost five shillings a bottle from the local army base and there were a couple of girls who enjoyed our company—Alice, a Dane, was my special friend. Looking back on it now, I don't know how we survived the filming. We drank far too much, slept far too little and misbehaved in every possible way. But the film didn't turn out too badly and later I was nominated for some kind of award for my performance. I never felt guilty about Alice; she was older than me and treated both me and the affair with hedonistic enjoy- ment, completely devoid of romance or sentiment. I responded in kind and, if ever assailed by guilty pangs for my infidelity, took comfort in the old film actor's motto, 'Out of the country, doesn't count.'

My brother Richard was now a literary agent, married and very keen to become a writer. I told him about my unionist story and together we nutted out the first draft script of what was now known as *The Angry Silence*—Bryan Forbes's title I think—and waited to see what would happen to it. It became quite a long wait as it turned out.

I was loaned out again to do a very boring film called *Life in Emergency Ward Ten*. It was yet another young doctor saga, a filmed version of a popular television series of the same name, which starred the Australian actor Charles (Bud) Tingwell. Like most filmed versions of television shows, it didn't have much success but it was a short schedule, only five weeks, and I was paid some overage, adding to my contractual salary. The only thing I can remember about it was working with Wilfred Hyde-White, who was adept at playing the quintessential English gentleman clubman, and the laziest actor I ever met. He never learnt his lines and I was horrified when we had to do an operation scene. He was the presiding surgeon and I was his up-and-coming assistant. He realised that, as we were all wearing surgical masks, it wouldn't be possible to see what we were saying, so he could record his dialogue later in the sound studio, reading it from his script. To provide me with my cues, he put the script on the operating table in front of him and performed the operation on that. He burbled away about nothing in particular—what was running at Ascot or Epsom (he was an inveterate race-goer)—and, when he felt it appropriate, he'd bark out a cue line from the script: 'Scalpel', or 'more suction', or 'what's his blood pressure?'

I had now made eleven films in three years and, in spite of my bolshie attitude, was considered to be a reliable performer. Domestically things were not good for Babs and me. The simple fact of the matter was that by the age of twenty-six, I had become a husband and a father and, as I saw it at the time, trapped. It was no one's fault, of course. We were conditioned by the customs of the times—it was unthinkable for Babs to be an unmarried mum. But it had not been the ideal way to start our marriage. Stephen was a lovely baby, having survived the first few weeks in his incubator. He is now a lovely chap of forty-seven with a twelve-year-old son of his own. I was a pretty good father but a terrible husband and my eighteen-year marriage to Babs was a failure. It was mainly my fault—I was consistently unfaithful after the first two years, which was bad enough. But I seemed to compound my infidelity by falling in love with my extramarital partners instead of just having an affair. I seemed to live a life of deceit and yearning, which put unbearable pressure on all concerned. This led to the inevitable break-up of our relationship. It was always terribly fraught, and neither of us had any fun. But we soldiered on for a long time—in Babs' case because she didn't know what else to do. She was prepared to tolerate practically anything as long as she could stay Mrs Me. She had given up living her own life after Stephen was born and seemed to live vicariously through me. It was not a good way to sustain a partnership—too much pressure on the one and not enough independence for the other. She was a wonderful and caring mother to both my sons, a very good manager and hostess, but my behaviour prevented her from being the kind of wife she wanted to be. Mostly my fault, I admit, but we really shouldn't have married when we did.

SEVEN

Overtime

I was next cast as a detective sergeant—complete with shabby raincoat, fedora hat and pipe—in a film called *Sapphire*. This was quite a breakthrough movie as it addressed racism in England through a murder investigation. During the course of the investigation it comes out that the murdered girl was coloured but had been passing herself off as white. It was a pretty good film for its time and the art department used an interesting design technique—everything in and on the sets was painted a shade of grey. Cornflake packets, tablecloths, wallpaper, furniture, carpets, bottles, all some kind of grey. One wasn't really aware of this greyness while watching but it *did* have a kind of alienating effect.

The film was produced by Michael Relph and directed by Basil Dearden for the Rank Organisation. They originally took it in turns to produce or direct and they had a well-deserved reputation for making well-crafted, innovative and interesting films. Basil wasn't an easy man to work for though—he had a short fuse and could be unbelievably rude. For example, on the first morning of the shoot, in the very first take, I discover the dead body of the girl, Sapphire, and I do my detective–sergeant bit. It was a cold morning on Hampstead Heath and I was a bit nervous, as one always is on the first day. The scene went well enough and I thought Basil would be pleased. One-take Wonder Craig! He looked at me and said in his dry, schoolmasterly way, 'Were you acting in that scene?' Now that was the unanswerable question. If I said no, Basil would say, 'What the hell do you think you're being paid for?' If I said yes, he'd say, 'Well don't. This isn't Drury Lane you know.' I decided that attack was the best defence. So, with what I hoped was a charming grin, I said, 'Fuck off, Basil'. He grinned back. I must have passed some kind of test because we never had any more problems and I did another film for him five years later.

In 1959 I turned thirty and rejoined the Betty Box/Ralph Thomas Club for a film called *Upstairs and Downstairs*. Not to be confused with the television series of the same name, which appeared many years later, it was a light comedy about the trials and tribulations of bringing up small children with the help of a succession of au pair girls and nannies. I think I was a young architect married to my boss's daughter, but the jokes and the situations were pretty much the same as in all the other Box/Thomas comedies I made. That's not surprising as they were mostly written by the same person and had the same casts. Sid James was with us again, as was Joan Sims and the ubiquitous James Robertson Justice.

James did a very good line in irascibility and pompousness—irascible pomposity or pompous irascibility, it was all the same to him—but, apart from that, he wasn't really an actor. He relied on his massive presence and booming voice, emerging from a bearded slab of a face, and got away with that in dozens of films for more than twenty years. I got on quite well with him in an uncle/nephew sort of way. He was an interesting man—a real Elizabethan, with an obsession with the rearing and training of falcons. He even had a tame, trained golden eagle, which was probably against the law. He was a friend of the Duke of Edinburgh and lived in the depths of the Scottish highlands in Sutherland.

My only problem when working with James was his insistence on having the real thing when required to eat or drink in a scene. I remember a dreadful occasion when I had to do an after-dinner scene with him first up in the morning. James insisted as usual on having real port and brandy to drink and he kept refilling my glass. I've always been a pretty competent boozer, but port and brandy at eight o'clock in the morning was pushing the envelope. Of course, James only had that one scene to do and he lurched off the set at about eleven o'clock to go home, or do whatever. I, on the other hand, had many more scenes to get through before I could put my feet up, and it was a very long day.

The film was quite enjoyable to make. I met my dear, now departed, friend, Daniel Massey, for the first time, and also a very young and inexperienced Claudia Cardinale, who had a small part as a promiscuous Italian au pair girl. My son Stephen gave his first and only performance as one of my children in the film. He was three at the time and it's nice to have a copy of the film with his walking, talking infant image in it. I have always been grateful that none of my children ever became, or wanted to become, actors. I did my best to discourage them by occasionally taking them to work with me. As anyone who has ever done it will know, there is almost nothing more boring and frustrating than spending a day hanging about on a film set. It's bad enough for the people involved, but for the onlooker or visitor it is absolutely un-riveting.

Meanwhile the storyline/treatment Richard and I had written for *The Angry Silence* had been transformed into a shooting script by Bryan Forbes and he and Attenborough had finally come up with the money to make it. Dicky had a great stroke of luck with the casting. After he'd finished *Sea of Sand,* he had done another film with Guy Green, called *SOS Pacific*, in which the leading lady was an Italian actress called Pier Angeli. She was extremely beautiful and had been snapped up by Hollywood, where she had a lot of success. She was a star, unlike the rest of us involved with *The Angry Silence*, and also a very good actress. While she and Attenborough were on location for *SOS Pacific*, she read *The Angry Silence* and told Dicky—who was madly but platonically in love with her, as was Guy and everyone else—that she'd like to play the character of his wife.

This part of course had been written as a working-class provincial English woman, but after a nanosecond of doubt and consideration, Dicky said it could easily be re-written for an Italian girl. He had to tell her that they couldn't pay very much—in fact we all did it for a thousand pounds each and a share in the potential profits. She didn't care about the money and agreed to the same deal as the rest of us. Armed with Pier Angeli's commitment to the film, Dicky and Bryan finally managed to make a deal with British Lion and others. They would fund the production if it could be made for £100 000. Even in those days that wasn't much of a budget, derisory in fact, but Dicky and Guy said it could be done—in the end I think we came in £4000 under budget. It meant, of course, basic money for the actors, a shortish schedule and hard work and dedication from everyone but that wasn't a problem.

Dicky had the ability to inspire real dedication and commitment from the cast and crew, and, as well as playing the lead character, was a wonderfully skilful producer. I was excited and enthusiastic for the first time in years—at last, a real character in a real story, a story that I'd helped to create. The Rank Organisation, however, didn't share my feelings. They hadn't spent four years building up my image as a romantic leading man to have me jeopardise that image by playing a moronic working-class randy yobbo in a film about a strike. It was definitely not their cup of tea—there wasn't even any money in it for them—and I was refused permission to make it.

Back to head office in South Street I went, back to Olive Dodds mediating between JD and me, back to threats of suspension and injunctions. There was no way I was going to miss this opportunity and I told them that if they persisted with their refusal I would go to the press and tell the whole story. The press was always critical of the Rank Organisation and its policy of making bland, family entertainment, and would have made a great story out of the company's refusal to let one of its stars make a controversial, ground-breaking film. My pathetic threat worked, I was allowed to do the film, but with the proviso that the ten weeks of my engagement on it would be added on to my contract. Fair enough—I'd have conceded much more than that.

We spent two or three weeks on location in Ipswich filming in a factory, and the rest of it was shot at Shepperton Studios. The cast included the marvellous Bernard Lee and Geoffrey Kean, with whom I'd worked so often, and a very young and inexperienced Oliver Reed. Ollie had just come out of the army and was almost embarrassingly fit and eager. He had no training but looked good and had connections in the film world—his Uncle was Sir Carol Reed, the famous director. Ollie was great fun and stayed with us in Wimbledon for a spell while sorting out his love life. He liked a drink, but knew how to behave himself and was nothing like the brawling drunken idiot he degenerated into later in his life.

Bernard Lee had been a really handsome up-and-coming leading man in the theatre before the war. He rather resented the fact that, while he had spent six years in the army, his contemporary Jack Hawkins had been making films and enhancing his career. Bernie was a really good actor and was hardly ever out of work, but by the time I knew him well his looks had gone. The booze had turned his face into a red-veined slab, and his nose was a makeup man's nightmare.

One morning we had an early call but Bernie didn't turn up for makeup. We were all staying at the Great White Horse Hotel in Ipswich, a pub that is described in *Pickwick Papers*. It was a big day for Bernie as he had to deliver the crucial speech that led to the unofficial strike and the eventual destruction of Attenborough's character. It was a long and complicated speech containing a lot of union jargon, and it had to be delivered with a passionate mixture of sincerity and guile. Bernie was eventually unearthed from a cupboard where he had spent the night. He had mislaid his room after leaving the bar the night before and then, finding the only door that would open to him was the linen cupboard, had dossed down in there. When located, he was still pretty pissed but he ordered two pints of Worthington for his breakfast.

Guy and Dicky and the rest of us were filled with dread. The canteen, which was the site of Bernie's speech, had been booked; extras had been called and we couldn't afford—literally—to lose any time. Bernie stood on the podium swaying gently, with his nose glowing through the powder. He refused offers of coffee and said he was ready to shoot. Guy sighed and the camera rolled. The clapperboard clapped and Bernie, who had been slumped in a haze of alcohol, came to life. He delivered the speech without the slightest flaw and with every nuance brilliantly in place. He finished and stood solid and belligerent until Guy yelled 'Cut!' and then slumped back into his previous glassy condition. 'Cut! Print!' A round of applause and Bernie was dismissed for the day. When we watched the scene at rushes, it was astonishing. Talk about Lazarus being brought to life by the sound of the clapperboard and then relapsing into death at the word, 'Cut!'

The Angry Silence went on to win the Silver Bear at the Berlin Film Festival and to get an Oscar nomination for best story and screenplay. We didn't win the Oscar—that went to *The Apartment*, which was fair enough—but it is one of the few things I've done in the film world of which I feel really proud and, more than forty years later, it still holds up well.

Bernard Lee became a great friend. I don't know why he liked me so much because he had a dim view of most of the actors of my generation but I worked with him on and off for the next twenty years and loved him dearly. In fact, I worked with him as soon as we'd finished *The Angry Silence* in another film called *Cone of Silence*. Also shot at Shepperton, it was about the aviation industry and I played a test pilot. Bernie was my father-in-law and, after he was forced to sleep on the set one night because he was too pissed to find his way out, I used to pick him up and take him to work each day and then take him home when we finished. He lived in Chiswick, which was a bit out of my way, but the pleasure of his company made up for it.

Cone of Silence was another loan-out for me so Rank were making up the money they hadn't made from *The Angry Silence*. I also go to work with Bud Tingwell once again on this film. It wasn't much of a film and did nothing for anyone's career. I remember watching it on television with my second wife Sue, not long after I'd come to Australia. We've been together now for over thirty years, but back then we didn't know a great deal about each other, and I suspect I was trying to impress her with my brilliant career. She wasn't that impressed, and had lost the plot towards the end of the movie. I had to explain to her that the television station had shown the last two reels in the wrong order, which hadn't helped. There was no apology from them on screen, and presumably no one rang them to complain, so I guess no one had noticed. It was that kind of film.

I rejoined the Box/Thomas club again—third time lucky, I hoped—to do the fourth of the 'Doctor' films, *Doctor in Love*. Dirk Bogarde had decided that, after his third Doctor adventure, enough was enough and it was time to move on to something more cerebral. However the Doctor franchise was extremely successful and profitable for Rank and they weren't going to abandon it just because Dirk wanted to do something else. I was next cab off the rank so I was called up to play the eponymous role. It was no sweat, a bit like a mildly pleasant piece of déjà vu. The same producer, the same director, the same crew and the same cast—Sid James, James Robertson Justice, Joan Sims etc.—but with the addition of my old friend Leslie Phillips, whom I'd first met during my early poker-playing days. The script was much the same as the ones that had gone before but it was a big success at the box office and was the top British money-earner the year it was released.

Ironically, the film that Dirk had chosen to do instead bombed at the box office—I think it was *The Singer Not the Song*, in which he played a sort of Spanish or Mexican bandit opposite John Mills' heroic priest. It wasn't a bad film but the British public preferred the tried and true, and queued up to watch Leslie and me go through the old routine rather than watch Dirk being wicked. I don't think *Doctor in Love*'s success had anything to do with me—King Kong could probably have played the part with the same result—but I never got the chance to find out. In the next Doctor film, which was made in 1962 after my contract had finished, Dirk was back in the saddle and the last two of the series, made later in the sixties, didn't include either of us.

•

Babs now felt like moving closer to central London, so some time in 1960 we bought a flat in Holland Park. I wasn't there long as I was off to Spain to do another loan-out film, this time for Columbia Pictures. *Mysterious Island* was an adaptation of a Jules Verne novel and, in those pre-digitally enhanced days, relied on something called Dynamation for its magical effects. Dynamation was invented by a charming American called Ray Harryhausen. It was stop-frame animation, using models instead of drawings, and, as far as the actors were concerned, necessitated a great deal of travelling matte. We spent a lot of time playing scenes with things which weren't there but which would be added later in the laboratory. I had to do a fight with a giant crab and to my great embarrassment was called upon to perform this action on the beach at Sagaro on the Costa Brava. Dressed in a tattered American Civil War uniform and armed with a rough spear, I stabbed and feinted and leaped and floundered in the sand while bemused and amused tourists looked on. They were bemused and amused because whatever I was fighting didn't exist. Ray added the crab many months later, after eating its good bits and wiring its joints together, and all the tourists could see during shooting was this demented figure—me—ducking and weaving with no opposition in sight.

My fellow actors were a mixed bag and included the charming and eccentric Joan Greenwood, plus Herbert Lom as Captain Nemo. The downside of the job was the director, a dismal arsehole of an ex-pat American called Cy Raker Enfield, who was so disliked by all and sundry that the crew had a sign made at the end of the filming reading, 'Sigh No More'. The producer was a real Hollywood suit called Charles Schneer. He was married to the boss's daughter and was the epitome of the old LA saying, 'The son-in-law also rises'. I was talking to him one day about the Oscars and Charlie said he wasn't interested. 'The day they give an Oscar for the best deal is the day I'll be in there pitching', was his attitude.

Charlie was a bit on the mean side as a producer and never provided anything but the absolute minimum. We had prop diving helmets designed to look like huge conch shells—well, it was called *Mysterious Island*—but only two of them were made of waterproof material; the others were made of plaster. On one occasion Cy wanted the whole band to emerge from under the sea and walk up the beach. Herbert Lom and I had the real helmets, and the others had the fake ones. We duly waded out into the sea, submerged ourselves, surfaced and marched up the beach. Herbert and I were fine, but Cy was almost sobbing with frustration and the crew sobbing with laughter as the plaster helmets dissolved and slid slowly down the faces of the rest of the cast. The film was quite successful and crops up fairly often on television.

I was loaned out again to do a film called *Payroll*, which was a sort of thriller. I was the leader of a criminal gang that hijacks a payroll van and during the course of the robbery the van driver is killed. His wife, played by Billie Whitelaw, vows vengeance and hunts us down. The director's name was Sid Hayers and I never had much of a relationship with him—I think he'd learned 'directing' from a manual. During the robbery scene, which took place in Newcastle on the Tyne Bridge and involved holding up traffic for an hour—not well appreciated by the Geordie civilians—he insisted on doing a second take. We robbers had nylon stockings over our faces and looked like a Mongol horde as we crashed the payroll van. I had to look into the driver's cab, see that he had been killed by the steering wheel impaling his chest, grab the money and take off. Take one had worked like clockwork, but Sid had to have his say: 'When you see that the driver is dead, Michael, I need to see it in your eyes.' Well I thought I'd heard it all! You couldn't even see my eyes, screwed up behind the nylon mesh, but Sid must have heard the phrase somewhere and we had to do the shot again. I did it exactly the same way as the first time but Sid had had his say and face was maintained.

On the homefront Babs was pregnant again. On medical advice, because she had had a series of prior miscarriages, she had a stitch put in her cervix and lay down a lot. Michael John was born a few days after Christmas 1960, six weeks premature. He was supposed to be called Matthew but while Babs was still in the labour ward she was asked what the baby's name was. She got it wrong as she thought they were asking for the father's name, so the baby went down on the record as Michael. Over the years he has always been called either Michael John—to differentiate him from me—or MJ, which is quicker and easier.

I suppose at the time I was a bit ambivalent about MJ's arrival. On the one hand it was enchanting to have a new baby in the house—Stephen was already five and becoming increasingly grown up and independent; but on the other hand it seemed like another link in the chain which I unfairly imagined Babs had placed around my neck. Still, MJ gave a new and proper focus to Babs' life, and that took some of the pressure off me, which was good for us all.

I was now into the seventh and final year of my Rank contract and was only obliged to do two films for my salary of £10 000 a year. Pretty good going; if only the two films hadn't been so naff. Actually the first of them, *No My Darling Daughter*, wasn't really bad. I was quite impressed when I saw it recently. It starred a very young Juliet Mills—John Mills' daughter and Hayley Mills' elder sister—and she was very good indeed. The two older actors, who played her father and my father respectively, were Michael Redgrave and Roger Livesey. They gave the proceedings a touch of class. It was another Betty Box/Ralph Thomas film—my fourth with them—and they provided us with a very jolly location in Loch Lomond.

Betty then employed me yet again to make my last film under contract. This was a dismal comedy called *A Pair of Briefs*. As the title suggests, it was about a pair of barristers—male me, female Mary Peach—who, in spite of fiercely battling each other in court, manage to fall in love and end up getting married. Ho hum, yawn yawn. We did our best but the material was pretty thin and, in spite of some extraordinary overacting by Ron Moody (the original Fagin in *Oliver!*) and Brenda de Banzie, there weren't many laughs. James Robertson Justice was, as ever, playing my prospective father-in-law and gave his irascible pompous performance (or perhaps it was the pompous irascible one).

It was a short schedule for those days—seven weeks—and by the end of June I was a free man. I was then asked to play the lead in a serialisation of AJ Cronin's *The Citadel* for commercial television and I accepted with thanks. A real job with a really good part for a change, and the money was quite good too. But JD at Rank got his revenge—he refused permission. He loathed television, considering it to be the enemy, and without permission I couldn't accept the job. I ranted and raved and explained that I had completed my contractual duties with *No My Darling Daughter* and *A Pair of Briefs*. Not so, came the legal response. I was contracted to Rank until 31 August and, even though they couldn't make me work for *them*, they could stop me working for anyone else. I went to Equity and took legal advice, but all to no avail and *The Citadel* was made with someone else.

I found it particularly infuriating as I had, in fact, done several television plays while under contract to Rank. In 1958 I had done a play called *A Guardsman's Cup of Tea* for Rediffusion. It was a light comedy which had had a certain success in the West End and it is memorable to me only because that was where I had first met and worked with Harry Fowler. Harry was the first choice for every loveable young cockney lad and had had, even then, a long and highly successful career.

I also did *Philadelphia Story* for Rudolph Cartier, who was the BBC's top drama director at the time. It went out live and the only time I've been more nervous was many years later on the opening night of *Funny Girl*. As well as these productions I went to Canada twice to do plays for the CBC. The first of these was in December 1959 and was called *The Beckoning Hill*, in which I played a shepherd with attitude in the wilds of Nova Scotia. It was made for what was called Kraft Theatre (as in Kraft cheese etc.) by the CBC in Toronto. It was the first time I'd been back to Canada since the summer of 1945.

I tried to use these precedents while arguing my case with JD and the rest at South Street after they refused my request to do *The Citadel,* but it did no good—my pleas fell on deaf ears. My time with Rank was drawing to a close. I had spent seven years, from 1954 to 1961, pursuing my professional life in a succession of unmemorable films, punctuated by stupid feuds with the Rank hierarchy. During this time of considerable social change— in which British society was moving from the greyness of its post-war existence into the rosy pink optimism of the 'swinging sixties'—my marriage was still spluttering along.

Babs and I entertained quite a lot, had friends to dinner, and were entertained quite a lot in return. We all smoked and drank too much, played a lot of poker and, in my case, carried on affairs whenever I thought I could get away with it. Just before I did the second of the Canadian television productions I had run away from home and began living in fair-to-middling bachelor squalor in a bed-sitter in Chelsea Cloisters. I was involved at that time with three separate ladies, as well as Babs, and felt I had to make a break from living under the same roof as my justifiably angry wife. I wasn't away for long, a few weeks perhaps—just enough time for my other ladies to get fed up with me and give me the push—and then I was back in the family home, sadder, but alas not much wiser. I don't know what the boys made of my absence; maybe they hardly noticed, as I was away so much working. But every so often Babs and I would go and stay with my mother and Roland at Gubbions Hall, and some of my London friends would sometimes come down with us for a day's rough shooting in the woods. We also went up to Scotland to see Pa whenever we could and he would kill the fatted calf and get stuck into the single malt with such enthusiasm that he'd be struck down by his chronic malaria, contracted in India in his army days, which always seemed to recur on these occasions.

As my Rank contract petered out in the summer of 1961 I could see that the writing was very much on the wall for me as far as the film business was concerned. La Nouvelle Vague had occurred in France and was echoed by a New Wave in England. It was the day of the working-class hero, and the gritty working-class, not to mention kitchen sink, type drama. Albert Finney, Richard Harris, Tom Courtney and the pre-nose-jobbed Peter O'Toole were the new and very talented leading men. The bland young good-looking professional men I had played—doctors, lawyers, architects or whatever—were *passé*. If I wasn't very careful, I'd be *passé* too. After seven years and twenty films I had a last drink with some mates at Pinewood and never went back.

I now signed a two-year contract with Columbia Pictures to make four films at a fair price and waited to see what would happen. The contract was non-exclusive and, in fact, lasted for nearly four years because it was voluntarily suspended for a year and a bit when I went to Stratford for the Royal Shakespeare Company in 1963.

EIGHT

Play time

As it turned out, I think I only made two films for Columbia, *Life at the Top* in 1965 and *Stolen Hours* in 1962. In between I worked for Basil Dearden and Michael Relph again in a film called *Life for Ruth* and for Peter Rogers and Gerald Thomas, the producer and director of the *Carry On* films, in *The Iron Maiden*. I also made the first of several Italian/Spanish/Yugoslavian/any-other-kind-of-European co-productions over the next few years. This was *The Captive City*, starring David Niven, the most charming and entertaining of men. I had a couple of brief sorties back into the theatre—in *Three Posts on the Square* at the Arts Theatre in London and *Whistle in the Dark*. I also did the occasional television play.

After I moved out of Chelsea Cloisters and back to the bosom of my family, who were on the whole fairly pleased to have me back, I tried to behave myself. The boys were growing up and I wanted to be a good father, even if I couldn't be a good husband. Stephen was six and MJ one and a half in 1962 when Babs and I decided we needed more room. So we sold the flat in Holland Park and bought a house in Chelsea. Eat your hearts out, twenty-first century home buyers—the five-bedroom house in Ormonde Gate, the best part of Chelsea, cost me £16 000 for a thirty-year lease. The sixties did truly swing for me.

The *Whistle in the Dark* experience was enjoyable and instructive. I first read the play, written in longhand in an exercise book, while I was holed up in Chelsea Cloisters. It was written by a man called Tom Murphy who at the time was teaching woodwork in a school in the west of Ireland. It was given to me by a friend called Brian Phelan with whom I had enjoyed many a pub crawl in London and Dublin. I read the play, thought it was great and, as a self-interested actor, thought it had a great part in it for me. I showed it to an agent/manager called Robin Fox (the father of the actors, James and Edward Fox). He had some sort of association with the Grade Organisation, by whom I was still represented in the care of Monty Lyon. Robin liked the play too and we decided to jointly present it at Stratford East. There was, of course, the little matter of finance for the production, but we thought that wouldn't be too hard. I put in £3000 of my own money and raised another three thousand from fellow drinkers at my local, The Queen's Elm, who kicked in amounts varying from £50 to £500 pounds. Sean Treacy, the governor of the pub, was very generous and I think the poet and author Laurie Lee shelled out as well. The money was raised over the weekend so we were formally in production.

We had a pretty good cast headed by a wonderful Irish actor called Patrick Magee. Pat was only in his late forties but looked sixty, which was just as well as he had to play the father of five sons. It required a cast of eight, yet we had to mount the production for £12 000, which needed to include the director's fee and the cost of building a set. We actors all worked for a straight fifty quid a week with no rehearsal pay. Pat's performance was truly magnificent. We had such a good reaction and such fun at Stratford East we decided to transfer the show to the Apollo Theatre in Shaftesbury Avenue. Sadly, we died a death over five or six empty weeks. Ken Tynan, who was the number one drama critic at the time, gave us a good notice as did one or two of the other critics, but the public didn't want to see a play about a warring Irish family coming to grief in Coventry, so we had to close.

The only person to make anything out of this production was Tom Murphy, the writer. He was on a percentage, of course, so he made two or three hundred pounds a week until we finally sank without trace. Tom gave up his school mastering and moved to London, where he continued to write plays. Robin Fox and I had an option on his next, which was called *The Morning After Optimism*, but we passed on it and I don't think Tom ever forgave me. He also resented the fact that I had played the lead in *Whistle*. He felt it should have been played by a real Irishman, not a jumped-up ex-film starling, and that the play might have been a hit if it had been. He could have been right, but he had no real cause for complaint. In the end he did pretty well out of the deal as he sold the film rights a couple of years later to producer Peter Rogers (who made all the *Carry On* movies), and who later sold them on to me. Tom also met and subsequently married a rich girl who drank in The Queen's Elm. They finally moved back to Dublin, where I think Tom became writer-in-residence at the Abbey Theatre.

I freely admit that my motives for doing the play were not entirely altruistic, but I did feel I was putting something back into a profession, which had been pretty good to me, by providing a shop window for a new young writing talent. However, it taught me that the fastest and easiest way to lose a friend is to do them a favour—they hardly ever forgive you for it. And *Whistle in the Dark* cost me a few quid, but it wasn't too damaging. I had quite a lot of work on offer and had returned home to Babs, so I no longer had to pay rent for the Chelsea Cloisters place as well as the family expenses. My relationship with Babs remained a touch delicate, but at least it remained. But there was something that was never quite right between us. I really tried not to wander and had had hoped I'd sowed the last of my wild oats. It was okay for a while—I was as discreet as I could be, and she was as oblivious as she could be—while we rubbed along in moderate affluence in the new house in Chelsea. But deep down we both knew it wasn't going to last.

The years 1961 and '62 were very busy. As well as *Whistle in the Dark*, which overlapped from 1961 into the new year, I made four films: *The Iron Maiden, Life for Ruth, The Captive City* and *Stolen Hours*. I remember the absolute hell of filming all day long on *The Iron Maiden* and then driving back to London to do *Whistle* on stage at night. You should never try to combine theatre and film at the same time. One or other, or more probably both, are bound to suffer. But greed and arrogance and youthful energy tell you that you can do it. In spite of the stress and sheer fatigue, I cheerfully burnt both ends of the candle, which in my case did *not* give a lovely light.

The Iron Maiden storyline involved a race between two steam engines—*The Iron Maiden* (mine) and *The Dreadnought*, belonging to a lovely Irish actor called Noel Purcell. There was an American girl in it, Anne Helm, who was my love interest and had been in a film with Elvis Presley. Her father was played by another American, Alan Hale Jr, who was most famous for being the Skipper in *Gilligan's Island*. He was a pretty irritating sort of actor. He had a big laugh and some other personal mannerisms, which he employed whatever the dramatic situation, and left it at that. The climax of the race took place at Woburn Abbey, home to the Duke and Duchess of Bedford. They both appeared as themselves in the film with a lot of old steam engines. As entertainment, the film was a harmless piece of rubbish.

Life for Ruth, which I did next, was a very difficult film to make. I played a Jehovah's Witness who allowed his small daughter to die rather than let her have a blood transfusion, so my character was charged with manslaughter. The film was made by Michael Relph and Basil Dearden, and written by Janet Green, the trio responsible for *Sapphire* five years earlier. I was rather surprised to be offered this film—playing a North Country working-class chap seemed against type—but I was very flattered and delighted to do it. My wife was played by Janet Munro, a lovely girl who had been under contract to Walt Disney and made several films for him when she was still a teenager. She later died tragically young of complications relating to alcoholism and never really had the chance to develop her great talents and personality.

We went to the north-east coast for the locations—we were based in Sunderland—and I remember having to plunge into the sea to rescue my drowning daughter. It was late autumn and I almost drowned myself with the shock of the coldness of the water. While on location I was invited to a party given by one of the local gentry and, for the first and only time in my life, I encountered the 'keys in the hat' wife-swapping routine. Fortunately, or perhaps unfortunately, Babs hadn't come on location with me (well, Sunderland in the autumn hadn't the same allure as Rome or Nice in the summer so who could blame her) so I had no wife to swap. How different life might have been if she had been there and pulled out the right set of keys and met a chap who could have made her happy!

For my next assignment, in 1962, I went to Italy with the entire family to make a film called *The Captive City*. As I said earlier, the star was David Niven. Babs and the boys and Saia, our Finnish au pair girl, adored being in Rome and spent a great deal of time on the beach at Ostia. One morning soon after we arrived, I told them I'd join them after lunch as I had the afternoon free. When I arrived, they were in a high state of excitement—a wonderfully debonair and handsome Englishman had chatted them up and was buying gelati for the boys, and camparis for Babs and Saia. A minute or two later Mr Niven hove into sight with the ice-creams and drinks. For the briefest of moments he lost his cool when he saw me, then the penny dropped. But David was the most urbane and sophisticated of men and we all became good friends.

David taught me a lot about filming independent productions on the Continent:

> Never ever shoot your last and, if possible, your most important scene until and unless you've been paid in full, Old Bean. It's all a bit of a game with them and, without wanting to screw

you per se, they will if they can. It's a question of 'face', as the Japanese would say, or *figura* as we say in Italy.

It was good advice and stood me in very good stead over the next few years when I worked in various dodgy co-productions in Yugoslavia and Italy and Spain. David was also an extremely generous and entertaining man, and his stories of his early life and times in Hollywood, which he later published in *The Moon is a Balloon* and *Bring on the Empty Horses*, I first heard over boozy dinners in the trattorias in Rome. There was one that made me laugh a lot but which for obvious reasons never made it into those books.

As a young actor in LA David was summoned to dinner by Joan Crawford, who was the reigning Queen of Hollywood. It was a summons he couldn't ignore but when he arrived at her mansion he discovered that what he had assumed to be a dinner party was in fact a dinner for two. His heart sank—he was in love with someone at the time—but, being the gallant chap that he was, he bravely soldiered on. They swam nude in the pool and she admired his manly figure—which he said had shrunk to peanut size in the cool of the evening—and then went in to dinner. They sat at opposite ends of a long dining table and were served by a butler in full evening dress. David found himself becoming more and more nervous and hysterical. After dinner she seated David in a large wing-backed chair, gave him a goblet of brandy and disappeared into the bathroom. He sat there considering his next move and a moment or two later looked up to see the Queen of Hollywood crouched above him on the back of the high chair, naked and ready for action. He excused himself politely, went into the bathroom in his turn and returned wearing her shower cap. He sat down again, prepared for the worst, but evidently the moment had passed for her and he was struck off her list forever.

Apart from David Niven, *The Captive City* starred a couple of Italian actresses, Daniela Rocca and Lea Massari, and featured Ben Gazzara, Martin Balsam, Percy Herbert and myself. The producer, or producers, were any number of Italian suits. One of them was alleged to be the head of Bel Paese cheese and was enjoying a liaison with Daniela Rocca. According to Niven, she persuaded the producer to put the hard word on the film's director, Joe Anthony, to include a death scene for her, which she would play with Niven and so earn an Oscar nomination. Both Niven and Anthony were reluctant to do this but even more reluctant to upset Ms Rocca and, through her, Mr Bel Paese. So the scene was duly written and shot. It was, needless to say, left on the cutting-room floor, as they say—or would have been if there had been any film in the camera while they shot it. However *bella figura* and goodwill were maintained at a very small cost in time and money.

The two American actors, Martin Balsam and Ben Gazzara, couldn't have been more different, in spite of the fact that they were both alumni of Lee Strasberg's Actors Studio in New York. Marty was a modest and funny man who, unlike so many American actors, didn't take the work or himself too seriously. He was very smitten by Lea Massari and wooed her as best he could. I don't know how successful he was but, after the filming wrapped and we all went our separate ways, he stayed on in Rome. I hope it all worked out as he wished.

Mr Gazzara, on the other hand, was a real pain in the arse. He took himself very, very seriously and behaved in an extraordinarily obtuse way. In the story, I was a British Army Captain (I turned out to be the traitorous villain as far as I can remember) and Ben was an American Lieutenant. In a particular scene he was supposed to salute me, but he refused to do so on the grounds that his billing in the film was superior to mine. One could but smile. The smiles turned to laughter when in another scene, in which the leading character briefs the other characters (and incidentally the audience) about what has happened and what will happen next, David Niven as the commanding officer gave the briefing and the rest of us were supposed to listen and take notice. Not Mr Gazzara—he was a physical actor, almost incapable of doing nothing. Simply reacting to someone else was not his bag.

He asked for a bread roll to eat while he listened, justifying the request by an invented 'back story' that he'd been on a mission of some danger and hadn't eaten or slept for three days. As the bread roll was produced, Marty and David and I looked at each other and smiled. I should explain here that these sorts of scenes are very tedious to shoot as they involve a wide shot (including the entire group), then mid shots (some of the group), then over-shoulder shots (most of the group and the principal speaker) and finally close-ups. By the time they got to Ben's close-up he'd gnashed his way through over a dozen rolls, his gums were raw and breadcrumbs were coming out of his ears. Every time there was a slight mistake by cast or crew we had to start again and the continuity clerk was kept busy gauging how much of the roll had been eaten before Joe Anthony called 'Cut'. The prop man would then appear with the appropriately sized roll, give it to the struggling Gazzara with a smiling *prego signore*, and sit back and watch.

It served the silly bugger right and reminded me of a story Nigel Patrick had told me when we were in *Sapphire*. He had done a film with Jack Palance and had found it very irritating to be kept constantly waiting to do a take while Palance gee-ed himself up to get into the mood for the scene. He bore with it for a week or two and then made his move. He was playing some kind of department head, to whom the Palance character had to report with a crucial piece of information. Paddy sat stoically in his chair in his make-believe office while Jack Palance ran around and around the studio until he felt sufficiently tired or inspired to do the scene. Each time the American actor entered the room and started his speech, Paddy would cough or drop something or give the wrong cue. He would then apologise profusely while Palance ground his teeth and swore and went out to run himself into the mood again. They did take after take until finally Palance ran himself to a standstill and waited quietly outside the door for his cue to enter, like any other sensible chap would have done in the first place. Paddy for some mysterious reason was then able to resist his coughing fits, refrain from dropping his fountain pen and get his lines right. Palance never said anything but for the rest of the film did his warm-ups on his own time and not on Paddy's.

About halfway through the shoot of *The Captive City*, Babs and the boys went home, leaving me alone and palely loitering on the Via Veneto. Rome was full of English actors, who were hanging about doing bits and pieces in *Cleopatra*, which was then filming at the Cinecitta Studios. I knew some of them. *Cleopatra* was originally supposed to have been shot at Pinewood Studios with Joan Collins as Cleopatra, Peter Finch as Caesar and Stephen Boyd as Mark Antony but it came undone in a big way. After five months of non-productive filming the whole thing was shut down and the studio started again. Elizabeth Taylor, Rex Harrison and Richard Burton were hired instead, and the entire production moved from Pinewood to Cinecitta. Many of the actors had been in Rome for weeks and weeks without ever doing a day's work. They were being paid, of course, and were enjoying an extended holiday in the sun courtesy of Twentieth Century Fox. So most evenings after the family went home I'd join them in their quest for the 'dolce vita'.

Our favourite haunt was a club called the Pipistrello where, full of goodwill and whisky, one night I was mistaken for a brilliant American dancer called Peter Genaro after I'd performed an impromptu tap dance on the tables and chairs. Now anyone who knows me also knows that I have two left feet, but the signorinas didn't seem to think so and one of them gave me the eye. It was summertime in Rome and I behaved a great deal worse than I should have. Babs was back in England; and the one evening I had spent with Ms Rocca had been a bit underwhelming due to her terror that Mr Bel Paese would find out and wreak a terrible vengeance on us both. However, luckily for me, I *didn't* fall in love for a change and when I finally returned to London I was tired but happy.

Columbia Pictures, who had me on contract, finally put me in a film called *Stolen Hours*. This was a remake of a famous Bette Davis tear-jerker called *Dark Victory*. It involved a youngish lady who gets a brain tumour, goes blind and finally dies coura-geously to the sound of an angelic choir. Along the way she falls in love with, and marries, the doctor who has diagnosed her condi-tion. In the Bette Davis version, the doctor was played by George Brent. In our remake he was played by me. Incredible as it may sound, I was even more boring than George Brent, who was never the most scintillating of actors. Solid, worthy, professional, but definitely not scintillating. In my case add *stupid*—in my final scene I watch my darling wife, who I know is terminally ill, stumble down the stairs, spill her drink all over the top of the piano and finally grope her way to the front door bumping into the furniture, without twigging that *this might be it*.

The dying lady was played by Susan Hayward, a redoubtable Hollywood star whom I had watched and lusted over while I was still at school. I remember seeing her in a film called *Reap the Wild Wind* back in the forties and was very struck by her looks and her cleavage. In 1958 she had had a huge success and won an Oscar for *I Want To Live,* directed by my later good friend Robert Wise. I don't know why she wanted to do *Stolen Hours* four years later. Did she owe Columbia a favour, did she want to show all those Bette Davis fans how it should be really done, or did she just fancy an all-expenses-paid trip to England? I never asked her. In fact, we hardly spoke to each other away from the set. This was not because of any antipathy between us, far from it. I liked her very much and I think she liked me too. It was just that she kept very much to herself, and had a personal dressing room on the sound stage to which she'd retire as soon as the director said, 'Print it'. She was charming and polite to everyone, unfailingly professional, but I never got to know her at all. We worked together for twelve weeks, in the studios at Shepperton and on location in Cornwall. We did love scenes, in-bed-together scenes, we even got married; but right up to the last day of the shoot I was still calling her Miss Hayward.

She was married at the time to an extremely unlikeable American who owned the Cadillac franchise for the state of Florida, and was thereby incredibly rich. He loathed England and everything English, especially the mixed blessings of Fowey, the little Cornish town where we spent three weeks on location. I was surprised to learn recently that yet another version of *Dark Victory* was made in 1976, starring Elizabeth Montgomery (*Bewitched*) and Anthony Hopkins. Perhaps he learned his doctoring in it—the doctoring he put to such good use as Hannibal Lecter. I suppose a good old-fashioned melodrama has a certain attraction, but I'm afraid that, of the three versions of *Dark Victory*, ours came in a pretty sorry third.

The rest of my family were pursuing their various lives of course but, apart from Richard, I didn't see much of them. A few years after becoming a literary agent, my brother became half-owner of Gregson and Wigan, which during the sixties represented most of the top writing and directing talent in the UK. Richard's personal life wasn't going so well, however, as his first marriage was disintegrating, in spite of the three children they'd had in a remarkably short time. He and Gareth Wigan, having made a lot of money, sold their business to EMI. Richard then got divorced and went to Hollywood, where he enjoyed great success as an agent and a producer and married Natalie Wood.

After *Stolen Hours* finished in the autumn of 1962, I did a couple of television plays for ATV at Elstree and then, to my great surprise, I got a call from Peter Hall, who was now top banana at the Royal Shakespeare Company (RSC) at Stratford-on-Avon. I hadn't seen Peter for the best part of ten years, not since he directed me in *A Man About the House* at the Oxford Playhouse. I had, of course, watched his rise and rise with great interest and some envy, but never really expected to work with him again. He asked me to come to Stratford to play the Earl of Suffolk in his monumental production of *The Wars of the Roses*. This was a version, edited and in some places re-written by John Barton, of Shakespeare's *King Henry VI*, Parts 1, 2 and 3. Barton compressed these into two parts, retitled *Henry VI* and *Edward IV*, and followed them with *Richard III*, the words of which he left untouched. I was extremely flattered to be invited. The part was quite a good one, and had the great advantage of playing opposite the wonderful Peggy Ashcroft. But I needed a new car to get me to Stratford.

One of the few disadvantages of living in Ormonde Gate was that I had no garage and we were uncomfortably close to the barracks in the Kings Road. Young soldiers on weekend leave would routinely steal cars in the neighbourhood, drive themselves home and then back on Sunday evening when they would leave the car in any old street, none the worse except for some extra mileage on the clock. This had happened to me a few times, but on one occasion my car just didn't turn up as usual. So I went down to Guildford, where I had bought three Jaguars over the years, intending to buy another. The dealer showed me a car, costing the same as a new Jag, which was unlike any I'd ever seen. In fact, I think only about five hundred were ever built, and this was one of them.

It was called a Facel Vega, a hard-topped gunmetal-grey sports car with two comfortable seats in the front, and two minuscule seats in the back. It had a French body and suspension, and a five-litre Chrysler engine in the old V8 configuration. The seats were of red leather and the gearshift was a small box with buttons protruding from it. The buttons were marked *1, 2, 3, 4* and *R*. It had a huge boot but this was mostly filled by the petrol tank which held thirty-five gallons. I should have been warned but I was entranced and bought the bloody thing. It was the first automatic car I ever owned. The fuel consumption was horrendous—about twelve miles to the gallon, less when travelling at high speed, which I did most of the time. There was no speed limit on the motorways then and I'd travel up the M1 to the Leamington Spa turn-off for Stratford at a conservative one hundred and thirty miles per hour (over two hundred kilometres in today's terminology).

I arrived in Stratford in the Facel Vega—the cynosure of all eyes, as they say—in May 1963. It was a bit like going to a new school. I knew no one in the company, except Donald Sinden, who had been under contract to Rank with me and with whom I'd worked a couple of times. He too had been co-opted by Peter

Hall for *The Wars of the Roses* and the press had a bit of a go at the idea of ex-Rank film actors joining the hallowed ranks of The Royal Shakespeare Company. They might have had some justification in my case ('Madam, I go with all convenient speed' wasn't much of a preparation for the world's premier Shakespearian company), but Donald had been a successful actor in the theatre long before he joined the Rank Organisation.

I was filled with an over-earnest determination to justify my inclusion in the company—it was my chance to validate my professional standing and finally lay to rest the ghosts of *A Pair of Briefs* and *Doctor in Love*. It was also a chance that had cost me quite a bit of money. Columbia Pictures, who were paying me £15 000 per annum, suspended my contract for a year (I think they were quite pleased to do this as they had no pictures for me to do at the time, but might have later on) and I was paid just £40 a week by the RSC. It was a considerable cut in earnings, especially as I had to pay for digs in Stratford for the eight-week rehearsal period, as well as keep Ormonde Gate up and running. But money isn't everything—*The Wars of the Roses* and the Stratford experience would be something different and important, something really special, I thought. Wrong! It was exactly the same as every other job, with the added irritation that it pretended that it wasn't. It took me a week or two to realise this and at first I was shocked and deeply disappointed. Later on it was a great relief as I was able to relax and go with the flow like everyone else.

We started the rehearsal process with a four-day seminar on the life and times of fifteenth-century England. Everything from politics, religion and royalty, to housing, cooking and education. I kept looking at my script to see how this affected my character, the Earl of Suffolk, but could find no link. Shakespeare had written the plays more than a hundred years after the events portrayed and had taken his material from the Holinshed Chronicles. He was never too fussy about anachronisms (e.g. the reference to a clock in *Julius Caesar*) and never let the real truth get in the way of a good story. Although the state of the drains in Plantagenet

England might have been of some interest to a history student, I was an actor and anxious to start the real business of rehearsal. I found a fellow spirit in Nick Selby and, after the first two days of lectures, he and I retired to the back of the conference hall to play Battleships. Nick was a very good influence. He refused to take anything too seriously except his beer and his pipe, and was instrumental in wiping the sillier stars from my eyes with his jaunty observation, 'It's only pretend, old plum'.

Nick played the Bishop of Winchester in a costume which made him look like a giant red lizard. He had some immensely long and complicated speeches about lineage and inheritance and church policy, and he delivered them with a wonderful mixture of wisdom and malice. At one matinee performance he finished the first of these speeches and then nodded off. It was one of the many council scenes in the play involving most of the nobles and, of course, the King and Queen, played by David Warner and Peggy Ashcroft. We were all positioned around a huge metal table in our armour and coronets and robes carrying on a fifteenth-century political debate. Very spectacular. The scene continued until it was time for the Bishop to speak again. Nick was sound asleep, his head propped in his hand with his cowl pulled down over his eyes. There was a pause and then Brewster Mason, who was playing the Earl of Warwick and was sitting next to him, nudged him savagely. Nick sprang to life—knowing instinctively that it was his turn, he started all over again—his first speech about Salic law, whatever it is. We looked at each other in horror. Nick droned on remorselessly until Peggy or David cut him off with a regal, 'Thank you, My Lord Bishop,' and swept off the stage followed by the rest of us. The audience was none the wiser. It is a curious phenomenon of play-going that, short of the set falling down or an actor dropping dead, audiences will accept pretty much anything that happens up there. Well, why not? They haven't seen it before and, even if they have, some productions are so wayward and arbitrary that practically anything goes.

When rehearsals finally started properly, I stood in the wings waiting to make my first entrance with Peggy. In the play I had just captured her in a battle in France and we had a nice little two-handed scene to kick off with. Peter Hall, who wasn't well throughout the entire rehearsal period, shouted from the stalls for us to come on. 'Where from, Peter?' we asked, expecting some kind of directive that was part of the great overall directorial plan. 'Where do you want?' he shouted back. Peggy and I looked at each other. Both our dressing rooms were prompt side, that is stage left, so it would be convenient to enter from that side. We shrugged and smiled companionably, and made our mutual decision. 'Prompt side, Peter,' Peggy shouted. 'Fine,' he shouted back. So that was what we did, and another star dropped from my ingenuous eyes. To be fair to Peter, his great strengths as a director were his ability to tell you what *not* to do, and to edit. He expected you to know what you should do, and his task was to make sure you did it at the right time with the right people.

It was a very long rehearsal period, eight weeks, because we were to open both plays, *Henry VI* and *Edward IV,* on the same day—a matinee of *Henry* followed by an evening performance of *Edward*. Initially I was only in the first play; I also played Jack Cade when we moved to the Aldwych Theatre later in the year, but at Stratford my involvement finished with my beheading at the end of *Henry VI*. I was supposed to be in *Richard III* as well, playing the Murderer of Clarence, but dipped out after a very disagreeable experience with Peter. He told me the part was mine, but I would have to 'appear' to audition for it as that was the standard practice in the company. There were half a dozen actors who were playing small parts and they all wanted to play the Murderer, so it had to seem as if they were being given the opportunity to try for it.

I couldn't believe what I was hearing. This was supposed to be a company in which every member had the same rights and status—one of Peter's proudest boasts—and yet he was clearly telling me that he was quite willing to bend the rules and bull-shit his actors if he felt like it. I didn't feel I could happily work and drink with these colleagues, busily working on their Murderer's auditions, knowing all their work was in vain because I already had the part. I told Peter this and he smiled his pussycat smile and let it go at that. That was the final star to drop for me, and afterwards I just got on with the job as if I were working for Ralph Thomas or Basil Dearden.

Many of the cast were appearing in the other productions running at Stratford that season—*Julius Caesar* and *The Tempest,* I think—and, after a long day's rehearsal of *The Wars of the Roses,* would have to kit up as a Roman or a sprite and labour on into the evening. All that for the basic salary of sixteen quid a week given for walk-ons and understudies. Meanwhile I was in the Dirty Duck, or whizzing back to Ormonde Gate in the Facel, depending on my next rehearsal call.

We finally opened to triumphant reviews after a dress rehearsal that seemed to last an eternity. David Warner, who was only twenty-three, had a huge success as *King Henry VI* and went on to have a curious and ultimately disappointing career. Perhaps it all happened for him too young and too soon, but in the summer of 1963 he had the theatrical world at his feet. We all came out of it pretty well and that *Wars of the Roses* became almost legendary, a landmark production for the RSC. Ian Holm, who had been in the company for years, finally got his chance as Richard III and we all know how he flourished after that.

I became good friends with John Welsh and Brewster Mason, who were senior members of the company and we used to play golf together. I'd also have a drink with Geoffrey Dench, Judi's brother, who'd worked with me in the company at York ten years earlier, and with Penelope Keith, Roy Marsden, Roy Dotrice and a couple of lads from Down Under, Ronny Falk and Rees McConochy. I kept out of romantic trouble by going back to London as often as I could. I found I could do stage door to London in ninety minutes if I put my foot down, so I would often drive home after the show. I enjoyed most of the whole time I spent on the play, apart from the anxiety of trying to make sure I got the dates right and didn't find myself on the golf course in Richmond on a day I was supposed to be losing my head in Stratford.

I came to adore Peggy Ashcroft, as well as to admire her enormously. No, no, no, nothing like that, a purely professional and cricketing relationship. She was a real cricket aficionado and when the test matches were being played she conspired with one of the cast to conceal a transistor radio under his helmet with an earpiece leading to his upstage ear, so he could keep her up-to-date with the latest score during the matinees. In a memorable local cricket match she and I were part of the Lancastrian XI, captained by Cyril Washbrook, ex-England and Lancashire opening bat. Our opponents were the Yorkists (Red Rose versus White Rose), captained by Sir Leonard Hutton, once captain of England and Yorkshire, and the maker of that historic score of 364 against Australia in 1938. The match was in aid of some charity and, while not to be taken too seriously, it was close and hard contested. I came on to bowl (rubbishy off-spinners, which didn't spin very much) against the great Len Hutton. He played studiously forward, the ball caught a leading edge and dollied up into the covers, where Dame Peggy clutched it to her ample bosom. There it was in the scorebook: 'HUTTON, L. Caught Ashcroft, bowled Craig.'

•

Peter asked me if I would do the London season (the RSC played the Aldwych Theatre for some of their productions) and he also asked me to work the next season at Stratford, playing the parts I'd be doing at the Aldwych—Suffolk and Cade plus The Constable of France in *Henry V* and Orsino in *Twelfth Night*. I thought I might as well do two seasons—the parts weren't bad and not too demanding—so I said I would if I could square it with my boss at Columbia. It was not attractive financially, even though my salary at Stratford would rise to £60 a week, but I had the fall-back position of the film contract, which guaranteed me fifteen grand as soon as I came off suspension. My agent and, more importantly, my wife thought it a good idea, so I went to see Bill

Graf at Columbia and got my suspension extended for another year. Again, I don't think they had anything for me. I wasn't required for *King Rat,* a film about prisoners of war in Changi, nor for their next production, so it was no skin off their noses.

A week or so later Peter called a company meeting at Stratford to announce his plan for the following year. I sat back in the comfortable knowledge that my future was already secured. That feeling of comfort was quickly dispelled as, avoiding my eyes, Peter elaborated. The success of *The Wars of the Roses* had persuaded him to change his original programme and replace it with all the Histories, starting with *Richard II,* followed by *Henry IV* Parts 1 and 2, *Henry V, The Wars of the Roses* and culminating with *Richard III.* Wasn't that exciting? The consensus was yes, it was very exciting but, when I knocked on his door half an hour later, he looked extremely shifty. 'Ah Michael,' he said, smiling that pussycat smile. 'I thought you might want to see me.' I asked him where I fit in to this new scheme of things and he asked me what parts I'd like to do. I told him, but they were all already cast. I had the choice of Hereford or Cornwall or Leicester or some other geographical location—the list read like the County Cricket Championship—but there was not a decent part amongst them.

I was devastated. I pointed out that it was only a matter of a few days since I had got myself suspended from my Columbia contract at great financial sacrifice—he must have known of his change of plans while I was doing it—and now I was put in a position of having to do crap parts or be out of work. He apologised and the pussycat smile grew thinner, but there was really nothing he could do about it. In that case, I told him, the sooner I left the RSC and returned to gainful employment—however I could—the better it would be for me. In the circumstances I would not be doing the Aldwych season, and would leave the company at Christmas, when the Stratford season finished.

This did not go down well. He said Peggy would be most distressed if I left; she enjoyed doing her love scenes etc. with me as Suffolk and wouldn't want to spend the Christmas break rehearsing them again with a replacement. I told him he could explain my reasons to Peggy, or I would. I was sure she'd be more than sympathetic. In the end I agreed to do the London season if I was paid a London salary, which was about £150 a week. After some haggling and compromise a deal was made.

It was a sad way to go out but it got even sadder when we reached London. Our contracts stated there would be no 'billing' except alphabetical, which wasn't too bad for me as a C, but not so good for my friends, John Welsh and Nick Selby, and terrible for David Warner, who was playing the title role. However, that was the agreement and it was the same for everyone. When I turned up at the Aldwych after the Christmas break, when I'd luckily earned some real dough by doing a television play with Arthur Lowe (later Captain Mainwaring in *Dad's Army*) I was enraged to see the posters outside the theatre. At the top of the bill they read: Peggy Ashcroft as Queen Margaret, David Warner as Henry VI, Ian Holm as Richard III, Donald Sinden as Duke of York, Roy Dotrice as Edward IV. Underneath was a list of all the other members of the company in strict alphabetical order; our names on the right and the parts we played on the left. I looked at this poster for about five minutes then went to see the company manager, Paddy Donald. I'd taken the precaution of ringing my agent and Actor's Equity first and was filled with righteous indignation. I told Paddy that I wouldn't be appearing that night as the RSC was in breach of contract. He looked a bit startled and I continued. 'The contract unequivocally states that there shall be no billing other than alphabetical, and this'— I pointed at the poster which had been printed on thousands of flyers—'this, according to Equity, according to my agent and according to me, is billing.'

Paddy had no answer to this and asked me what I wanted. I told him that the posters had to be changed or there'd be no show. I wasn't just fighting for myself, I was thinking about Welsh and Selby and all the others further down the alphabetical list. I was sure they'd feel the same. Poor Paddy was in a bind. He knew management was in the wrong, but thousands of the flyers had been distributed and he couldn't get them back. I conceded the difficulty and told him I'd settle for changing the posters on the front of the theatre. I can't really remember now whether this was done or not, but I'd made my point and given the bastards something to think about.

We opened the season by doing all three plays in one day, starting with *Henry VI* at 11 a.m. and finishing with *Richard III* at about 11 p.m. A long day for some. I had a vision of one of the walk-ons and understudies, who played everything from a French peasant or an English bowman to a London beggar or a you-name-it with a constant change of costume and props, getting out of sync—spending all day changing into or out of the wrong character and never actually getting on stage until the very end, when he rushes on to ruin Richmond's final speech in *Richard III*.

Nick Selby, John Welsh, Clive Swift and I shared a dressing room and of the four of us only Clive was in all three plays; the rest of us were in the first two only. I was now doing Jack Cade in *Edward IV* (he also got his head cut off) as well as Suffolk in *Henry VI,* but at the first performance we were told we had to return for the final curtain call at the end of *Richard III*. This was a bad management decision and was never implemented again. While *Richard III* was being performed, Nick and John and I went to the pub and, when we returned to take the call, we'd had an absolute gutful. I remember the three of us trying to get into our costumes—chain mail and boots and breastplates etc.—and finding it almost impossible. We settled on a sort of hybrid disguise of cloaks and boots, and did our best not to fall over when we bowed.

The season was a huge success but there was a lot of ill feeling in the company. Towards the end of the run, on one of the days when we did all three plays, a notice was posted on the board backstage announcing who would be playing what in the upcoming season. For every cheerful satisfied actor who had got what he'd hoped for, there was a desperately unhappy one who had learned for the first time that he was surplus to requirements and had better start looking for another job. Not a good way to start a day that seemed to go on forever.

We closed in April 1964 and I thought I'd done my dash with Peter Hall and the RSC. Not so. A couple of years later I was asked to take over in Harold Pinter's *The Homecoming* and then to do the play in New York and Boston. Peter was ever the pragmatist and, when we met again to rehearse, it was as if nothing had ever come between us.

NINE

Showtime

Soon after I finished at the Aldwych, I started rehearsals for the play *I Love You Mrs Patterson* at St Martins Theatre. It dealt with the infatuation of a teenaged schoolboy for the wife of his schoolteacher. I was Mr Patterson, the schoolteacher, and my namesake, Wendy Craig, was the subject of the infatuation. A very good young actor called Jeremy Bullock played the teenager. Another member of the cast, playing my headmaster, was Peter Collingwood, who I would again meet and work with twenty years later, after we'd both moved to Australia. It was the only time I ever worked for the legendary 'Binkie' Beaumont, and he lived up to everything I'd ever heard of him. He came to Brighton to see a performance before we opened in London and, with the polished urbanity and thinly disguised malice for which he was famous, delivered his judgement: 'A little snip-snip perhaps', he said, making scissoring movements with his fingers, smiling benignly and shimmering away to be chauffeur-driven back to his offices in Shaftesbury Avenue. He might well have been right. The play got respectable notices but didn't catch on and we closed after five weeks.

While I was playing *I Love You Mrs Patterson*, I had a curious call from Monty Lyon about meeting Jule Styne, the legendary composer and songwriter responsible for *Gypsy*, among other notable Broadway hit musicals. I was to meet him and an American producer who wanted to talk to me about a Broadway musical. I had an initial meeting with the producer followed by a concentrated period of singing lessons, during which the long-suffering teacher taught me to sing a song called *Just in Time*. This had been written by Jule Styne and was thought to be an ideal number with which to impress him when we met a fortnight later.

We met, I sang and they asked me what I knew about an American Broadway star called Fanny Brice. She had been the toast of the town in the twenties and thirties, and they were going to do a musical based on her life. They told me they had seen me in *The Wars of the Roses* and thought I'd be right for the part of Nicky Arnstein, Fanny Brice's first husband. I naturally asked why they didn't want an American actor and they told me that Arnstein was an international gambler and in their view should be played by a European. Also I looked a bit like him.

I was intrigued and asked who they had in mind to play Fanny. They told me they had signed this fabulous, but as yet not very well known, girl called Barbra Streisand. The name meant nothing to me but I thought I might as well keep my options open. We agreed to keep in touch. I read the script, which was the size of a telephone directory, and saw that Arnstein was a pretty good part. I had grave reservations about my singing abilities but they didn't seem to be worried, so we left it at that. A few months later they told me that American Equity had refused permission for a non-American to play the part; they were very sorry but there was nothing they could do about it. I wasn't too bothered and forgot all about it but, as it turned out, they didn't quite forget about me.

I had plenty of other things to think about. I did a couple of television plays—one for ATV and the other for Thames Television—and played a lot of golf and cricket. In fact, I was on the golf course one day in July when the club secretary came running out to tell me I had, what he described as an extremely important phone call from my agent. Monty was almost incoherent on the phone. He told me that I was to go to Rome the following day to meet with Luchino Visconti, who wanted me to appear in his next film, scheduled to start shooting in a couple of weeks. I would be in Rome for two days only while they organised my wardrobe for the film, and could then return to London to make any arrangements I needed to before returning to Rome for the start of filming. 'Are you interested?', Monty asked. Was I! Visconti was one of the major directors in Europe, if not the world. His films included *Rocco and His Brothers*, *The Leopard* starring Burt Lancaster and a very young Claudia Cardinale, *The Earth Trembles* and *Senso*. He was also a great stage and operatic director who worked many, many times with Maria Callas. Later he was to make *The Damned* with Dirk Bogarde and perhaps his most famous, if not best, film *Death in Venice*, again with Dirk Bogarde. He was right up there with, if not above, people like Fellini and de Sica—icons. I couldn't imagine why he wanted to employ me.

I hastily got my ass to Rome, where I had lunch with him and then went on a clothes buying spree along the Via Condotti with his production designer. Luchino could speak a bit of English, but chose not to as he hated doing anything that he couldn't do well. I spoke my brand of 'kitchen Italian' and schoolboy French and he replied in fluent French and/or Italian. We got along very well and I loved him from the start. He told me he'd seen me in *Stolen Hours* and felt I would be right for the husband in his new film, which was called *Vaghe Stelle dell'Orsa*. The title was a quotation from some famous Italian poet and, literally translated, means 'the vague stars of the bear', an astronomical reference which lost whatever meaning it might have had when the film was released as *Sandra*.

I have a feeling that Columbia Pictures had some sort of involvement in the production or its distribution, as the film was ticked off as one I had to do under my contract. The star of the film was Claudia Cardinale, who had come a long, long way since we first met in *Upstairs and Downstairs*. I played an American married to her, and the story involved an incestuous affair between her and her brother, played by the French actor Jean Sorel, when she and I revisit her old home in Volterra. Others in the cast were Marie Bell, a famous, senior French actress; a German called Fred Williams, who had made a bit of a name making spaghetti Westerns and was Visconti's current friend; and a then well-known Italian actor, whose name I forget. It was all very gothic and spooky as we prowled around a fifteenth century castella in the old part of Volterra, lost in the Tuscan hinterland.

Visconti, or Luchino as I was allowed to call him—he called me Mikie—was a master craftsman. He enjoyed enormous respect from his crew, many of whom had worked with him on all of his films. The filming went very smoothly, in spite of the fact that the actors were speaking in four different languages. I spoke mainly in English, although sometimes in Italian if it wasn't too difficult. Cardinale, Marie Bell and Jean Sorel spoke their lines in French (Claudia had been born and raised in Algeria). The Italian actor spoke Italian and Fred Williams spoke German. It didn't matter what we spoke as in those days Italian films were always dubbed into the language spoken in the country into which they were released. There was a thriving industry in Rome doing nothing but revoicing films. I had the same actor do my voice in several films—he had a great voice; much better than mine. So I sounded really good in Italian, not too bad in German and Dutch, but pretty moderate in French.

Not shooting direct sound made filming a lot easier—you didn't have to bother about where the microphones were placed, or worry about intrusive boom shadows. It also allowed the director to speak to his cast while the camera was rolling. This was a bit unnerving for me at first—I was used to total silence on the set while the camera was turning. The first time I heard Luchino talking to Claudia while we were playing a scene, I thought something must have gone wrong and stopped. Luchino explained the situation and after a few days I got used to it. He never spoke to me personally during a take, but constantly to Claudia. Little things like, 'raise your right arm a little', or 'a touch more right profile', 'turn your head away . . . now'. The amazing thing to me was that, while doing everything else in the scene—like kissing me or crying or laughing or eating and drinking—Claudia was able to do exactly what she was being directed to do almost instinctively.

Another of Luchino's techniques was to rehearse long scenes, as much as ten minutes, as if for television. We might spend a day and a half on some of them and then actually shoot the scene in a couple of takes. So the time factor was as productive as if we were shooting the then average of maybe three minutes per day but we had a lot more rehearsal time. Quite often he used three cameras—two ordinary Mitchells and a hand-held Arriflex with a zoom lens. His number one operator was on the Arriflex and Luchino would tell him where to go and when to zoom in throughout the take. I once asked him why he did this and he said that the best acting always took place in the wide shots, when everyone was engaged in playing the whole scene and not worrying about cameras and angles. He said:

> An actor will do one of two things when it is his close-up. He will either get nervous and do too little, or think *Ah ha, this is my moment* and do too much. I zoom in on him when he doesn't know I'm doing it and then I get what I want.

I asked him how the film editor would know where to cut the film with all the material to sort out. He replied, 'Mikie, the film is already edited, in my head. All the editor has to do is *assemble* it.' A wonderful way to make pictures, but not a popular one with the moneymen. Three cameras running at once used up a lot of film stock, but no one was likely to challenge Il Conte.

Luchino looked like one of the great Caesars and moved with a sort of gravitas, which was most impressive. He was a strange mixture; an avowed communist but also an aristocrat of the highest rank. The Viscontis were one of the oldest and noblest families in Italy and Luchino was often addressed as 'Count'. His younger brother had taken the title when Luchino had disowned it for some reason (his communist beliefs, I suppose), but that hadn't made much difference to his status. One evening during the shoot we were invited to the Visconti Castle for a dinner, hosted by Luchino's brother and his wife. It was mind-blowing. Every worker on the estate, including the household staff (nearly a hundred I suppose), was lined up to greet us when we arrived for dinner. Luchino led us into the castle and every one of those men and women bowed low and kissed his hand as he went by. It seemed to be a peculiar brand of communism, but the dinner was sumptuous, with truffles sprinkled on the pasta with the same abandon as if they were Parmesan cheese.

Babs was with me that night as the whole family had joined me for the ten weeks in Volterra, and it was probably the best and happiest family time we ever had. Good work, good weather, good food, and good behaviour from me. When we returned to London I completed a couple of television plays for ATV at Elstree and Thames Television at Teddington, and then I went to Nottingham to do *Richard II* at the Playhouse. This was another example of the random way in which careers are built. I happened to be in a pub in Drury Lane one lunchtime and ran into John Neville. John had been a matinee idol in the early fifties, when he and the young Richard Burton had filled the Old Vic Theatre with their talents and sex appeal. They did a season in which they alternated in the same parts. At one performance John would play Romeo and Burton would play Mercutio, and at the next performance they'd swap. They did this doubling in *Othello* as well, trading Othello and Iago at alternate performances. There's a famous story that at a matinee they found themselves in the backstage gents just before curtain time. To their horror they realised they were both blacked up and costumed to play the title role. Needless to say, they both thought themselves in error and raced away to change . . . only to confront each other in the wings dressed and made up as Iago. I don't know how they resolved the matter—perhaps they spun a coin—but the curtain was a little late going up.

Anyhow, when I ran into John in the pub in late 1964 he was running the Nottingham Playhouse. He was the artistic director and leading actor and he had made the Playhouse one of the major theatrical centres in the country. We had a beer or two and exchanged notes. He was about to do a production of *Richard II* and had hoped to have my old friend Donald Houston join him to play Bolingbroke. For some reason Donald couldn't or wouldn't do it, so John was in London looking for someone who could and would.

'Look no further,' I told him. 'What about me?'

'Fair enough,' he replied, and that was that.

It was a very jolly atmosphere at Nottingham, with a great deal of drinking and carousing after the show. The bar would stay open as long as there was anyone left standing. Certain members of the company, myself included, took advantage of this liberality. One evening after a performance and a long stint at the bar, I offered an actor called Norman Rodway a lift back to our digs. The Facel Vega was parked nearby but for some reason wouldn't start—luckily probably, considering the condition I was in. 'Not to worry,' I told a giggling Norman, 'I'll fix the fucker. I'll do what I do to myself when I don't feel too good—I'll give the bugger a Bisodol tablet.' (Bisodol were and are antacid pills taken for indigestion.) Norman saw the logic of this and we opened the bonnet and took the cap off the carburettor. I solemnly placed two Bisodols inside and closed everything up again. Magic did not happen; the Facel remained resolutely immobile and we had to walk home.

The next morning I vaguely remembered what I'd done, but hoped desperately that maybe I hadn't. I called the AA road service and eventually a solemn, dedicated, highly skilled mechanic arrived to sort out the Facel's problem. He'd never seen or heard of a Facel Vega but, undaunted, went through his checks and balances until the moment I'd been dreading arrived. He looked at the carburettor, which was now filled with a sort of glutinous substance consisting of Bisodol and petrol, and confessed that he was stumped. I did my best to carry it off with a certain insouciance, suggesting the mixture might be 'er . . . er . . . Bisodol?'

He looked at me as if I was the idiot I actually was. 'How the fuck could Bisodol get into the carburettor?' I had to confess it had seemed like a good idea at the time and I was extremely sorry. He shook his head and muttered something, which I fortunately didn't hear, and did what had to be done. I offered him a fiver for his trouble when the car was up and running again, but he shook his head, barely refrained from making the sign of the cross and went on his way, still muttering.

John Neville was the definitive *Richard II*—he'd had a huge success with the part ten years earlier and was even better second time around. We shared a dressing room and a great many bottles of Guinness, which he told me solemnly had been recommended by his doctor to help him put on weight: 'All you need to sustain life is Guinness and the occasional bit of greenstuff to prevent scurvy.' Well you don't argue with that sort of medical advice.

We were sitting in our dressing room one evening after the performance, helping him keep his weight up and congratulating ourselves on what we felt had been *the* definitive performance of the season, when there was a knock at the door. The director of the next production came in to ask John some question about rehearsal times. John told him and then asked the question no actor should ever ask: 'Out front were you? What did you think?' We sat back awaiting the adulation we felt was our due. The poor man shuffled uncomfortably for a moment, smiled apologetically, and replied, 'Could see you were both a bit tired . . . but . . . but it was good.' He disappeared. John and I looked at each other. There was absolutely nothing to say.

In spite of our 'tiredness', the season was a huge success and I enjoyed every minute of it. My only worry was the boots I wore as Bolingbroke. They had been hired from the Royal Shakespeare Company's wardrobe department, and had been worn by an actor called Eric Porter (later the original Soames Forsyte in the hit TV series *The Forsyte Saga*) in a production of *Henry IV* at Stratford. I don't know if Mr Porter is a short man or if he had to appear as an extremely tall Hotspur or whoever he was, but the boots had built-in two-inch lifts and high-ish heels. By the time *Richard II* was finally despatched at Pomfret and I became king, my feet were killing me. I promised myself that I would never play any Shakepearian role that wasn't a king again as kings were the only ones who ever got to sit while everyone else did a great deal of standing around. Not a promise I kept, of course, because since then I've played both Prospero and Julius Caesar—but *The Tempest* and *Julius Caesar* are mercifully two of the shortest plays in the canon.

I got an extremely bad notice in the *Manchester Guardian* but, luckily for me, the critic got the name wrong and ascribed the performance to Michael Goodliffe. I wrote to this prat of a critic, pointing out the error, and told him he owed Mr Goodliffe an apology. It was bad enough to get a bad notice for something you were in, but to get blasted for something you *weren't* in was unforgiveable. I heard later that he did in fact apologise but I'd stopped taking *The Guardian* seriously by then.

There were a lot of dedicated fans of the Playhouse, some of whom would stay and drink with the actors after the show. One of these was married to the vicar of a nearby village and, to John's great amusement and with his active encouragement, she and I enjoyed a casual but jolly liaison. Neither of us took it too seriously and there were no hard feelings or sadness when we eventually said goodbye. I felt mild guilt about my infidelity, but as long as Babs didn't know, there was no damage done. I extended the dictum of 'Out of the country, doesn't count' to 'Out of town, doesn't count' and let it go at that.

The season finished and I went back to Chelsea to make *Life at the Top,* the only film I ever made under my contract to Columbia, or at least the only one which went out under the Columbia Pictures logo of the Statue of Liberty. It was a sequel to *Room at the Top*, the highly successful film that had been made in 1959, which was partly responsible for the new wave that radically changed the style of British films. The sequel had the same leading actor, Laurence Harvey as Joe Lampton the anti-hero, and Donald Wolfit as his father-in-law, but hardly anyone else from *Room at the Top*. Heather Sears, who had played the wife in the original film, was replaced by Jean Simmons; the wonderful Simone Signoret appeared only in flashbacks and Jack Clayton was replaced by Ted Kotcheff as the director.

Apart from the pleasure of working with Larry again, the great attraction for me was Jean Simmons. As a teenager and young sailor I'd been madly in love with her after seeing her in *Way to the Stars*. I'd even written and sent a poem to her with a request for a signed photograph. I don't think I ever received a reply but that in no way diminished my adoration. Now, twenty years later, I was working with her. Part of that work was to play a love scene with her. In the story she is married to Larry and I, as his best friend, have an illicit affair with her. The love scene had to be as near explicit as the film code would allow in those days.

At the time in real life she was married to the American film director Richard Brooks, who happened to be shooting *Lord Jim* on the soundstage next door to us at Shepperton Studios. He used to lob onto our set every now and then, and it always seemed to me that Jean got very uptight when this happened. As a matter of fact, so did I—he was quite a scary man. On yet another sound-stage someone was making another Sherlock Holmes film with John Neville as Holmes and Donald Houston as Watson, so there was something of a party atmosphere in the bar when filming finished each day. Donald knew Larry well and had been in *Room at the Top*, but for some reason his character didn't appear in the sequel. John of course knew everyone and he and Larry arranged an elaborate practical joke to amuse the crew and cast and, incidentally, annoy the shit out of the Columbia brass.

For some plot reason Sherlock Holmes was disguised as an old beggar—John was almost unrecognisable. Larry persuaded him to come onto our set while we were in the middle of filming some sort of boardroom scene. A very good but 'stitched' Australian actor called Alan Cuthbertson was playing the part of the company secretary or treasurer, and was holding forth to the Board, which included Larry and me and one or two others. He was laying down the law, when Neville in his beggar's guise burst into the board-room and delivered the immortal cliché line: 'There's trouble at mill.' He and Larry had a brief discussion about the 'trouble' and then Larry told him to 'foook off', which he did.

Poor Alan Cuthbertson, who wasn't privy to this jape, maintained a wonderful stoicism and soldiered on as though it was some sort of last-minute script amendment that the production office had failed to give him. It was a remarkable demonstration of a truly professional actor's ability to cope with unforeseen distractions. He got a well-deserved round of applause when he completed the speech that had been so dramatically interrupted.

Ted made the mistake of including the scene in the daily rushes which, by some unlucky chance, were viewed by some suits from head office. They were not amused and an angry memo was sent to us all, advising us to stop wasting Columbia's time and money. Larry didn't care—he was courting, or about to marry, Joan Cohn, the widow of the great unlamented Harry Cohn, the former head of Columbia. She had more power than all the suits in the London office put together.

We went on location to Bradford and I misbehaved in a desultory fashion with one of the ladies of the company—not Miss Simmons, I hasten to add—and when we got back to London I had a tricky time explaining why a phone call from Babs to my hotel room had been answered by a female voice. I don't suppose she believed my explanation but was sufficiently resigned to my behaviour to turn a blind eye. The film didn't turn out very well and wasn't successful at the box office, and that was the end of my career with Columbia.

After I'd done another television play for Associated Rediffusion, my brother persuaded his good friend the producer Joe Janni to cast me in a film called *Modesty Blaise*. This was supposed to be a pop art, witty send-up of the secret agent genre, and was based on a very popular comic strip of the same name. The two stars were Terence Stamp as Willy Garvin and Monica Vitti as the eponymous heroine. The villain was played by Dirk Bogarde in a white wig. Harry Andrews and I were a pair of bumbling officials from MI5, or possibly MI6, on the trail of the naughty people. The director was Joe Losey, who had recently re-invented himself with his two big successes, *King and Country* and *The Servant*. Dirk had been in both of these films and I suppose he felt he was in safe hands.

Wrong. For some reason Losey decided that Terence Stamp, who was dark-haired and skinny, should play Willy Garvin, who was written as a blonde and a muscular karate expert. Monica Vitti, who was blonde, slender and spoke very little English, was cast as Modesty Blaise, who was dark-haired, voluptuous and English or American. It was wilful miscasting of an epic nature, but for some reason Twentieth Century Fox went along with it. It was part of the joke, I suppose—a joke that included extraordinary sets and costumes and bizarre special effects. If that *was* the case, it was a joke the audience neither got nor shared and the film was a bit of a disaster.

As far as I was concerned it had its moments—foreign locations in Amsterdam, Taormina, Pompeii and Rome, and a little bit of uncomplicated misbehaviour when the family wasn't with me. (They *were* with me for most of the time and we had a very jolly time in Sicily for about three weeks.) Most of my scenes were with Harry Andrews, which was good fun, but some of them were with Miss Vitti, which was painful. She refused to be photographed in profile, seemed unable or unwilling to learn her lines, and by the end of the shoot even Joe Losey was sick of the sight of her. I had to do one very complicated sort of love scene with her, involving the switching of sleeping draughts, plus some witty badinage and mild acrobatics on a swinging sofa. As I said, she didn't speak much English and Losey spoke no Italian so things weren't going too happily. Finally it was over to me, so I asked Joe what he wanted me to do. He fixed me with a tired and jaundiced eye and gave me this immortal piece of direction: 'Be inventive.' Thanks very much, Joe. This was the director idolised by French cineastes, who rated him second only to Renoir or Orson Welles.

Soon after this, I was asked to do a two-handed television play called *La Musica* for ATV. The other 'hand' was Vanessa Redgrave, who was very much the flavour of the month at the time, in spite of her revolutionary politics and behaviour. She was married to the film and stage director Tony Richardson, who was away in America during filming. They lived in a huge house in Chiswick. She was also extremely attractive and sexy and I feared the worst—or best—when I discovered that we'd be going to Le Touquet for two or three days of location shooting. The play was by the French writer Marguerite Duras, who had outstanding success in the eighties with her novel, *The Lover*, later made into a successful film of the same name.

La Musica involved a married couple who have to finalise their divorce by attending some kind of judicial hearing in the small town where they lived. Of course when they meet up to do this, old lusts and loves reawaken and you can imagine the rest. The characters had no names, just 'him' and 'her', in that rather irritating and pretentious continental fashion. We rehearsed for ten days and all was well, except that in the second half (television plays were divided into two acts in those days) our characters seemed to alter radically. Being actors, we battled on making the best of this incomprehensible change, assuming that Ms Duras had her reasons and it was all very French.

The director was happy enough but Vanessa wasn't. Over the weekend she flew to Paris, had a chat with Marguerite Duras and returned to Elstree on the Monday morning in a high state of excitement and amusement. Whoever had printed out the scripts had made a small but basic error on the second page of Act Two. The last speech on the page was a 'HIM' speech that should have logically been followed by a 'HER' speech on the top of the next page. However the typist had followed the 'HIM' speech with another 'HIM' speech and for the rest of the script I was speaking Van's lines and she was speaking mine. Once this was established, life became a lot easier. If Vanessa hadn't gone to Paris that weekend the play would have gone to air in an even more enigmatic form than it did. I suppose the viewers would have simply thought, how *très, très français*.

Actors on the whole are trusting loons who honour the written word, but I've been wary ever since when a director tries to convince me that it's not for me to question the playwright. 'He or she knows what he or she is doing, Michael—it's up to you as an actor to make it work.' Yeah, okay, the playwright knew but did the bloody printer?

My worst fears or hopes about the Le Touquet location were realised and I was besotted once again. It was impossible of course. The demands of family, work, career and my obsessive demands for reassurance and commitment led to her total disenchantment and it all ended in tears as far as I was concerned, but I had other things to occupy my mind and the wounds healed soon enough. I returned to Nottingham; this time to play the scheming and lecherous Horner in William Wycherley's immortal *The Country Wife*. Like all Restoration Comedies, it is a bitch to learn but a pleasure to play, especially if you have Dame Judi Dench— or Jude, as she was known to most of us who knew her from York, and Jude, she will always be to me—in the title role. We had a lot of fun but it was tempered slightly by the fact that Jude had been having a long-standing relationship with John Neville, which seemed to work well enough when it existed at a distance, but became a bit tense when she was on view, as it were, twenty-four hours a day. John's family, which included his wife of many years and their assorted children (some natural, some adopted), were all staying in their Nottingham house. John went home every day after the work was done. I think Jude found this difficult, but she must have known what she was getting into when she agreed to go to Nottingham because she did Shaw's *St Joan* as well as *The Country Wife*. She was in Nottingham for quite a while in fact.

John directed the production with great style—good sets and costumes and an outstanding cast. We were a great hit. Even the *Manchester Guardian* approved, although they didn't give Michael Goodliffe credit for my excellent Horner, which would have been only fair after slating him for my dreadful 'Bolingbroke' the year before. The fans gathered in the bar after the show and one evening John told me with a glint in his eye that he had a surprise for me. Sure enough, there nursing a gin and tonic was my former friend the vicar's wife. She was great with child and I did some speedy mental arithmetic. Hmmm. She didn't say anything about the approaching birth so, in spite of John's sardonic smiles, I relaxed and thought, 'Good for the vicar.' Some weeks later she rang me up and asked me to tea at the vicarage. When I arrived she showed me the baby, which was a girl aged three weeks. 'I'm calling her Michele,' she said. 'I thought you'd like to see her.' I asked the usual questions and got unusual answers. Yes, I was the father. No, the vicar wasn't in the least put out. No, she didn't want anything from me, not even for Michele. She'd just thought I'd like to see the child and, now that I had, I could forget about it. Not that easy to do but it was what she wanted. I did send her a thousand pounds to buy something for Michele a few months later, but I've never seen either of them again. Michele would be thirty-six now. I hope she's well and happy and bears me no ill will, if in fact she even knows of my existence. If she doesn't, its best that it stays that way, so on the odd occasion when I've wondered if I should seek her out and make contact, I've rejected the idea and left that particular boat *un*rocked.

While all this was going on I got a call from Monty to say that Bernie Delfont and the producer Arthur Lewis were going to present *Funny Girl* at the Prince of Wales Theatre with Barbra Streisand. They wanted to see me. It didn't click at first but then I realised that *Funny Girl* must be the musical about Fanny Brice's life that I'd discussed two and a half years earlier. My first reaction was to say, 'No bloody way', but then I thought, 'Well why not? What have I got to lose?' The following six months answered that question.

My meeting with the producers was amiable enough. They explained that Ms Streisand had looked at me in a couple of movies and was satisfied that I was suitable for the part of Nicky Arnstein. I must have looked a little quizzical at this news because Arthur then explained to me Ms Streisand's pivotal importance. During the two years that she had been playing *Funny Girl* in America, she had risen from relative obscurity, known only to a coterie of fans in New York, to megastar status. She had won awards, was married to Elliot Gould and was signed to make the movies of *Funny Girl* and *Hello, Dolly!* when she had completed the London season. All very impressive, and when I glanced through the script I noticed a big difference from the phone directory-sized tome I'd read in 1963.

Firstly, it was much shorter and, secondly, the part of Nicky Arnstein had been reduced from 'leading' to 'supporting'. The whole show had been re-vamped as a vehicle for Ms Streisand. I was, of course, dimly aware of the huge success the show had had on Broadway, but I hadn't quite realised how powerful Barbra had become. The New York scene didn't figure prominently in my life and, apart from having heard the song *People* occasionally played on the radio, I was blissfully unaware of what I might be getting into. To be fair to myself, I wasn't the only person in England to be unaware of Barbra's status and talent. I heard later that she hadn't wanted to do the London season—she was pregnant and, reasonably enough, wanted to take things easy—but she was told by the film producer, Ray Stark, that if she didn't play London and establish a more international reputation, he wouldn't be able to guarantee her the part in the film.

I don't know how much truth there was in this rumour but it was pretty obvious, when Barbra finally showed up, that her heart wasn't entirely in it. I was told that she and the two other American leads wouldn't be joining the London cast until the last two weeks of rehearsal. In the meantime the rest of us would be rehearsing. I decided to give it a go—it was a short season, to accommodate Barbra's pregnancy, and Monty made a deal which allowed me to leave the show if and when Barbra and the other Americans did.

Rehearsals for musicals were a strange new world for me. They were held at the synagogue in Dean Street, which was often used as a rehearsal venue for West End musicals, with dancers in one room, singers in another, and me in a third going through my scenes with the director and whoever else was available to stand in for Barbra. The scenes were simple enough, basic you might say, but the singing and dancing were something else. I only had three songs to cope with and when I went through them with my singing teacher I had no problems. It was in the wider context of doing them with the full Company that my nerves were put through the shredder.

I was supposed to do a bit of a top-hat and cane routine while singing my first number, *I Want To Be Seen With You*, but I continually dropped the hat or the cane, or sometimes both, as I was supposed to glide elegantly about the stage. It was a crucial scene, coming early in the show and conceived so that Barbra as Fanny could fall in love with my frilly shirt, my urbanity and charm. She had to go off stage singing, 'Nicky Arnstein, Nicky Arnstein what a beautiful guy' etc. etc. I felt she could hardly do this in the face of my ineptitude. I told the director that my character was supposed to be a gambler, not a dancer, and in the end I got my way—I did a token spin of the cane, doffed my topper and sauntered, rather than danced, away into the wings.

Finally the great day arrived and we were joined by the American stars. Barbra was clearly on the defensive; she'd become rather irritated by some of the London showbiz writers, who tended to take themselves more seriously than they had a right to. Arthur Lewis invited Babs and me to dinner at the Caprice restaurant to meet and greet Barbra and Elliot the night before she was due to start rehearsals with the English cast. It wasn't a happy occasion. She and Elliot arrived about an hour late and, to fill in the time, I'd drunk a great deal more than I should have. There was a lot of reshuffling of chairs so she could sit where she wanted to and then she instructed the head waiter on how to make steak Diane. The Caprice was, and probably still is, one of the best restaurants in London, and the maître d. didn't take kindly to being instructed in his duties by a twenty-three-year-old American girl who referred to *wore-cester shyre sauce* as if it were something from an alchemist's laboratory. I excused myself to go to the lavatory and while there I split the seat of my trousers. I was unaware of this until one of the waiters passed me a note telling me that my bum was hanging out, and 'PS I love you'. (Not really the PS . . .)

The dismal evening dragged on and when we finally got home I knew the next few months might prove to be more than a little fraught. This feeling was reinforced the next day when Barbra arrived at the rehearsal rooms swathed in leopard skin and, after meeting the English cast, looked about her with some distaste. 'Why,' she asked, 'are we rehearsing in a synagogue?' I thought I'd lighten the mood with a touch of humour and said with a light laugh, 'Why what's the matter, Barbra, are you anti-semitic?' She looked daggers at me. 'Whaddya mean? I *am* Jewish.' My heart sank—not a lot of irony or humour there. I mean, at the time, she would have been second only to Golda Meir as the best-known Jew in the world. 'Just kidding, Barbra,' I muttered and slunk away.

We finally got out of the synagogue and into The Prince of Wales Theatre for the 'band call'. All through the rehearsals my musical accompaniment had been the piano and sometimes drums, and I'd had no difficulty picking out the tune and following it more or less correctly. Now suddenly there was a forty-piece orchestra led by Marcus Dodds from the BBC Symphony Orchestra, playing so many twiddly bits and complex arrangements and I couldn't recognise my music or my cues at all. To make matters worse, the music for my first number struck up while I was still speaking—four *da-dum-de-dums* over my dialogue, and then I was supposed to start singing.

I was used to musicals where there was no attempt to blend the dialogue into the songs. The chap would finish what he was saying and then turn to the audience; the orchestra would play and he would launch into song. No problem. But there was no such luxury for me here. In my growing panic I lost the ability to count up to four and speak and move at the same time. I inevitably came in after the third *da-dum-de-dums* or, even worse, waited for a fifth, by which time the orchestra had launched into whatever followed the *da-dum-de-dums* and I was left straining in its wake. I eventually came to an accommodation with Marcus, who was an extremely nice and long-suffering maestro—I would race through my last couple of speaking lines and then casually glance at him in the pit while he counted me down and gave me the signal to start singing.

Barbra was phenomenal and could recognise a misplaced 'ting' on the triangle from the other side of Leicester Square. She was a wonderful performer and, even when she did her own little improvisational riffs, she was always in complete magisterial control. Marcus had a little problem with her during the run because, when she sang the big hit of the show, *People*, she tended to elaborate on what was in the written score. This made things very hard for him as he was under strict instructions to stick utterly and faithfully to the dots. One evening he decided to have a word with her. I should point out that he was a very talented and experienced conductor, not just your run-of-the-mill 'pit jockey', and *she* was doing her first starring role at the grand old age of twenty-four. He told me in the pub after the show that he'd mentioned the problem he was having with *People* and she'd looked at him blankly. He'd floundered on, attempting to be both conciliatory and deferential, but had finally told her regretfully that sometimes he found it extremely difficult to accompany her as she was doing it wrong. 'She fixed me with a steely glare and said, "I may not always be right, Marcus, but I am never ever *wrong*."' He took another swig from his drink and smiled almost lovingly. 'And you know what, Michael? Musically, she never ever is.'

As we approached the opening night my panic changed into a cold dread, which I almost enjoyed. I knew I was going to stuff things up; I knew there was nothing I could do about it and, the sooner we got it over with, the better. I maintained a cheerful British sangfroid despite my jangling nerves, and this seemed to irritate all the Americans involved; and there were plenty of them. They adored the drama and terror of Opening Night and, when I seemed completely impervious to the increasing hysteria, they were at a loss. 'Just another show,' I'd say airily. 'Just another show. It'll be fun.' They'd look at me in horror at this sacrilege and walk away shaking their heads. Little did they know.

Above: Little furies at the bottom of the garden—Richard, me and Hilary, 1935. *(Author's Private Collection)*

Below: 'Coming the raw prawn' with siblings and Ma, 1937. *(Author's Private Collection)*

Above: Pa with his 'ladies', 1937. *(Author's Private Collection)*

Right: Hello Sailor—in my merchant navy uniform at age 16, 1945. *(Author's Private Collection)*

Above: E.R. saving me from falling on my face at the Royal Premiere of *Les Girls*, watched by Anne Heywood on my left. *(Author's Private Collection)*

Left: As a Rank 'starling', trying to do beefcake. More muscles between the eyes of a kipper. *(Author's Private Collection)*

Above: A bad hair day for Susan Hayward and me, on the set of *Stolen Hours,* 1963. *(Author's Private Collection)*

Left: Babs and me with Stephen, circa 1958, during the earlier—and happier—days of our marriage. *(Author's Private Collection)*

Below: Whodunnit? The cast of *The Homecoming*, New York, 1967. Faces of note include, back row, L to R: Paul Rogers, Terence Rigby, Ian Holm. Front row, L to R: Harold Pinter, me, Lynne Farleigh, Michael Jayston, John Normington. *(Author's Private Collection)*

Right: With the incomparable Ms Streisand in the London production of *Funny Girl.*
(Author's Private Collection)

Below: Waiting for the chariot to carry me home. *Uncle Tom's Cabin* at the Royal Court Theatre, Warrington, 1952.
(Author's Private Collection)

Above: Julie Andrews looking miffed—I forgot to dress for the party. Robert Reed about to faint in the background. *Star*, 1967. *(Author's Private Collection)*

Left: Corporal Major Kidman tidying me up while the 'gin bearer' smirks and holds my horse in *Star*. *(Author's Private Collection)*

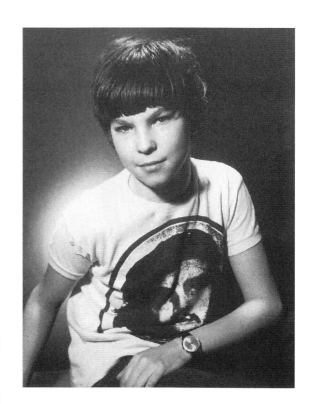

Right: Stephen (and Che Guevara) aged about ten. *(Author's Private Collection)*

Below: MJ aged five. *(Author's Private Collection)*

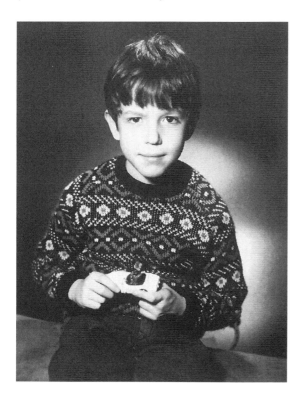

Above: Paddy Doolan and Mrs Doolan, a.k.a. Robin Nevin, *The Irishman*, 1978. *(Author's Private Collection)*

Left: Reverently dancing with my Great Dane in *The Danedyke Mystery*, 1979. *(Author's Private Collection)*

Above: As the naughty Stephen Mannion, with Nicola Paget (as my wife) and Angela Punch McGregor (mistress), cooking in the Kellyville sun, *Timeless Land*, 1981. *(Author's Private Collection)*

Left: The eternal and lovely triangle: Sue and Jessica and me, 1988. *(Author's Private Collection)*

Below: 'You're not really going to put that in the book, are you?' My brother Richard at home at Whitebrook Farm, UK. *(Author's Private Collection)*

Above: 'and another thing …' Stuart Wagstaff amusing John McTernan and me in *GP*. *(Courtesy ABC Television)*

Below: Episode 99 of *GP*, written by me, with Michael O'Neal and me about to commit Peter Collingwood to the grave. What a good jape. *(Courtesy ABC Television)*

We did a 'gala' preview attended by Princess Margaret and her then husband, Antony Armstrong-Jones. Even Barbra seemed a little awed by this, but refused to bow or curtsy and chewed her gum vigorously as she shook the Royal hand when the Company was presented after the performance. HRH passed me by with a cursory nod on her way to chat with Barbra, leaving me to exchange inanities with Antony Armstrong-Jones. He was very affable and pleasant, but it wasn't hard to work out that he'd rather have been somewhere else.

To my surprise and great relief the opening night came and went with a remarkable lack of drama. Barbra had a great success although some of the critics commented on how small her voice seemed in the theatre, compared with what they had heard on her recordings. She was the only one on stage who was 'miked'— the rest of us had to make do with lung power and shotgun mikes directed at the stage from the spot rail. I rather liked that, feeling that the less the audience heard of my singing the better it would be for all concerned. I did have to be a bit careful in my more intimate moments with Barbra and make sure I didn't speak into her personal mike, which was hidden in her cleavage, but apart from that I started to really get the hang of it.

The rest of the Company was pleasant enough and they even tried to teach me a rudimentary tap routine, but to no avail—I remained resolutely un-terpsichorean. Business was phenomenal; we were the hottest ticket in town. The scalpers outside the theatre were getting ten times the price of a ticket and I could have made a tidy little profit if I'd cashed in on the two tickets which were available to me for each performance. Alas, my conscience wouldn't let me so I'd let the box office know each day that they could sell my seats when I didn't need them.

When we were well into the season Barbra announced that, because of her pregnancy, her medical advice was that she shouldn't do two performances in one day. We were only doing seven shows a week anyway, no midweek matinee, but being the ruthless pragmatist she was, she elected to do the Saturday *matinee*, rather than the evening show. Well, why not?—it made her weekend that much longer. However, the rest of us were faced with the anti-climactic prospect of doing the Saturday night show, which was traditionally the big show of the week, using her understudy and playing to a half-empty house. There was nothing we could do about it, but one evening I managed to lose it completely.

It was very hot and in my first scene, when I was singing *I Want To Be Seen With You* to a supposedly entranced Fanny Brice, Barbra went off-stage, sat down in the wings and fanned herself until it was time to return for the little bit of a duet which ended the number. I was mortified, I was singing 'I want to be seen with *you*' and there was no one bloody well there. It was like doing the balcony scene in *Romeo and Juliet* with no Juliet up there on the balcony. I pointed this out to Barbra at interval, when I stormed into her dressing room to vent my fury. She was unimpressed by my logic.

'It's your number, Michael,' she said.

'No it fucking isn't,' I replied. 'It's *our* number. You're supposed to fall in love with me while I'm poncing around in my white tie and tails. Jesus, you go off singing "Nicky Arnstein, Nicky Arnstein, what a beautiful guy". How can you do that if you've been sitting in the wings while I'm doing my thing?'

I don't think she was used to being spoken to like that, although I'd heard that Elliot Gould was a pretty straightforward kind of guy. Anyhow she didn't say anything, so I went on.

'If you ever do that again, I'm going to walk off the other side of the stage and you can explain to the producers why they had to bring the curtain down.'

•

Well she never did do it again, but there was never much love lost between us for the rest of the run.

She used to send me a note after every performance pointing out what she felt had gone wrong in her scenes with me and how I should put it right. Her dresser would knock on my door as I was getting into a stiff whisky and hand me Barbra's crit.

I took it seriously at first—I read the note, thanked the dresser and asked her to pass on my gratitude to Barbra. Finally, however, I got sick of it—after all, I was thirty-seven years old with quite a long track record and she was this twenty-four year old kid with a huge talent but not a hell of a lot of experience. In the end I used to take Barbra's note, write 'Bollocks' on it and return it to her dresser. I don't know what the dresser said or did but Barbra went on sending the notes, up to and including the night we closed.

Towards the end of the run, which was only about fifteen weeks, I got a bit bored and started to do little things to see if Barbra would notice. In the story Nicky goes to prison for two years for fraud. In the scene when he has been released and meets Fanny again, I started to limp on one leg. After six or seven shows, with a gradually increasing 'limp', Barbra finally noticed and asked me if I'd hurt myself.

'No, no,' I said. 'It's part of the performance.' She looked at me and I continued.

'It's 1922 Barbra, right? Well back then it was the old ball and chain, and I thought that after two years of ball and chain bizzo, you'd have a pretty sore leg.' She looked at me with dawning respect.

'Jeeze, Syd Chaplin [who'd played Nicky in New York] never thought of that. Terrific!'

I had a quiet laugh and used to limp on different legs at different performances to see if she'd notice, but she never did.

I suppose it had something to do with her pregnancy, but she became less and less interested in doing the show. In spite of this, we continued selling out at all performances except Saturday nights and the management wanted to extend the run. Barbra wouldn't and, in spite of being tempted with the prospect of maybe Liza Minnelli or Lanie Kazan joining the show, I invoked the clause in my contract which said I could leave when and if Barbra did. A funny peculiar time with a funny peculiar lady. I admired her talent enormously—still do—but back then her profession-alism left a lot to be desired.

TEN

Bigtime

Late in 1966 I was startled to get a call from Peter Hall asking me if I'd like to take over from Michael Bryant in Harold Pinter's *The Homecoming*. This was a Royal Shakespeare Company production that had been a great success at the Aldwych Theatre in London. An American producer called Alex Cohen now wanted to present the play in New York. Mike, who had previously played the part of Teddy, didn't want to go to America but the rest of the cast were hot to trot to the Great White Way. To say I was startled is a bit of an understatement. I hadn't seen or been in touch with Peter since our somewhat acrimonious parting of ways in the spring of 1964. However the theatre is nothing if not expedient. Both he and Pinter thought I'd be right for the part and the production, so we all let bygones be bygones and got on with it. My taking the job had some interesting repercussions, however; one of which dropped me deep in it and in some way led to my coming to Australia and a whole new life.

Rehearsals were interesting and speedy. The rest of the cast had been doing the play for some time and knew exactly what to do and when, so it was only a question of getting me to fit in. I was allowed some leeway; I didn't have to slavishly follow what Mike Bryant had done; in fact I invented a piece of business that so pleased Harold Pinter it became part of the stage directions, printed in the published text. Wow! The hardest part for me was learning to respect the 'Pinter pauses'. I hadn't done a Pinter play before, although I'd seen several, and some of the pauses seemed to me to be arbitrarily long and unnecessary. Still he was the writer and, as he was present at most of the rehearsals, I wasn't going to argue. His then wife, Vivien Merchant, was playing my wife, or perhaps I should rephrase that, I was playing her husband, as hers was by far the more important role. I found her very hard to get to know. She was the leading lady in most of her husband's plays and did them very well, but in real life she was more enigmatic than the characters he wrote for her.

Our New York opening, on 31 December 1966, went well and was respectfully received, but I don't think New York was actually ready for Pinter. The audiences seemed more mystified than entertained. For a few weeks it seemed we mightn't even do the six months planned as takings were very moderate. Then the Tony Awards came along and the show won five of them. Business immediately picked up and we were suddenly a hit. Peter Hall had gone back to England soon after we opened, but he came back briefly to accept his Tony and give us a pep talk.

Harold stayed on with Vivien and their twelve-year-old son Daniel in their grand apartment on the Upper East side and kept an eye on the production. I got a bollocking from him for not holding my pauses long enough and tried to explain why I was shortening them. New York audiences were used to pace and quick-fire chat on stage, and you could feel their puzzlement and restlessness when things ground to a halt while one of us stared off into the distance or lit a cigar before answering a perfectly normal question. You could hear the whispers—'What's going on?' . . . 'Someone's missed an entrance' . . . 'Someone's died.' There's nothing worse than being on stage knowing you're losing the audience. To try and prevent that, I started to speed things up. Harold wouldn't have a bar of this. 'Fuck the audience,' was his reaction. 'It's my play and that's the way I wrote it. Christ, you wouldn't muck about with a Mozart sonata would you? So don't with Teddy.' There's no arguing with that kind of certainty, but he didn't have to stand there eight times a week and feel the audience dialling out.

Winter inched slowly towards spring. As the wind blew less cruelly you could almost see the end of our run in sight. My sister Betty and her husband Bill came down from Toronto to see the show and their visit coincided with a party at Harold's apartment to celebrate his birthday. It was held on the Sunday night so there was no show to worry about, and only the cast and crew with our significant others were invited. The three exceptions were Betty and Bill and Robert Shaw, who was an old friend of Pinter's and mine and was on his way to LA. He had to catch a midnight plane so he wasn't there when the roof came down. Lucky old Robert.

The Pinter apartment, as I have said, was very palatial. It was on the tenth floor of one of those grand buildings that overlook Central Park from the East Side. It was serviced by a uniformed hall porter on duty day and night. The living room occupied the full width of the apartment, with windows overlooking the avenue below and the bare trees in the park. Behind this was a long corridor, with bedrooms and a bathroom coming off it, and at the end of it lay the kitchen and the dining room. The windows in the kitchen and dining room looked down into a service area a hundred feet below, in which the garbage cans and odds and ends were kept. The geography of the apartment had a significant bearing on the events that occurred later that evening.

To begin with, we all gathered in the living room on our best behaviour, sang 'Happy Birthday, Dear Harold', and drank to his health before moving to the dining room for a sit-down dinner. Daniel, Pinter's son, didn't join us for dinner—he had eaten earlier and, feeling a bit excluded, I suppose, rather sulkily retired to his room, leaving the adults to themselves. The dining room was furnished in a sort of mock-Spanish style—a long refectory table, heavy carved chairs with leather seats, complete with two even larger and heavier carver chairs at each end of the table. Everything in the room was ornate and heavy—the silverware, the crockery and the large brass candlesticks on the table and sideboard. I think a dozen of us sat down to eat and lingered over a splendid meal accompanied by a great deal of wine.

The mood lightened as the wine was drunk, but nobody overdid it. We were all relatively sober and well-behaved when we finally returned to the living room for coffee and a nightcap. Betty and Bill and Babs and I excused ourselves soon after midnight—we had to get back to relieve the babysitter who was looking after MJ, who was six, (Stephen was at boarding school in England)—but the rest stayed on swapping the usual sort of actors' stories.

Soon after nine o'clock the next morning I got a telephone call from the company manager telling me to get down to the theatre right away. When I got there, it was like walking into a morgue. The rest of the company, with the exception of Vivien, was already there. I asked what was going on but nobody seemed to know. People were looking at each other oddly and it was obvious that something momentous had occurred. Finally Harold emerged from the manager's office and told us to sit down. He looked exhausted and deeply worried and, when he told us what had happened, I understood why.

At about 1.30 a.m. the night porter had come to his apartment to enquire about certain articles that had fallen into the service area at the back of the building. These had been identified as coming from the Pinter apartment. We all looked at each other as Harold continued. The two carved armchairs from the dining room, plus a large brass candelabra and assorted pots and pans from the kitchen, had been thrown from the window and had smashed to pieces on the concrete far below. Disregarding the cost of this vandalism for the moment, it was a criminal offence in New York to drop things from high-rise buildings—people could be injured or killed. The night porter had called the police, who had concluded the culprit must have been one of the guests. Harold needed to know which one. He didn't intend to pursue the matter—the insurance would take care of the cost of replacement—but clearly whoever was responsible was in need of some kind of counselling and help. He would wait in his office and hope the guilty party would come and see him, and give some sort of explanation. He dismissed us and disappeared into the office. We retired to the nearest bar to try and work things out.

We looked at each other and jokingly made our accusations. The actor Terence Rigby was a bit of a law unto himself and had become even more eccentric than before as the season progressed, so he seemed the obvious suspect, but he maintained his innocence so vehemently and emotionally that he had to be believed. He'd never left the living room; neither, it seemed, had anyone else. I was in the clear, of course—I'd left before the crime had been committed—so who the hell could it have been? There had been no rows; nobody had got upset or even drunk; nobody had any motive to do such an arbitrary and bizarre deed.

Apart from the lunacy of the deed, it was fraught with the danger of discovery. It would have taken some time and a little strength to open the windows and throw the chairs out into the night. Anyone might have come into the dining room while the deed was being done and caught the culprit *in flagrante*. Besides, what was the point? Whoever was responsible had presumably left the living room, ostensibly to use the loo, gone down to the kitchen and dining room, committed the crime and then returned to the party as if nothing had happened. If they had done it to make some point, they had clearly failed. You can't make a personal point if you remain anonymous so, until and unless they fronted up to Harold in his office, it would remain a completely empty gesture.

I left it at that and went home, where I told my riveted family what had happened. When I returned to the theatre for the evening performance I was met with the news that Lynne Farleigh, Vivien's understudy, would be playing that night for Vivien, who was too distressed by the previous night's events to be able to appear. Needless to say, no one had confessed to Harold and the matter remained unresolved, and remains officially unresolved to this day. Vivien returned to work a couple of days later, but both she and the rest of us were never quite the same again. Someone had done it; it had to be one of us—nobody else had been there—and a faint whiff of mutual suspicion tainted the rest of the season. Its ongoing repercussions in my life came a few years later.

As I wrote earlier, after the Tony Awards, business picked up and we became minor celebrities for five minutes. We were invited by a New York actress called Rita Gam to attend the Actors' Studio as observers. She was a member and so was her husband, whose name was Rip Torn. I wasn't all that eager, but one of my fellow-*Homecomers*, Johnny Normington, wanted to go so we went together. Lee Strasberg, who ran the Studio, was an egotistical little bugger with a contempt for English actors, whom he considered effete and lacking passion. No doubt some of them were, but at least they were professional—they learned their lines and spoke them audibly, which is more than could be said of some of his students. As observers, Johnny and I weren't allowed to join in the general discussions that followed a performance piece given by one or two of the students. Every time somebody did a scene or a speech with wit, timing and expertise, Strasberg would destroy them: 'No heart! No balls! It's all on the surface. Where's the dynamic? Where's the journey?' and all the other buzzwords used to elevate a not-too-difficult craft to the status of an art. I bit my lip as Strasberg demonstrated the superiority of The Method and the American way to the detriment of the British way, with a mocking bow in our direction.

Finally, he asked Johnny and me to make a comment. We had just sat through an appalling rendition of Hamlet's 'To be or not to be' given by an earnest young Texan called Pete. He had stuttered and muttered, farted and belched and scratched his way through one of the best-known speeches in the English language, frequently getting the text wrong and, worst of all, being barely audible in a space no bigger than a church hall. When he finished the speech—it had taken the best part of ten minutes with all the pauses for scratching and belching etc.—Strasberg gave him a big tick: 'Great work, Pete, you really nailed it.' Pete blushed and beamed and Strasberg turned to Johnny and me. 'We have two members of the Royal Shakespeare Company with us;

perhaps they might like to comment.' This was said with heavy sarcasm and a nudge-nudge wink-wink delivery to the rest of the class who, to their credit, refused to reward him with the obligatory snigger.

I'd had enough of all this tripe, so I delivered my considered verdict. 'Number one,' I said, 'Pete should make sure he gets the words right. A large number of the audience will know the speech and every time he makes a mistake they will register the fact, and Pete will lose their attention while they try to think what the correct word should have been.'

'Not important, it's the feeling that counts.' Strasberg grunted.

'Number two,' I continued, 'I couldn't hear him very clearly and this isn't a big auditorium.' Strasberg grunted again, even more fiercely.

'Doesn't matter, it's the journey that's important.' I sighed softly and tried again.

'Number three, if Pete is going to play Hamlet at that speed the audience better bring lunch boxes and sleeping bags because the performance will last twenty-four hours or longer.' Strasberg stopped grunting and told me to leave, which I did with some relief and never went back.

What a load of old bollocks, I thought, and how unfair to Pete. I could imagine him auditioning for some Broadway producer, such as David Merrick or Alex Cohen, and launching into 'To be or not to be . . .' By the time he'd scratched his bum the second time and belched his way through 'to suffer the slings and arrows . . .' he'd have been on his way out of the theatre and quite possibly out of the profession. He would have been heartbroken and totally at a loss. The great Lee Strasberg had praised his reading, so he'd wonder what he had done wrong.

Some time in late March I got a call from my brother Richard in Los Angeles. Bob Wise and Saul Chaplin, who had made the hugely successful *The Sound of Music*, were about to make a new film with Julie Andrews, based on the life of the great English star of the twenties and thirties, Gertrude Lawrence. There was a very good part on offer to me as Sir Anthony Spencer, one of

Julie's/Gertie's lovers, which I ultimately accepted even though it meant getting out of my *Homecoming* contract two weeks early.

Julie turned out to be a model of professionalism and charm in a slightly remote kind of way. As with Susan Hayward, I never got to know her very well. In spite of doing love scenes and hate scenes with her, she remained a cool, charming, totally professional mystery. This was partly due to the fact that she had such a huge load in the film. When she wasn't actually filming, she was rehearsing the half dozen or more big production numbers she had to shoot when the rest of us had finished. Clearly she had no time for idle conversation or a winding-down drink after the day's work was done, but I do wish I'd got to know her better as I admire her very much.

For some reason to do with taxation she couldn't or wouldn't come to England, where a large number of my scenes with her were suppose to take place. This was no problem for the art department, who recreated the interiors and some exteriors of English locations at the Fox studios in LA. But we needed some long establishing shots, which I had to shoot with a double. In the story, Sir Anthony was a Captain in the Lifeguards, so I had to be fitted out with the full dress uniform befitting such a person. As well as being instructed on how to wear all this spectacular but uncomfortable clobber by a Corporal Golightly, I had to pass a riding test to ensure I didn't disgrace the Brigade when I appeared in public. I spent a happy enough morning at Chelsea Barracks trotting round a sawdust ring under the tuition of an eagle-eyed senior warrant officer, Corporal Major Kidman, who was an imposing but jovial man who liked me and liked a drink. I was arrayed in all my splendour and sitting on my horse in the grounds of the Royal Chelsea Hospital, waiting for my troop of genuine Lifeguards to arrive, when Mr Kidman asked me if I would like a drink. Without thinking, I said, 'Yes, I would'. I was thinking along the lines of a cup of tea or coffee, but Mr Kidman had different ideas. He ordered the trooper who was standing by my horse to double away to the mess and fetch Mr Craig and himself a large pink gin. The trooper sprang into action and remarkably soon returned with a tumbler full of gin faintly tinged with a drop of angostura bitters and a teaspoon full of water.

Mr Kidman handed me my glass and grasped his own. 'Your very good health, Sah', he boomed, and tossed it back without blinking. I tried to do the same and managed most of it without splashing my cuirass. 'The other half, Sah?' Mr Kidman asked. I nodded weakly and the trooper doubled away to replenish our glasses. I took the second glass slightly more slowly, but even so by the time we set off down the Kings Road, all jingling and creaking, I'd had about a quarter of a bottle of gin in ten minutes and was drunk in charge of a horse. Luckily my horse—his name was Ocean and he was the horse that Lord Mountbatten always rode on ceremonial occasions—was well used to London traffic and rattling sabres and cuirasses.

•

When the location shooting was completed, the whole family flew off to Los Angeles, where I found a comfortable house in Beverly Hills, about ten minute's drive from the studio. It was alleged to have belonged to Greta Garbo at one time but I rather doubt that. It had a swimming pool and all the mod cons. Babs and the boys settled into it very cheerfully. We went out a good deal as Richard knew a great many people in the business and was heavily involved with Natalie Wood (whom he later married) at the time. She was very hospitable, sweet and beautiful, but lived in another world to most people. She was then, and had been for more than twenty years, a major movie star, with all the privileges that stardom afforded. She had servants and managers and secretaries and minders, and never had to involve herself with the mundane facts of life. She had only to pick up the phone, express her wish and it was done. This had its drawbacks of course.

Some years later she brought a custody case against Richard after they divorced. My brother had committed the ultimate solecism of sleeping with someone else while she was away on a long location shoot. That, of course, was unforgivable—I mean, how could you fancy anyone else if you were blessed and lucky enough to be married to Natalie? She was justifiably pissed off and tried to prevent Richard's access to their baby daughter Natasha. She and her lawyers tried to prove that he was an unfit father and shouldn't be allowed to see his child. Richard told me she turned up in court dressed as if for a great 'trial scene' in a movie, and confidently awaited a favourable verdict. When the judge refused to allow her claim, she was affronted and dismayed. She reacted as if someone had got the script wrong and almost asked for another take to get it right. Poor Natalie, she died tragically young and unnecessarily. She was always good to me and mine.

Filming on *Star* was easy and pleasant under Bob Wise's sympathetic and expert direction. We were given number one status at the studio. We were top of the pops, expected to repeat if not surpass their previous triumph. Unhappily it didn't work out like that. The public wasn't interested in the life and times of some half-forgotten theatre actress, and we died a death at the box office all over the world. It was a pity because Julie did great work in the film and so did my old friend Dan Massey as Noel Coward, who was Dan's godfather in real life. I was okay, if a little fatter than I should have been, and it was an entertaining musical. Too bad.

ELEVEN

Departure time

Looking through the bare record, the list of jobs and their dates, in the back of my script cover I see that, in the four years between returning from LA and *Star* in 1967 and departing for Australia in 1971, I made seven films and appeared in sixteen television plays, two of which I wrote. I also scripted *The Night of the Chairs*, my version of the Pinter apartment mystery, which never went into production. Some of those sixteen television plays were fairly routine productions, but there were some which in their way were original and important. Well, they were to me.

Simon Gray's *Spoiled* was made for the BBC and it portrayed the first homosexual act ever shown on television. I played a schoolmaster with a pregnant wife, who was giving extra tuition to an adolescent schoolboy played by Simon Ward. This was before Simon entered the film world and played the young Winston Churchill in a film of the same name. I had to kiss Simon on the lips and then sink down onto his bed and, mercifully, out of shot. Fade to black. Neither Simon nor I were practised in the art of kissing our fellow man in that kind of way, so I asked the director, an Indian prince called Waris Hussein, for any hints. I think he was slightly offended that I should assume he'd know, in spite of the fact that he clearly would and did. He refused to help us with the benefit of his experience. We rehearsed around the kiss for two weeks, but the moment finally came when we had to do it for the camera. Simon and I looked at each other and decided we'd each imagine that the other was the girl of our dreams and let rip.

I got some peculiar fan mail after the show went to air, but neither Waris nor the BBC held it against me because a few months later I was employed to play the Earl of Warwick in Shaw's *St Joan*, a major production. Janet Suzman, with whom I'd worked at Stratford, was St Joan and Sir John Gielgud played the Inquisitor. He was a lovely man and I had the pleasure of working with him on two subsequent occasions. He never got the Inquisitor's speech right in all the long rehearsal period (it's a very long speech) but as soon as the cameras rolled he delivered it faultlessly and brilliantly in one sustained take. For my next gig I had to age twenty years and had the experience of seeing what I might have looked like at sixty—bald head and pot belly which, though I say it myself, I've managed to avoid.

In between these television shows I did two films in Spain. One of them was *Royal Hunt of the Sun*, the adaptation of Peter Shaffer's monumental stage play about the conquest of Peru by Pizzaro. The original concept of the production was very grandiose. It was meant to have been shot in Cinerama—a wide, wide screen technique occasionally used at the time for major epics—and the locations were to have been in the Andes in Peru and Chile, and in the actual places where the events had occurred. In the end the money didn't eventuate and we shot the film in a studio in Madrid with locations in the Sierra Nevada mountains north of Granada, and on the beach at Almeria. There is a vast ridge of sand between the land and the sea at Almeria, and it had become a favourite location for Westerns and 'Easterns' ever since David Lean used it for the capture of the train in *Lawrence of Arabia*. You had to book the location well in advance. While we were doing our version of appearing over the skyline of the dunes, there were two other American productions hanging around awaiting their turn.

At the end of the year I wrote and then appeared in a television play for Yorkshire Television. It was called *Tiger Trap* and it was based on my experiences of having my car nicked by the local soldiers going home on a weekend pass. Then the BBC employed me to do a peculiar play by George Bernard Shaw, called *In Good King Charles' Golden Days*. It was written when Shaw was eighty-three. John Gielgud was King Charles, and it was good fun to be working with him again. He was very helpful in his own way, which was really no help at all. He would happily give me an inflection or line reading when I had a problem, but his suggestions were always so idiosyncratic and personal that they were useless. A friend of mine was directed by him at Stratford and had a very difficult time coping with Johnny's direction. At one moment my friend had to arrive in haste, deliver some bad news and then depart at speed to rejoin the battle or whatever it was. Johnny told him to kneel down and pray for a moment before he delivered the message and my friend tried to do this. It didn't work for him—urgency was the watchword, no time for praying—and he finally gave up and asked Johnny why he wanted him to do it. Johnny looked at him benignly and in his inimitable way told him, 'You look so pretty on your knees'.

Johnny and I had a common bond in our addiction to the *Times'* crossword puzzle, which we both did every day. Johnny would often ask if I'd solved a certain clue. 'Have you got 18 Across, Michael?' he'd ask. I'd tell him it was 'Accomplice', or whatever it was. He'd peer at his puzzle and back at me as if in wonder.

'*Accomplice* . . . hmmm, I've got *Alcibiades*.' I'd ask him how he'd managed to deduce *Alcibiades* from the clue and he'd smile that sweetly tortured smile.

'It fitted, dear boy, it fitted.'

I looked at his puzzle one day, after he'd supposedly finished it. It was finished all right, but half the answers bore no relation to the clues and in some cases weren't even words. A harmless and loveable pretence, which he still maintained when I last worked with him in Jerusalem nearly twenty years later.

Johnny was notorious for inadvertently putting his foot in it. We were having a drink after the end of recording and I told him how much I'd enjoyed working with him again. He returned the compliment and told me it had been his idea to cast me.

'I was discussing the play with Cedric [Cedric Messina, the producer] and he was wondering who to ask to play James. I told him it's a terribly boring part, you must get Michael Craig.' He said it with great affection and I'm sure he didn't mean to hurt my feelings. He might even have meant it as a compliment, but I'll never really know.

Summer arrived and with it an offer to do a film in Ireland called *Country Dance,* or *Brotherly Love* as it was subsequently called. This suited me very well as I had a reasonably good part opposite Peter O'Toole and Susannah York. Other members of the cast were Brian Blessed, Judy Cornwell (now known for being Hyacinth Bouquet's fat sister, a gorgeous looking girl) and Harry Andrews. The script included a naked bed scene with Susannah and me, a country dance (full of reels and strathspeys etc.), a duck shoot in which we were supposed to shoot live and flying ducks, and various comings and goings of a decadent and incestuous kind. We had an absolute ball. The weather was brilliant, the hottest and driest summer for many years, and, being on British Summer Time, the sun didn't set until nearly midnight.

O'Toole had a place in the west of Connemara, where his wife Sian Phillips and his two daughters were spending part of the summer holidays. I knew, and had worked with, Sian and she invited me to spend a weekend with them. It was the most spectacular ambience, looking due west across the Atlantic to the east coast of America three thousand miles away. We sat on the verandah, drinking pints of Black Velvet, and watching the sun sink very, very slowly into a dead flat ocean that looked like it was on fire. Peter was still on the booze in those days and, in spite of being built like a hat rack, was surprisingly strong and fit. He chain-smoked Gitane of Gauloises French cigarettes, as I did then too, the difference being that mine were filter-tipped and his weren't. He regarded this as affectedly wimpish behaviour on my part and got extremely ratty when I refused to do as he told me, smoke the unfiltered kind. He could be autocratic and domineering when he felt like it—well, he was the star and I wasn't—but he could also be wonderfully generous and sympathetic.

My father died quite suddenly while I was in Dublin and I got a phone call telling me of his death while I was having dinner one evening with Peter and Susannah. I was far more saddened by the news than I had expected to be and Peter could see I was in no state to organise what had to be done. He gave me a double brandy and took over, calling the production office and getting them to book me on a plane to Edinburgh the following day. He also laid on a car to take me to Dublin airport and another to meet me at Edinburgh. He then persuaded the office to rearrange the shooting schedule so I could have enough time off to go to Pa's funeral, and then he sat with me while I drank my brandy and maundered on about how I'd neglected the Old Man and now it was too late.

I'd like to pretend that my behaviour in the subsequent weeks was prompted by my father's death, that my extravagant lechery and boozing was inspired by the intimations of mortality awakened at Pa's funeral. I'd like to pretend that, but I can't. I behaved the way I did because I wanted to, and there was nobody to tell me I shouldn't. I had the hots for Susannah, but she wasn't having any of it, so I went where the girls were less choosy; and there were plenty of them that long hot Irish summer.

My heart was really no longer in my marriage. I loved the boys and was fond enough of Babs, but I felt chained to a life with which I could no longer even pretend to conform to. I suppose it was the cliché of the male menopause, reaching the age of forty. Whatever the reason, I became more and more reckless with my indiscretions and infidelities until even my mother and Roland felt obliged to comment. I was making myself and everyone else unhappy, but felt unable to make a clean break. The boys were growing up fast and couldn't help noticing that something was wrong, however hard Babs and I tried to preserve the status quo. So that summer I carried on recklessly, as did others. Peter got arrested one night for fighting in a nightclub (not his fault really as he was defending himself from a guard dog which had bitten him on the bum) and spent a night in the slammer, arriving at makeup the next day with a black eye and a very sore leg. Nothing stopped him, however, and we filmed and partied on for another several weeks.

One day we decided to go to the races in Kildare. We'd had very little sleep for the previous few days and none at all the night before because of an all-night shoot, but booze and adrenalin kept us going in a high state of euphoria. The racecourse was packed, but money was no object and we managed to get ourselves into the Member's Stand. It seemed like half the Republic was in attendance and amongst the locals was a sprinkling of shell-shocked actors on the run from the endless schedule of David Lean's *Ryan's Daughter*, which was still bogged down in 'The Dingle'. They had been there in the wilds of County Kerry waiting for the perfect wave, or for the precise moment for the seagull to shit on the requisite rock at the exact second that the sun shone on the right piece of coast, for what, to some of them, seemed an eternity. David Lean knew what he wanted and didn't mind spending Sam Spiegel's money to get it.

I heard that Trevor Howard, after some months of incarceration in a pub in Dingle, while waiting to be called to work ('Stand by until noon, Mr Howard, and we'll advise you') had finally cracked. Apparently the owner of the pub had a pair of lovebirds in a cage over the front door, and the squawking of these birds along with the boredom and frustrations of downtown Dingle, had tipped Trevor over the edge. He begged the landlord to do something about the birds and, when the host refused, persuaded him to sell them to him for a large sum of money. Having made the purchase, he had the birds destroyed and, conscious of a job well done, sat peacefully in the bar under the empty cage until the next irritation came along to drive him to distraction.

•

For some reason to do with international monetary exchange, American film production in Europe and specifically England dried up at the end of 1969. I was spared the ramifications of this for a few months longer as I was engaged to do an Italian/Yugoslavian co-production, originally called *Appointment with Dishonour*. I played an intrepid but ultimately stupid army officer under the command of an even sillier general, played by the ageing and almost senile George Sanders. We had a director who couldn't direct, and an Italian co-producer who couldn't produce. But I didn't help my cause with the latter by seducing his girlfriend, Ljuba, who was the Yugoslavian production secretary.

When the film was over and we made our way back to London, I told Babs that I had to have some breathing space and moved into my friend Brook Williams' flat next door to The Queen's Elm. A few days later Ljuba joined me, but within twenty-four hours we both knew we'd made a terrible mistake. The shared hell of *Appointment with Dishonour* was no foundation for an on-going relationship in London. Ljuba found me shallow and frivolous, and I found her boring and lacking in humour. After a fortnight she returned to Dubrovnik and I crept back to Ormonde Gate. Babs was exceedingly gracious about it—a few 'I told you so' remarks and looks—but on the whole she was prepared to write the whole business off as a middle-aged aberration. Luckily I became extremely busy through 1970. I did five television plays, one of which I wrote, and two films. So I had, as it happened, a great deal of breathing space, which I put to good or bad use depending on your point of view.

In the first of the television plays I worked with a charming, if slightly drunken, young actor called Mark McManus. He had been working in Australia for a number of years and his stories of Sydney and Melbourne reinforced my urge to go there before I was too old to enjoy it. When I finally did go to Australia and met my wife-to-be, I discovered that she and Mark had been an item in the mid-sixties. I could only admire his taste. I worked with Mark eight years later in a television series my brother wrote. He was already showing signs of Olympic boozing and somehow he managed to miss his flight back to London from a location shoot in Venice, which lost him some brownie points as he was due on the set the next day. He survived and thrived for at least another decade, and made a name as the eponymous television detective, Taggart. It couldn't last, of course, and it didn't—he died on the job, as it were, in his early fifties.

My next film, *The Fourth Mrs Anderson*, was a Spanish/Italian co-production starring a Spanish comic actor, whose name I don't remember, Carroll Baker of *Baby Doll* fame and myself. Carroll's boyfriend at the time was the Italian producer and, according to her, he had a very jealous disposition. He and she got very steamed up one evening when a phone call from him to her was put through to my hotel room rather than hers. As it happened she was in my room at the time, not what her lover wanted to know. So we moved to her room down the corridor. Mr Italian Producer rang again and, without thinking, I answered the phone, forgetting that we were now in her room, where I wasn't supposed to be. There was a great deal of shouting down the line from Rome and a great deal of explaining, and blaming of the incompetent hotel switchboard operator, but I don't think Mr Italian Producer was convinced. He turned up in Madrid the following day and Carroll did a lot of loving TLC and smoothing of ruffled feathers. I kept well out of the way, just in case, but happily the feathers stayed smoothed and there were no further repercussions.

Safely delivered from whichever Mrs Anderson it was (I never saw the film and perhaps nobody else did either), I returned to Ormonde Gate and wrote an Armchair Theatre play for Thames Television. It was called *Father's Day*, about a divorced father who gets lumbered with his twin ten-year-old sons when his ex-wife does a runner. It wasn't a bad piece of work—a few laughs, a few tears and a little bit of something about responsibility. I played the father, of course, and behaved rather shamefully by insisting that Thames cast an actress I was having an affair with as my love interest in the piece. It was miscasting and bad casting and it was autobiographical enough to really annoy

Babs. I was ashamed of myself, but I did it. The play was received well enough and prompted Lloyd Shirley, the Head of Drama at Thames, to ask me to write another play for their Armchair Theatre series. I promised to think about it.

I received the supreme accolade from the BBC a few weeks later when I was asked to read the story on *Jackanory*. It had rankled with me for some time that I had never been asked to do this show on Children's Hour, and I kept hinting to my agent that I wanted to do it. All kinds of actors, from the very grand and important to the merely skilful, had appeared there and posed the immortal question, 'Are you sitting comfortably? . . . Then I'll begin.' Anyway I got my chance and was put through my paces by an extremely fierce lady producer.

The BBC was a law unto itself in those days. I could never understand why the BBC arbitrarily decided that fees for children's shows should be only half those for non-children's drama. I had a conversation with a producer along those lines and asked him why he was offering me so little money, simply because the show he wanted me to do was for children. Was I supposed to learn only half the lines? Or spend only half the time at rehearsal and recordings? If not, why was he prepared to pay only half my normal fee? Because that's the way it is, he responded, and that's the way it was.

At least I was paid properly for *Hotel in Amsterdam*, which was my next engagement. A television adaptation of the stage play written by John Osborne which had enjoyed a respectable run in the West End. It starred Paul Scofield, whom I found charming, diffident and brilliant. While I was finishing that show in late November, I got a strange call from a man called Benny Fisz. He was a soi-disant American film producer scrubbing along in London. He wanted me to go to Madrid for two weeks to appear in a film called *A Town Called Bastard* with Robert Shaw. Apparently the film had come in at only eighty minutes long and they had decided to shoot a flashback sequence of about fifteen minutes to increase the running time to the more commercial ninety-five minutes. I was to be in the 'flashback' as

Paco, a Mexican bandit. My only scenes would be with Robert
Shaw and they were written to explain why his character turned
out the way it did. I was entranced. I'd never played a Mexican,
had never expected to, and the chance of a couple of weeks in
Madrid in the depths of the English winter was very seductive.

I was kitted out with a mustard-coloured suit (vintage 1890s),
a pair of yellow lace-up boots and a drooping black moustache.
Equipped with this and my own clobber, I flew to Madrid. It
was very cold—I'd forgotten, if I'd ever known, that Madrid is
built on a plateau—and the temperature was well below freezing.
We were to shoot mainly at night—all night—because the sets
for *A Town Called Bastard* had been cannibalised long since and
turned into something else, the town of El Paso to be exact. During
the day, the streets and bars of 'El Paso' were being used by
another film but we could have the use of them through the nights.
The film is a real stinker, but I treasure it in my CV because, in
a dreadful Mexican accent, I spoke the immortal line . . . 'to be
poor in Mehico is to be dead señor . . .' It was all so bizarre.

By the beginning of 1971 the slump in the film industry
brought about by the withdrawal of American money was really
beginning to bite. I had no film work in sight and, to make things
even worse, many of the television roles that I might have expected
to come my way were going to actors with greater clout than me
but who previously would have refused them because they were
doing better-paid film jobs. I managed to keep going in a desultory way but I stopped driving big cars and settled on a Mini
Cooper, which had the advantage of great acceleration and excellent fuel economy. With no work in the pipeline I decided it was
time to take up Lloyd Shirley's earlier offer and write another play.

I provided Lloyd with the rough outline of the events that
had occurred at Harold Pinter's birthday party in New York and
he was immediately intrigued. I was commissioned to write it
by Thames Television and did so under the title of *The Night of
the Chairs*. I did advise them that perhaps they should check with
the Pinters to make sure they had no objections but Lloyd
assured me it wasn't necessary. I wasn't going to name names

or identify bodies; it would be a fiction to which nobody could object. A rattling good story of mystery and suspense, ironically not unlike the sort of story that Harold had made his name writing.

Over the two and a half years since we'd been in New York with *The Homecoming*, I'd run into fellow members of the cast on odd occasions and, of course, the opening gambit was always, 'Have you found out who did it?' The answer was always 'No', but I'd developed a theory that the only person with a real motive and the opportunity was Vivien herself so I wrote the play that way. It was in two acts and at the end of the first, we learn that the vandalism has occurred and the host says, 'I'm not so concerned about *who* did it, but *why*?' The second act dealt with a sort of investigation, which led nowhere, and in the end the host and his wife are left alone after everyone else has gone. 'Well,' he says, 'that settles it. If none of them did it, it had to be you or me, and I know it wasn't me.'

Lloyd Shirley was pleased with my efforts; a cast was engaged and a start date announced for rehearsals. A couple of the *Homecoming* cast were to appear as their own well-disguised characters and I had conferences with the director about one or two things in the script. I was sitting at home in Chelsea two days before rehearsals were due to start when I got a summons from Lloyd to get my sorry ass down to the studios forthwith as there was big trouble at mill. When I got there I was told that Lord Goodman, one of the most fearsome 'legal eagles' in the country, had issued a libel writ on Harold Pinter's behalf and Thames Television and I were going to be sued for punitive damages.

I tried to point out that the story was known only to a tiny number of people and that the only way it could be linked to the Pinters was if they actually sued. That didn't wash so I asked what exactly they were objecting to. Everything in general, but in particular the fact that I'd pointed the finger unequivocally at the wife. 'Okay,' I said, 'I'll change it. When he says, "I know it wasn't me", she can look him straight in the eye and say, "And

I know it wasn't me." Let the audience work it out.' That didn't wash either and the production was cancelled with apologies all round. The libel suit was dropped, but I received a letter from Lord Goodman advising me that if I ever repeated the story I would find myself in court quick sharp. Well I have repeated it here on these pages, but Lord Goodman is dead, and sadly so is Vivian, so maybe the writ won't be delivered. As far as I'm concerned, the story is true and part of my life, so *I* think I'm entitled to tell it. Hope I'm right.

The actors who were booked to work on the television play and I were paid, of course, and the director and anyone else who'd signed a contract; and I suppose the whole debacle cost Thames television a considerable sum of money. Naturally I carried the can even though I *had* warned Lloyd Shirley at the beginning, and I became very much persona non grata at Shepperton. Even worse, I had inadvertently and innocently made an enemy of Harold Pinter, who was a powerful influence in the business. When the film version of *The Homecoming* was made, Teddy was played by Michael Jayston instead of me.

The irony of the whole debacle was that, far from keeping a lid on the story, it made the Diary column in the *Times*. I was telephoned by some hack who asked me why my play had been cancelled by Thames Television. Mindful of Lord Goodman's strictures, I told him I had no idea. They had the right to produce or not produce the play, I had been paid and had no further control over what I'd written. The next day the whole story was there in black and white. The names of everyone who had been at the birthday party, an exact description of what had happened, all laid out on the pages of the *Times*. Murder will out, so they say, and it did in this particular case.

In subsequent discussions with Johnny Normington, he told me he'd worked out who'd chucked the chairs from the window and why Harold had gone ape at the thought of the production of *The Night of the Chairs*. 'It had to be Daniel,' he said. 'He wasn't part of the birthday party but he *was* in the flat, sitting in his room, pissed off about not being part of the party. Harold and Vivien must have found out later, but kept it to themselves.' It made sense but we'll never really know.

All this happened in 1971 and it was influential in my decision to get out of London for a while and seek my fortune in Australia. Ten years later I was back in London and was invited to some kind of celebration at the Guildhall to honour Richard Attenborough. I ran into Harold at this do and we had a minor sort of reconciliation. He was no longer married to Vivien by then, but to Lady Antonia Fraser, and was even more successful than when I'd last seen him. Quite rightly, as he's one of the major playwrights of the twentieth century.

•

Just before things got too desperate, the BBC employed me in a television version of Moliere's *Tartuffe*. Michael Hordern played Tartuffe with marvellous, eye-rolling, lip-smacking hypocrisy; I played Orgon, the duped husband, and Patricia Routledge played the small but showy part of the maid. We had splendid costumes, sets and wigs, but I found the text horrendously difficult to learn. It was a new translation by some American professor and it was written in rhyming couplets. Shakespeare had the good sense and consideration for his actors to restrict his rhyming couplets mostly to the last two lines of a scene. When I did *Tartuffe* I understood why. A page-and-a-half speech, of which I had several, no matter how cleverly rhymed and wittily written in rhyming couplet after rhyming couplet, is a bugger to memorise and even harder to invest with dramatic life. We got away with it but I have no wish to repeat the exercise.

Post-*Tartuffe*, the phone stopped ringing and my agent might have died for all I knew. It was high summer so I concentrated on my golf and a bit of cricket and tried to keep my pecker up. September arrived and with it the soccer season. I played for a team called the Coughin Casuals, based at the Queen's Elm Pub. We played our home fixtures on one of the public pitches in Hyde Park and our team was made up of a random selection of actors, writers, journalists and regulars from the pub.

One Sunday morning in early September I turned up at the park to play and met Maurice Kaufman. He was an actor of about my own age and at the time he was married to Honour Blackman. I hadn't seen him for a while and asked him what he was doing. He told me that he and Honour had been asked to go to Australia to do a play called *Move Over Mrs Markham*. This was a successful farce by Ray Cooney and had been running in London for some time with Moira Lister and Tony Britton. I assumed that Honour would be playing the name part, so I asked Maurice if he was going to play Mr Markham. He said no—he was playing the 'friend' and that the producers were still looking for a 'Mr'. It is at such moments that one's life can change forever.

I told Maurice that I'd always yearned to go to Australia and he was delighted. 'Give them a ring tomorrow, old boy,' he said. 'Honour would love it if you came too.' It couldn't have been simpler—I made the call, met Ray Cooney, got the okay from JC Williamsons, who were presenting the show in Sydney, and left for Australia two weeks later.

It's self-indulgent and silly to dwell on these things. But if I hadn't turned up to play football that morning and met Maurice Kaufman there, I'd never have known about the job, probably never have gone to Australia, wouldn't have met my wife-to-be, and wouldn't have conceived my beautiful daughter, Jess. In my view it is one of the strongest arguments in favour of sport that anyone could have and, when people knock the importance of soccer in our society, I know a hell of a lot better.

TWELVE

Dreamtime

I left England for Australia in the middle of September 1971 and arrived in Sydney on a Saturday morning. My first view of the city was the absolute traveller's cliché—the pilot flew us over the Harbour Bridge (the Opera House hadn't been completed by then) and up the harbour before turning south again and on to Mascot airport.

My employers were JC Williamsons, the long-established theatrical management chain, whose Sydney office was run by a man called Sidney Irving, a rather dour but decent enough old pro. With a staff of about four, he ran a business that would now have a staff of forty, if the Sydney Theatre Company is anything to go by. Sid met me at the airport and drove me to my serviced apartment in McMahon's Point, not very far from where I now live. He gave me a couple of hundred dollars on account, so I could buy provisions, told me that my call was for 10 a.m. on Monday at the theatre, and left me to it. I was travel-weary but excited. My flatlet was on the sixth floor with a panoramic view of the harbour with its non-stop traffic of ferries and merchant and naval ships, and boats of all descriptions.

I turned on the television and watched with some mystification something called the Bathurst 500. It was the most boring kind of motor race. To me it looked like ordinary saloon cars going on and on and on, their frenetic progress intermittently interrupted by even more boring commercials. There was nothing much else to watch so I walked up the road to the nearest pub and had a few beers before finding a small supermarket. I spent some of Sid's advance on necessary staples and strolled back to the Florida Harbourside Apartments to unpack my bags. I felt an extraordinary sense of freedom and exhilaration—I was as far away from home as it was possible to be, and anything could happen.

I rang Babs in Chelsea and discussed our situation. In view of the distance and cost of the journey to Sydney, it seemed prudent to wait and see whether we were a hit before bringing her and the boys out to join me. We'd know in a month or so and, if all went well, she and Stephen and MJ could look forward to Christmas and a few months in the sun away from the bloody awful English winter. Babs seemed agreeable and I went to bed conscious of having done the right thing—knowing I had covered my bets both ways. I resolved to put Babs and the family first, to be faithful, and resist any and all temptation, whether real or fanciful.

My contract with Williamsons was for three months, I think, with an option for a further three months, which they could exercise if business warranted it. We were to play the Theatre Royal in Castlereagh Street for the first three months, and then move to the Comedy Theatre in Melbourne for the second three. We would rehearse for three and a half weeks and open towards the end of October. Ray Cooney, who was the author of *Move Over Mrs Markham*, was to direct the show. Apart from Honour Blackman, Maurice Kaufman and me, the cast would be Australians.

I couldn't wait. I rang my old friend Ronnie Frazer, who was back in Sydney after his adventures with HM Tennants and the Theatre Royal in York, and we had a drink or two in his flat in Macquarie Street. He gave me scotch and the local showbiz gossip, but it didn't mean anything to me or interest me very much. Back home on his native turf, Ronnie had shed his English circumspection and reverted to his 'flaring' worst, or best if that's your bag. I discovered Hegarty's Ferries, which ran from the dock under my window in McMahon's Point to Circular Quay, and decided they were the way to travel to and from work. It was only a ten-minute walk from Circular Quay to the theatre and there was no risk of being breathalysed on the harbour.

On Monday morning I arrived at the theatre and was directed to the rehearsal room. This was a mirrored space towards the top of the building, tucked away behind the Circle Bar. I said hello to Ray Cooney, who had been in Australia for some time casting the other parts, and chatted to Honour and Maurice. They were renting a house in a posh part of Sydney, big enough to house them and their two small children and a nanny. I hoped for their sakes that we were a success, or it was going to be an expensive exercise for them. I was introduced to the Australian actors: Colleen Clifford, an elderly expatriate British actress with a sweet smile; Charles Little, an eager juvenile cast as the 'camp' interior decorator; Brian Blain, a nine-foot-tall lanky eccentric with a lantern jaw and great charm; Olwen Cook, a skinny blonde girl who startled me by asking for a pernod and Coke (I'd never heard of such a thing) when I bought a round of drinks at lunchtime; and Coralie Neville, a slightly worn looking woman, somewhat like a leading lady of a twice-nightly North Country rep company.

I checked my script. We were missing someone—the someone who was to play 'Miss Wilkinson', the someone who had to appear in her underwear in the second act and with whom I, as Mr Markham, had some mildly intimate moments. The door opened and in she came—the most gorgeous girl in a leather mini-skirt, boots and a jacket—and I was a gone goose. Her name was Sue Walker and she had a smile that would make the angels sing. All my good resolutions about fidelity and family priorities went hurtling out the window—I was enchanted, captivated, spellbound and lost.

Ray Cooney called us together for a quick pep talk and we started to rehearse. It was a real learning curve for most of us, certainly for those unfamiliar with the technique of farce. Ray was a master of the genre, as actor, writer and director—he knew exactly what he wanted, exactly what worked best, and he put us through an intensive three weeks of instruction. I personally enjoyed it immensely—I'd always been more interested in the nuts and bolts of performance than the more esoteric arty side, and this was nuts and bolts with a vengeance. Three and a half weeks later it really paid off. I had never heard laughs like it in the theatre, some of them went on for minutes. Everything Ray had predicted and made us work towards came good, and the twelve hundred people filling the old Theatre Royal had one of the best nights of their lives.

We were a huge hit, bookings were sensational, the options were exercised and I was in deep trouble. There was no way I could go back on my decision to bring Babs and the boys out, but by now I was hopelessly in love with Sue and, to my great surprise and happiness, she with me. I knew a lot of people were going to get hurt. I knew there wasn't going to be any easy way of sorting it out, but I also knew that I would soon be forty-three and, if I didn't behave like a grown-up person for a change, I wouldn't have much of a future.

Babs duly arrived with MJ—Stephen had to wait for the end of term before joining us. We moved into a larger apartment in the Florida Harbourside and MJ started school in North Sydney, something he didn't much like. As planned, Stephen arrived just before Christmas. The show was a huge hit and, as is the way of the world, everyone wanted to know us.

I was made an honorary member of the Royal Sydney Golf Club, where I played with an Admiral Gatacre and a surgeon called Dick Opie who really impressed me one day with his nonchalance. He got a message on the fourteenth tee to come to the hospital to carry out some kind of emergency surgery. This was before the days of mobile phones so Dick told the messenger to advise the hospital that he was on his way, and promptly hit his drive down the fairway. I asked him if he shouldn't be on his way to this emergency but he checked his watch and remarked that, by the time the poor bugger was 'prepped' and ready for *his* expertise, we'd have time to finish our game and have a drink. Echoes of Francis Drake playing bowls on Plymouth Ho with the Spanish Armada approaching up the Channel! When I came to play the surgeon in *GP* twenty years later, I modelled some of my attitude on Dick. I was then accused in some quarters of being overly unfeeling but, with Dick's example as a guide, I knew I was being realistic.

Jack Lee, an English film director whom I had known in my Pinewood days, was now living in Sydney and he and his wife, Isabel, entertained us generously. She was one of the Kidman heiresses and they lived in a grand house with all the mod cons, including a swimming pool, in Woollahra. Most Sundays they held open house in a wonderfully lavish manner. We were taken sailing on the harbour by Admiral Gatacre and I bought a second-hand Holden Kingswood from our production's head mech. The weather was great and life should have been great too. The fact that it wasn't was entirely due to me.

Sue and I were carrying on a clandestine relationship that made us both unhappy and unsatisfied, and I was bad-tempered and unloving at home. Christmas came and went, as did Stephen, back to school in London. Business continued to boom, so much so that not a week went by without my making an extra three or four hundred dollars from my small percentage. Our three-month season was extended to five months.

Finally we closed in Sydney in February 1972. We were the penultimate show at the old Theatre Royal, which was demolished soon after we left and became a cavernous pit for several years while the developers got their act together. Babs, MJ and I drove down to Melbourne and rented a house in Albert Park, where poor MJ was put into yet another school. He loathed it even more than the one in Sydney, where at least he hadn't had to play Australian Rules football.

The play didn't have quite the same success in Melbourne. The old Sydney/Melbourne rivalry didn't help our cause— Melburnians were usually reluctant to embrace a Sydney hit with open arms, in case they might appear to be influenced in any way by their northern neighbours. Still business was more than respectable and we played on for two months. Sue and I continued to see each other away from the theatre as much as we could, but it continued to be an unhappy and frustrating situation.

Towards the end of the Melbourne season we were asked if we would go to New Zealand for seasons in Wellington, Auckland and Christchurch. Honour was agreeable and so was I. Maurice went back to England with their two children and I persuaded Babs that I'd be a lunatic to leave the show, which was proving to be such a goldmine. I told her I should make the most of the New Zealand opportunity to top up the bank account, while she went back to Chelsea with MJ. I sighed with relief as I waved goodbye to them at Melbourne Airport—I now had three months to be with Sue, and that was as far ahead as either of us were prepared to look for the moment.

In Wellington we packed them in and we became the toast of yet another town, even though we got off to a bit of a dodgy start—Colleen Clifford was ill and her understudy had to play the first few performances. Back in those bad old days (and this might interest young actors who complain about paying their union dues), if actors were unable to perform because of illness, they didn't get paid. 'No play, no pay' was the order of the day. So poor old Colleen, who was in her late seventies, was stuck in her digs in Wellington, paying rent and doctor's bills, with no money coming in. The cast had a whip-round and raised a couple of hundred dollars, which management, under considerable pressure from Honour and me, matched. So Colleen was able to pay her way until she was better and performing again.

Sue and I shared a motel room and were happy as the flowers that bloom in the spring. Then we moved on to Auckland, which was a bit of an anti-climax because we met some competition there. A show called *Charley Girl*, starring Anna Neagle and a young John Farnham, was packing them in across the road and affecting our business. However, we did okay and the five weeks passed by without problem. Honour decided to leave after the Auckland stint so Sue, as her understudy, was delegated to play Mrs Markham when we went to Christchurch. Everyone was delighted for her, in spite of a poster announcing our season in Christchurch reading, 'And Introding Sue Walker as Mrs Markham'. She and I were blissfully happy, sharing accommodation and everything else. She knocked them dead when we opened, and the only shadow over all this was that the New Zealand tour was coming to an end; and I was due to return to England.

We went back to Sydney and the day that Sue and I had been dreading arrived. I returned to England, home and heartache at the end of August 1972, and to the worst four months of my life. I ached for Sue and we kept up a furtive correspondence through my old friend Dan Massey, who acted as a poste restante for me. I was lucky enough to be kept busy with work but my heart wasn't in it and life at Chelsea was strained and horrible.

I did a low-budget film called *Vault of Horror*. It was one of those anthology films, where five dead characters gather in limbo and tell their stories before returning to their graves. The cast included Terry Thomas, Curt Jurgens, Glynis Johns, Dan Massey and Tom Baker, later one of the famous Dr Who's. I also did three television plays. I don't remember much about any of these ventures as my heart and what was left of my brain were back in Sydney with Sue. Finally I knew I had to make the break.

I booked a one-way ticket to Sydney, took £1000 in cash out of the bank, told Babs that the house and the rest of the money was hers and broke the news to Stephen and MJ. Stephen was seventeen and involved in his own world of Westminster School, football and art, so he took it pretty well. I promised that I'd always be around and would be back and forth from Australia so we'd see each other often. Even though I suppose we both knew that wouldn't be quite the case, we let it go at that. MJ, who was not quite twelve, took it really hard. I remember breaking it to him while we were taking the dog for a walk in Hyde Park one Sunday morning. He looked at me in horror and wailed a long drawn out 'Nooooo'. It brings tears to my eyes even now, but I'd made up my mind and I had to leave. At the beginning of February 1973 I flew back to Sydney with the £1000 in my pocket, an overweening feeling of guilt and expectations of a new and happy life with Sue. It was just a few days after my forty-fourth birthday and I was ready and eager to start again.

Sue was living in her own flat in Cremorne, on Sydney's lower north shore, and was working in a revue at the old Chevron Hotel in Macleay Street, earning a reasonable salary. The star of the show was Ronnie Frazer and the others in the company were John Derum, Judy Morris and Dawn Lake. I worked, and became friendly, with them all in later years. I bought an old Fiat 1100 from Sue's brother, Tony, who was also doing a runner from his wife and leaving for Tasmania with his new love, another lady called Sue. It only cost me $200, and it did me very well for the next three years. Because I had more or less decided to give up acting for a living and try to make my way as a writer, I felt I really had to see a lot more of this huge new country I was now living in rather than just the bits of Sydney and Melbourne that had been my compass up to then.

I met a fellow ex-pat English actor-cum-writer called Don Barkham and over some pot-fuelled meetings, we decided to co-write a television series called *The Outsiders*. It would be about itinerant workers in outback Australia—cane cutters, fruit pickers, fish gutters, drovers, whatever, from the Gulf of Carpentaria to the Great Australian Bight. The leading character and driving force for the series was a young city bloke looking for, and finding, his grandfather, and of course himself, in the great university of hard work and experience. In order to learn at least a little of what it might be like, I decided to drive up to far north Queensland and have a look at some of the sugar towns. I hadn't a clue really—just what I'd read in the guidebooks in the library—but I liked the sound of the names and the Pacific Highway went all the way from Sydney to most of these places, so I could hardly go wrong.

What I hadn't properly sussed out was quite how far it was to Cairns. There and back was about 3500 miles (5600 kilometres), and that wasn't allowing for any detours. I packed a small bag, filled the Fiat's tank, told Sue I'd be back in a few days and headed north. I'd got just south of Taree when the petrol pump packed in and I spent the night on the side of the road waiting for assistance. By an extreme piece of good luck a petrol pump for a 1965 Fiat 1100 was found in Taree and the next morning I was on my way again. My confidence was slightly dented by this breakdown but, apart from a couple of punctures, I had no other problems. The old Fiat chugged resolutely along at seventy miles per hour (or one hundred and ten kilometres per hour) for the rest of the journey.

I duly checked out the towns on my itinerary—it didn't take long as they were all pretty much the same and deadly dull. I made a few notes and kept pressing on. I spent one night in a hotel in Rockhampton, where I was charged seven dollars for a shared room. I could have had the room for five dollars if I'd been prepared to share the double bed, but that seemed a bit too close. Just as well I decided on the deluxe price as I was woken at 2 a.m. by a very large and drunken man falling into the double bed and roaring obscene abuse into the night until he collapsed into a catatonic state. I pulled the blanket over my head and pretended I wasn't there. I got up very early and had a shower, which ran out of water just after I had thoroughly soaped myself. I had to drive on with the dried soap cracking on my body until the sweat dissolved it into my shirt and trousers.

On and on I went. I ate and drank in pubs where, against the warnings I'd been given, my pommy status caused no offence. I was treated with good-humoured kindness wherever I went. I slept in the car, which I covered in mosquito netting, and washed and abluted in the petrol stations when I filled the tank. Once I had reached Cairns and the Atherton Tablelands, there seemed to be nothing to do except turn round and head back to Sydney.

I decided to do the return journey in two days and, at the end of the first, stopped on the side of the road just south of Rockhampton. It was already dark, so I wrapped the mosquito net round the Fiat, had a slug of scotch and went to sleep. An hour or two later I was woken by the sound of a train whistle and looked out of the rear window to see the blazing headlamp of a train approaching at speed. 'Christ!' I thought. 'I've parked on the fucking railway line.' I fumbled for the door handle in a panic as the train whistled again and the headlamp grew ever brighter. The mosquito net wrapped itself around me and I lay gasping on the back seat, struggling to get out. The train seemed to be only a few yards away and the inside of the car was lit by its light as I steeled myself for the crash. At the last moment it veered away and disappeared down the track, and I slowly pulled myself together. I'd parked on the apex of a bend and in fact, was at least ten feet (three metres) from the edge of the rails, but it had been one of the scariest moments of my life.

I didn't bother trying to go back to sleep—my heart was still pounding as I drove on and headed towards Sydney and Sue, eleven hundred miles (nearly eighteen hundred kilometres) to the south. I did the trip in one hit and arrived at the flat at about 4 a.m. the next morning. I was tired but, apart from hallucinating on the last stretch from Newcastle, when I seemed to be travelling *up*hill all the time in spite of the fact that I could see I was going downhill, I hadn't found it too difficult. When I took my shorts off they stood on the floor in the shape of my bum, as if they had been bronzed and mounted, and I slept solidly for twelve hours.

I'd driven about 5000 miles (8000 kilometres) in seven days and learned a little about Australia, but not much about itinerant workers. I'd have to bullshit when it came to writing the scripts, and ultimately did so without too much difficulty. What I did learn was that, apart from the occasional stretch of sugar cane or banana or pineapple plantations, much of the countryside was interminably the same. When in due course *The Outsiders* was filmed, with German participation and a German actor playing the young man in search of himself, we took advantage of the sameness of the Australian countryside and shot most of it in and around Sydney. Nobody knew the difference and it saved a great deal of time and money. However, that didn't happen for a couple of years and in the meantime I had to earn some money.

As soon as I'd recuperated from my epic drive, I decided to write something quite different. In those days most television series consisted of thirteen episodes so I racked my brains to find the perfect subject which would divide into thirteen parts. Finally I came up with what I imagined to be the perfect answer—the Twelve Apostles, plus a thirteenth episode to tell what happened to them. No one seemed to know much about this famous dozen, not much more than their names, so I felt free to indulge my imagination and had a ball inventing lives and adventures for each of them within the loose context of the Gospels. I felt it had a good chance of being snapped up, especially as it could all be shot in Australia. There were deserts and camels available, and plenty of ethnic types to play the Egyptians, Romans, Palestinians etc. when required. However, although several people showed interest, in the end it never got the green light and remains in my dusty file of things that might have been.

In the light of this double failure to make a living through my writing, I had to think again. I had quite heavy financial commitments to Babs and the boys. I'd agreed to continue to pay the outgoings at Ormonde Gate as well as the school fees for Stephen and MJ so I needed to earn a minimum of seven or eight thousand pounds a year before I could buy myself a beer or help Sue with the rent. I'd kept a pretty low profile since my return to Australia. I'd seen Jack Lee and Isabel occasionally, but I think I was a bit on the nose as a runaway husband, and of course I wasn't starring in a hit play. There was no more golf at the Royal Sydney, no more harbour cruises with the admiral and, worst of all, no more fat pay packets every week. Sue introduced me to her agent, Faith Martin, and I signed with her for employment in Australia. I still had an agent in London, but he was unlikely to find me a job in Sydney, and I had no intention of limping back to England as a failed emigrant.

As it happened, Sid Irving at JC Williamsons came to the rescue. I was offered the lead in a play called *Suddenly at Home*. This was a rather creaky whodunit, which had been a minor hit in London. As was customary then, Williamsons reckoned that what was good enough for London was good enough for them and were planning a production in Melbourne. The money wasn't bad, not as good as for *Move Over Mrs Markham* but enough to put me solidly back in the black. I was the only Pom in the cast, but the director was English and he had directed the play in London. It was a good cast, but the play didn't work. Australian audiences are a more cynical lot than their West End counterparts and they have never shared the English liking for the stately formalities of the detective play. Hercule Poirot and Lord Peter Wimsey are not for them and *The Mousetrap* wouldn't run fifty weeks in Australia, never mind fifty years plus. In the event we closed after five fairly dismal weeks and I returned to Sydney. I was glad to be back, though. I hated being away from Sue, and the Melbourne winter had been more than usually unkind.

Although *Suddenly at Home* was a flop, it did do me some good by re-establishing me in Australia. I got some publicity and it became known that I was no longer a visiting English actor, but a resident Australian who just happened to be English. I was offered a part in a film called *Inn of the Damned*, aka *Death Hunter*. It was a period piece written and subsequently directed by a man called Terry Bourke. I think he had an advertising company. He was a nice enough chap, but he didn't know much about writing or directing films. It was based on the old story of the lonely inn where travellers disappeared, killed in a huge four-poster bed whose canopy descended in the night and smothered its sleeping occupants. The innkeeper's wife was played by the illustrious Dame Judith Anderson, who for some extraordinary reason agreed to return to her homeland to appear in this piece of rubbish. I suppose, in her defence, she had nothing left to prove. At her then great age she was probably quite pleased to get a free trip back to Australia and some money in her pocket.

She was quite intimidating and took it all very seriously, which was more than I could do.

Her husband was played by a very dear man called Joseph Furst and the inevitable American 'star' was an actor called Alex Cord, who'd had a successful television series in the States playing some kind of cowboy character. He obviously fancied a trip Down Under. He paid no attention to the fact that our story was set in colonial Australia in the mid-nineteenth century and did his bounty-hunter *shtick*, as if he was on the Chisholm Trail rather than the Road to Gundagai.

It was a really cheap production. In the last big scene, when Alex and I had to attack the wicked innkeepers and save some poor traveller's life, I was supposed to have a shotgun with which to despatch poor old Joseph Furst before he could blow me apart with *his* shotgun. On the day, the props department had only provided one shotgun, which Joseph and I had to share. I had it in my hand as I crashed through the window . . . 'Cut!' I gave it to Joseph, who raised it and pointed it at me . . . 'Cut!' He gave it to me and I blew him away . . . 'Cut!' I gave it back to Joseph, who was lying in a pool of blood clutching the gun, which he hadn't had time to fire . . . 'Cut!' I retrieved the gun and walked out of shot.

Another actor in the cast was the late great John Meillon. I'd known him slightly in London and admired his talents enormously. He had returned to Australia a few years earlier and established himself as a sort of icon for his performances and his drinking. He was a few years younger than me but we had a lot in common, and in the desperate desolate evenings on location on Mangrove Mountain we became very good friends and remained so until his premature death in 1991 at the age of fifty-five. He introduced me to a lot of his friends, most of whom are now dead, and I found myself part of a circle which socialised at The Oaks pub in Neutral Bay, the Mosman Rowing Club in Mosman, and in what was then the number one watering hole for television actors and staff, the Seven Two Nine Club at St Leonards. It was in this last club that I met Eric Tayler, who was the 'gun' drama director for the ABC. Eric employed me constantly for the next five or six years, and we too became very good friends. We golfed and drank, went fishing and drank, played snooker and drank, but also worked long hours for not great money for the Drama Department of the ABC which, in those good old bad old days, produced a consistent stream of high-class drama, as good as any in the world.

I did a three-part television series called *Three Men of the City*, directed by Eric for the ABC. While I was working on this, I told him that I'd like to write a three-part series myself. In the late sixties I had worked with a writer and film director called Bill Fairchild, who had written *Star* and written and directed *The Silent Enemy* ten years earlier. We had become fairly good friends and while on holiday together in Madeira in the late sixties, Bill had told me about the Hollywood actor Red Skelton who, when his young son was diagnosed with incurable leukemia, had taken the boy around the world and given him anything and everything he asked for in the final year of his life. An understandable effort to soften the impending tragedy for them both. It was a very moving story, but it had occurred to Bill and me that such a gesture would only be possible if you were rich and successful and could afford to take a year off work. What would you do if you were an ordinary working man without much money and were told that your twelve-year-old son had only a few months to live?

Bill and I had kicked the story possibilities around over the years but had never got very far beyond that initial premise. However, while surviving the longeurs of *Inn of the Doomed*, as it became known, I'd discussed this idea with Meillon over a beer or two. He was greatly excited by its possibilities. I asked Eric if he thought it might be a goer and he too was very enthusiastic. So I sat down and wrote what was finally called *The Fourth Wish* with Meillon in mind as the battling Aussie father. In my scenario the father asks his son what he would wish for if he had three wishes—nothing fancy or magical, but things he'd like to do or have. The boy doesn't know he is dying and wishes for a dog, to see his mother and to meet the Queen. I know it sounds really corny and even maudlin, but it didn't play like that. The wishes were difficult for the father to achieve but not impossible. Each episode dealt with the father's attempts to make the wishes come true. The 'fourth wish' of the title came at the end of the last episode when the boy, having had his wishes granted, asks his dad what he would wish for if *he* had three wishes. The father says he doesn't need three, he has only one.

I wrote the three episodes in about six weeks and they were barely changed from my first drafts to the final production scripts. Amazing really, especially when you consider each episode was a full hour in length and the third one over-ran by about ten minutes. Nobody cared in those more carefree days and I had no script editors to sit on my back and urge their largely unwanted suggestions. The programme was a huge hit for the ABC and all concerned and, in an unprecedented piece of programming, they repeated it within a year. I'd had a small problem with the brass at the ABC about Meillon being the man for the job as he had a bit of a reputation for 'unreliability through drink'. However both Eric and I held out for him and guaranteed his good behaviour. Meillon fully justified our faith and in a way re-created his career with his performance and his behaviour during and after the production.

The only downside to the enterprise was my inability to get Bill Fairchild's approval and/or his involvement. I wrote to him to let him know what I was doing, but he either didn't take it seriously or couldn't be bothered to respond until it was too late and the show was in the can. It caused a bit of a rift between us for some time, but eventually he admitted that I hadn't deliberately excluded him and that it was his fault that he'd never been part of it.

While Meillon and Eric were shooting *The Fourth Wish*, I did a couple of one-off dramas for the ABC wearing my acting hat. One was called *Payoff*, a murder mystery in which I played the bad guy opposite Cornelia Francis. The other was a wonderful piece called *Essington*, written by Tom Keneally. It dealt with a bizarre moment of Australian history in the 1840s, when a military garrison stationed at Port Essington in the Gulf of Carpentaria to defend Australia against Russia was left to rot for twelve years without contact with the outside world. It was a surreal story of a mad commandant trying to maintain full military discipline and procedures in an environment where only the local Aborigines, and those who imitated them, could survive and thrive. It was a wonderful script; macabre, funny, tragic and optimistic, and extremely well directed by Julian Pringle. The cast included Wynne Roberts, Jacqueline Kott, Melissa Jaffer, Chris Hayward, Justine Saunders and Drew Forsythe. I was taught how to throw a boomerang by one of the Aboriginal actors and, apart from a scene in which one of the ladies blew her brains out over my face, I enjoyed myself greatly. It was beautifully shot and won some international prizes, but for some odd reason has never been repeated by the ABC. Someone gave me a tape of it but, as far as I know, I'm one of the very few people who has one. Pity.

I don't know where I found the time or the energy but, as well as performing in these productions, I also wrote another two-hour pilot for a television series, again to star my friend John Meillon. It was called *Arena* and was about a failed businessman who sets himself up as an agent for sporting celebrities. It also starred Ray Barrett but, alas, the option wasn't exercised. Although the pilot went well enough, we never did the series. Many years later a series *was* made based on a similar idea, also starring Ray Barrett, but I had nothing to do with it. Since the idea is in the public domain I couldn't really claim plagiarism.

It was at about this time that a bloke called Jim McDonald asked me to direct a production of *Move Over Mrs Markham*. Jim was the booker and producer of entertainment at the St George Leagues Club in Kogarah. The money was very good and I was allowed to cast the play as I wished. Sue played Mrs Markham, and I cast two of her co-cast from the revue, John Derum and Dawn Lake, as the camp interior decorator and the mad old lady. I quite enjoyed the experience of directing, but I don't think I'm really cut out for it. My impatience with an actor's failure to learn or remember lines made me bite my tongue too often for comfort. We were a big success with the patrons, but the club wasn't happy. It seemed that the bar and gambling takings slumped considerably while the show was on, so we closed after six weeks.

Another little earner which came my way that year was to fly to Hildersheim in Germany to shoot a commercial for Blaupunkt. They were about to introduce this Rolls Royce of television sets into Australia and I was chosen to front the campaign. I've no idea why I was chosen, but I had no hesitation in saying yes. I was paid a good fee, and I received a television set from the top of the Blaupunkt range. It was absolutely brilliant, with great colour and one of the first remote controls. It lasted for at least twenty years and was given a decent send-off when it died. The odd thing about this venture was that Blaupunkt never ran their advertising campaign in Australia or ever actually sold any television sets here.

THIRTEEN

Full-time

As well as all my non-stop activity on the work front—Sue was flat out working too—we managed a hectic social life with parties and fishing trips and golf and poker, and visits to Sue's parents at Wentworth Falls in the Blue Mountains. From time to time people from my life in England dropped in. Peter O'Toole came to Sydney in some play at the new Theatre Royal and we had an evening together. I hadn't seen him since our days of country dancing and was looking forward to a night of revelry. It was not to be. Poor Peter had suffered some vile stomach disorder, contracted in Venezuela while filming *Murphy's War*, and wasn't able to drink any more. He had a sort of substitute in a cigar-sized joint, but smoking isn't as sociable as drinking and the evening wasn't a big success.

Jack Lee's brother Laurie came visiting. Laurie Lee, the poet and author of *Cider with Rosie* and *As I Walked Out One Midsummer Morning*, was a member of the Chelsea Arts Club and he played darts in The Queen's Elm pub by blowing his darts through a bamboo tube like some jungle hunter in the Amazon. I knew Laurie quite well from my Chelsea days and was very pleased to see him. He had grown tired of staying with Jack and Isabel in Jersey Road, said he found it all too genteel, and wanted to see some *real* Australia.

I'd driven to Lightning Ridge the previous year to look for locations for a story-line for *The Outsiders* and I felt it was about as real as Australia gets. An image I had retained vividly in my memory from that trip was of its scrub and red earth landscape, dotted with heaps of tailings from hundreds of mineshafts and encampments of old trucks and buses and corrugated iron shanties. From my car I had seen a straggle of sweating half-naked miners of every nationality heading to their local, The Diggers Rest, exactly as I had expected it. Then, as I turned a corner, I had glimpsed the timeless gentility of a ladies bowling match taking place at the local club. Every lady was appropriately dressed (totally inappropriately in the circumstances) in white stockings and shoes, a white blouse and skirt and the pudding-bowl white hat of the lady bowler. Their polished bowls gleamed on the green sward (probably carpet) and the stately ritual of bend and roll and the checking of the 'head' was accompanied by little encouragements of 'Good shot, Madge', or 'Not quite a toucher'. They carried on as if they were in Wimbledon or Bath, and I had been enchanted. Oh yes, I thought, Lightning Ridge is the place to take Laurie.

It was early February 1974 when we set out in the old Fiat. Laurie was unsuitably dressed in a panama hat, a tweed jacket and grey flannel trousers over a set of long-johns which protruded from his shirt sleeves at one end and were tucked into his socks at the other. He had a small Gladstone bag containing a change of clothing and a large paper bag containing a pre-mixed bottle of whisky and soda. Very little soda. I kissed Sue goodbye, told her we'd be back in four or five days, and drove west to the foot of the Blue Mountains. I'd told Laurie it was a long drive and would involve an overnight stop in Gulargambone or Gilgandra. Laurie looked at me and lovingly savoured the names of the towns—Gulargambone . . . Gilgandra—in his Cotswold burr, but I don't think he fully realised the extent of our journey. After about an hour and a half on the road and a few reflective pulls from the bottle in the paper bag, he asked me mildly if we were nearly there. We'd barely reached the foot of the mountains and my heart sank.

Memories of taking my children on journeys when they were small flooded back and depressed my spirits. 'Are we there yet, Daddy?', 'Can I have a drink, Daddy?', 'I need to do potty . . .' We'd soon be playing I Spy With My Little Eye if I wasn't careful! In a quiet but fervent tone I told him we had at least 400 miles ahead of us and I'd let him know in plenty of time before reaching our destination. He grinned amiably, had another pull from the bottle and went to sleep. He became a little more animated after we'd got west of the mountains and were travelling through wilder country. At one point we drove through a small watercourse, startling a flock of budgerigars, which flew off in a cloud of squeaks and bird shit. He asked me what they were and, when I told him, shook his head in disbelief. 'You get budgies in Harrod's pet department,' he said. 'Are we nearly there?'

We arrived in Lightning Ridge the following morning after a brief stop at the pub in Walgett, where the publican showed us his collection of rare clocks. Laurie was enchanted and wanted to stay, but I was going to get him to Lightning Ridge if it killed him. When we *did* get there he went straight to the Diggers Rest and, in spite of all my efforts, refused to leave and look at whatever else was on offer in the neighbourhood. I finally dragged him out of the bar at about 2 p.m. and headed south.

In the middle of nowhere he suddenly told me to turn off up a side track leading to infinity. He had seen a name on a letterbox at the corner of this by-road and told me that his brother Jack had told him to look in on whoever it was if we were passing. Whoever it was would be desolated if he didn't do as Jack had asked. Five miles up this track we arrived at quite an imposing homestead. We knocked on the door but there was no answer, so I turned to go. Not Laurie. He pushed the door open and went into the house. It was obvious that no one had been there for some time because there was a pile of unopened Christmas cards lying on the floor by the front door. Laurie was unstoppable and thirsty. Old whoever-it-was would want us to make ourselves at home, he said, pulling a couple of bottles of beer out from the fridge in the kitchen. His thirst somewhat slaked, he wrote a note of thanks, expressing his regret at his host's absence and passing on his and Jack's best wishes for the New Year. We then drove away, Laurie in a comfortable doze and me in a state of high nervousness about our breaking and entering. I dropped him off at Jack's place the following day and I heard later from Jack that we had gone to the wrong house.

Some time later I was interested to see on television that Laurie had been knocked unconscious by a flying beer can during the tea interval on the notorious 'Hill' at the Sydney Cricket Ground. Apparently he'd been given the 'kiss of life' by an attractive New Zealand nurse and the inference was that, had it not been for her, Laurie might very well have snuffed it. He chatted to the interviewer expressing his thanks to this lady, looking pained but noble with a large dressing on his forehead. I took him to the airport the next day and asked him how his head was. He grinned his sly grin and lifted the plaster holding the dressing to his brow. Not a mark on him. Dear old Laurie, 'By Appointment. Bullshitter to The Queen.'

My lucky streak continued and towards the end of the year I got a call from my agent in London. The BBC wanted me for a thirteen-part comedy sitcom called *Second Time Around*. I didn't need to be asked twice—it was nearly two years since I'd been in London and I looked forward to seeing friends and family again, especially as my trip would be paid for by the BBC. I'd kept in touch, of course, by letter and phone, and had been as generous as I could afford to be at birthdays and Christmas. But I knew it would be pretty traumatic when Babs and the boys and I finally met up again. Still, it had to be faced sooner or later, and at least I'd be back in London to do a reasonably well paid job, rather than as a failed runaway, looking for forgiveness. Also, I had Sue's love and support to give me strength. Sue decided to come too—it would be her first trip to Europe—and she and her mother joined me in London after I'd been there for a couple of weeks.

I don't think I was very good in the show. Perhaps I was trying too hard, but I found it difficult to perform enthusiastically in scenes with dragon-like mothers-in-law, fierce ex-wives and the full gamut of seaside postcard grotesques. I also found it extremely difficult to do the show in front of a studio audience. Not because of any kind of stage fright, but because of the timing compromises involved, and the general unpredictability of the audience. The actors had to keep to the timing of the camera script, already written in stone by the director/producer, and, if a laugh came at a non-scripted moment, you had to ignore it and press on to the next camera cue. When anything went wrong, which it inevitably did because of technical or acting booboos, we'd stop and do it again. Needless to say the invited audience grew more and more disenchanted at each repetition, and a line that might have generated a good laugh the first time it was heard would be greeted by a deathly hush at its third or fourth appearance. It didn't matter in the end as a laugh track was added in the editing process—even the feeblest quip could generate a belly laugh if the producer and editor felt like it.

It worked the other way around too. On one occasion an extra in a scene with me said 'Thank you', when I tipped him for carrying my suitcase. Before we started to record the show, the warm-up man introduced us all and explained a little about the show. He also alluded to the 'extras', who were under strict instructions not to speak. If they did, the BBC had to pay them a bigger fee, and with a coy smile he referred to the tightness of BBC budgets. Well, of course, when the extra thanked me, it got the biggest laugh of the evening and with a weary shrug we had to do it all again.

I went to Ormonde Gate quite often to see the boys and Babs, but it was always difficult. MJ hadn't forgiven me and Babs hadn't either. She still believed it was just another of my aberrations, like my stays in Chelsea Cloisters, and I'd soon come to my senses and return to the nest. It wasn't going to happen—I knew by now my commitment to Sue was rock solid and wasn't going to change. However, neither Babs nor I had plans to remarry so divorce wasn't a necessity and I was happy to leave things as they were.

The first seven episodes of *Second Time Around* were finally in the can and we went back to Australia for Christmas. I was due to return to London in January 1975 to do the last six, so I had no compunction about missing a few weeks of the English winter. When I did get back to London it was evident that *Second Time Around* wasn't going to be a success—it was clearly past its use-by date in style and content. Still, we were committed to doing the other six episodes, so we went through the motions as best we could.

While we were grinding out these last six, I got a call from BBC Radio. They asked me to present a series of programmes called *The Showmen*, dealing with some of the great theatrical impresarios of the previous hundred years. It was the first radio work I'd ever done and I found it pretty easy. All I had to do was read the stuff and, if I made a mistake, I read it again. It wasn't going out live so there was no pressure. I did twenty-six programmes in batches of three a day and took the money and ran.

My lucky streak continued in spades. While staying in London to do these recordings I got an offer to do a Walt Disney film in Australia. Originally titled *Ride a Wild Pony* (but I think it was also called *Born to Run*) it was about the love of a little girl for a Welsh pony. We shot all the family interiors and one or two establishing exteriors at Belltrees near Scone in the Hunter Valley. It is the historic home of the Whites, a traditional pastoral family whose most famous descendant was the novelist Patrick White. In one scene I was required to round up some cattle and separate certain beasts out of the herd—camp drafting it's called in Australia. I could ride okay but I'd never done anything like that, so I was naturally a little nervous that I'd stuff it up. Michael White, whose horse I was to ride, told me not to worry. 'Leave it to the horse,' he said. 'You'll be right.' So I just sat on this miracle animal, which twisted and turned and nudged and guided the animal of choice in the right directions with absolutely no prompting from me. Michael told me later that the horse had won many camp drafting competitions at rodeos and agricul-tural shows, and I could well believe it. My only problem had been to stay deep in the saddle as it spun and accelerated in different directions. I just about managed it and on screen it really looked as if I knew what I was doing.

We had an animal trainer from Hollywood to train the Welsh ponies to do what they were supposed to do and I found him fascinating, if a little difficult to understand. His name was Jim Breen and he was from Texas. Big in the beam and gut, about seven-foot tall, he had a drawl that made John Wayne sound like Noël Coward. He'd worked on dozens of movies, including Hitchcock's *The Birds*, 'Which was a real doozey, Michael'. He told me that one of the hardest animals to train for the movies was a horse. A horse's natural instinct, when faced with the unknown, is to run like hell, and there is nothing more unknown to a horse than a movie set. The easiest animal to train, according to Jim, was a pig—easier than a dog and more intelligent than most people. The only drawback with pigs was the speed of their growth. They had to be constantly replaced and retrained as the weeks went by and they grew out of their roles. Cats were the hardest to train because cats only do what *they* want to do, and when they *want* to do it, if at all.

We had several different ponies, all identical, because, according to Jim, you could teach a pony only a limited number of tricks. So we had the 'riding' pony, the 'kicking and bucking' pony, the pony which could open the latch on the gates, the pony which would lie down and the pony which drove the car (well, not quite). Jim trained them with a mixture of food (apples and carrots) and force (a cracking whip, which never touched them), and dried peas shot from a catapult to give them their cues.

John Meillon was in the film and its director, Don Chaffey, took a great shine to him. They became good mates, except for one afternoon when John had been in the pub too long at lunchtime. He had great difficulty speaking his lines as he walked down the street, which had been dressed with a flock of sheep. I saw the shot in the rushes and begged them to keep it in—it was the only funny scene in the whole epic as John ricocheted from sheep to sheep, trying to retain his dignity and his feet, not to mention his bowler hat, which kept falling off his head. Alas, they decided to re-shoot the scene and Meillon was on everyone's bad boy list for a couple of days. He wasn't on the outer for long because he did another Disney film with Don a few months later and also got Don very interested in making a feature film of *The Fourth Wish*.

As soon as shooting wrapped on the pony film we went back to Sydney. Sue had to rehearse as she had the title role in the musical *Gypsy*, and she was bloody marvellous in it too. I did a seven-part television series called *Company Men* for the ABC, and then an episode of *Rush*, which was a sort of Australian Western set in the Gold Rush days. I played a French con-man who gets into trouble in the goldfields and did nothing very memorable except for fighting a duel with sabres against the leading hero, played by John Waters, another ex-pat Brit. All should have gone well, I suppose—we were well rehearsed—but neither of us could see clearly without our glasses. Of course glasses were not worn on the goldfields in 1880, or whenever it was. We hacked away at each other, avoiding death or mutilation by millimetres, and in the end it didn't look too bad.

This episode was directed by a man called Rob Stuart, nick-named Rocket Rob for his speed of shooting. I worked with him again three or four years later in *The Timeless Land* and he was even speedier then with his 'Action!' and 'Cut!' He hated rehearsing anything except the camera moves, and subscribed to the Basil Dearden School of Direction—leave the actors to act and the director to shoot the pictures. If the two activities coincided here and there, so much the better; if they didn't, Rocket Rob would sort it out in the cutting room.

Sue had a big success with *Gypsy* when it opened in Melbourne. Then the show moved to Adelaide for three weeks before it came to Sydney. This was a lucky break for me as I had to go to Adelaide to do some re-writes for the film version of *The Fourth Wish*. Don Chaffey, John Meillon and I had formed a company to produce the film but, because it was being funded by the South Australian Film Corporation (SAFC), we had to set the action in Adelaide instead of Sydney. I'd never been there so I needed to suss out the city before writing the scenes in their new locations.

Sue and I decided to drive from Sydney to Adelaide in a new Honda I had acquired. It was an easy drive of about 800 miles (1200 kilometres) through the backblocks of New South Wales on the Hay Road. We broke the journey in West Wyalong and stayed at the True Blue Motel, which was of such an awfulness that one could only laugh. The fibro cabins had all the wiring on the outside of the walls. Swags of electric flex festooned our room like cut-price Christmas decorations. The water seeping from the shower was a bright rusty red, and harder than the pipes through which it ran . . . or crawled. Still, it was only one night and we were tired.

Gypsy went well in Adelaide, and so did my writing. Well, I got it done and it was accepted by the SAFC, which was the object of the exercise. When Sue's short season finished, we drove back and *Gypsy* settled into its run at Her Majesty's Theatre in Sydney, where once again Sue enjoyed a big success. I filled in my time while waiting to be called to Adelaide to do my role in *The Fourth Wish* by writing some episodes of *The Sullivans*, which was in its heyday on television. It was a breeze of a job. The story-line was given to you, with who did what and to whom and when already plotted. All I had to do as the writer was join up the dots. I think it took me five days to do. The hard part was having to watch the show to identify the characters, one of whom was Lorraine Bayly as Grace Sullivan.

Lorraine had worked with me in *Suddenly at Home* and had also played my wife in *Ride a Wild Pony*. She belongs to the school of acting which seems to believe the audience should be shown how difficult it is, and she spares no effort in demonstrating the wheels going round. A very nice woman and extremely professional, but not my kind of actor. Years later, when I was working with her in an episode of *GP*, she made me laugh a lot by asking the director what face she should make when having to show some kind of emotion in a scene. I mean acting isn't— or shouldn't be—about making faces. Maybe she was joking. Still, on the other hand, perhaps it doesn't really matter if it's what the audience likes?

I got the call from the SAFC and flew to Adelaide to do my stint on *The Fourth Wish*. A couple of days on location, a couple of drinks with Meillon and Chaffey; pleasant enough but also an odd experience. Apart from John, it was a completely different cast from the television version and I missed the originals. I especially missed Noeline Brown, who had played the wife/mother originally and whose part was now being played by Robyn Nevin. Robyn is a superlative actor—she is now artistic director of the Sydney Theatre Company and, a couple of years after *The Fourth Wish*, played my wife in *The Irishman*—and I had nothing but admiration for her performances, but it just wasn't the same. I held my tongue, did my scenes, and flew back to Sydney for Christmas.

Acting jobs at the beginning of 1976 were in short supply, but once again my financial bacon was saved by some writing commissions. *The Outsiders*, which I'd co-written with Don Barkham two years earlier, was going into production with German finance and a German star. I forced myself back to the typewriter. Together Barkham and I churned out an opening episode called 'The Dropout'. I'm not sure now if they used the script but we were paid and both our names ended up on the credits. I also wrote an episode for some kind of cop show starring Paul Cronin. Then I was asked to go back to London to do another series of BBC radio programmes—*The Impresarios* this time instead of *The Showmen*, but pretty much more of the same. Fifty programmes at fifty quid a go, so it was worth making the effort and paying my way to England for a few weeks. When we got back to Sydney our acting slump continued.

Sue's success in *Gypsy* had proved a mixed blessing. Because she'd played a stripper (in the nicest possible way), the only jobs she was being offered were more of the same—a commercial for a paint stripper, plus a role as a stripper in an episode of a show called *Bluey*, and not much else. We were both getting a bit toey when lightning struck twice.

The ABC in cooperation with the BBC was about to do a four-part series called *The Emigrants*. This dealt with the fortunes and misfortunes of a British working-class family which emigrates to Australia. Two episodes were to be shot in England, the first and fourth, and the middle two in Australia. Eric Tayler was the director and he cast me to play the father of the family. The start date was July and I was thrilled to get another trip to England which someone else was paying for.

Then the second lucky bolt came down. For some unaccountable reason I was asked to play an Italian concert pianist called Alberto Reggiani in an Italian spaghetti romance called *Per Amore*. There were locations in Rome, Parma, Milan, Venice, Paris and New York. Sue and I looked at each other—it was too good to be true. I had a lot more courage then and the fact that I couldn't play the piano, hadn't read the script apart from an outline, and didn't know any of the people involved didn't bother me. I remembered David Niven's advice about how to ensure you got paid for films shots on the Continent, brushed up my kitchen Italian and flew off to Rome. Sue was to join me a couple of weeks later, after I'd sorted things out and settled in.

I realised I was in for a bumpy ride as soon as I arrived at Rome airport. There was no one to meet me or to tell me where to go. I took a taxi to the production office, whose address was luckily on my letter of contract, and hoped for the best. It was not to be. The director was a man called Mino Giarda and his wife was the costume designer. He seemed more concerned with pleasing her than shooting the picture, but as long as he didn't give me a hard time I wasn't too bothered. The producers were two brothers called Maietto. I'm not sure what their track record was but they were a tough pair of buggers and not people one would either trust too much or want to upset. The leading actress, the object of my *amore* in the film, was a beautiful

Scandinavian blonde, and I discovered she was also the girlfriend of one of the Maietto brothers. Oh well.

The other main character, my wife, from whom I ran away for love of the Maietto girlfriend was the lovely Capucine, a French actress who had worked in Hollywood and had been unfairly labelled a transsexual. She became a great friend of Sue's and mine, and we kept in touch for some time after *Per Amore* was no more than a grotesque memory. She made what became a horrendous shoot almost enjoyable, and both Sue and I were terribly sad to hear some years later that she'd jumped from her apartment in Switzerland and killed herself.

I was fitted for a tailcoat, given a cassette of Chopin etudes played by Maurizio Pollini—the music I would be 'playing' in the various venues of my tour as Alberto—and filming began. It went well enough, apart from a love scene I had with the Scandinavian blonde. It was quite a steamy scene for those days—both of us seemingly naked in bed etc., etc. It shouldn't have been a problem, but it was made a great deal more difficult by Signor Maietto's presence on the set, glowering at me every time I came up for air. Not a relaxing or romantic atmosphere in which to perform.

There was a small hiccup in the filming at Milan. I did my concert okay—close-ups of my concentrated brow and someone else's nimble fingers on the keyboard. I'd learned the music fairly well and knew enough not to be leaning over the treble keys when the bass chords were rippling forth. However, the day before we were to leave for Venice, I had to do a scene in a car with my blonde lady. There was only room in the car for the two of us in the front and the cameraman and a grip in the back. So the director gave us our orders, rehearsed the dialogue and sent us on our way.

Unfortunately the way he sent us on was the autostrada from Milan to Turin. We bowled along with the traffic, did the scene, did it again and couldn't stop. There was no exit road from the autostrada for the best part of fifty miles, so we had to keep on going. We got back to the others two hours later to find them in a state of panic and Signor Maietto looking at me with blood in his eye. Not my fault, of course, but try telling that to a Maietto.

As we were about to leave Rome for filming in Paris and then in New York, I learned from my agent that I hadn't been paid for several weeks and that I was owed about US$12 000. I knew very well that, if I finished the film, I could kiss that money goodbye. I told the production office that I wasn't prepared to leave Rome or carry on working until I was paid in full. Some hysterical conversation ensued—veiled threats, urgent pleadings, fervent promises. I was adamant: no pay, no play. The next day Sue and I packed our bags and prepared to check out of the hotel. The Paris flight was due to leave at 3 p.m. and by noon nothing had happened except for a visit from Maietto, who told us he'd be back with the money.

He left it until the last minute. At about 1.30, as we sat on the balcony of our room having a farewell drink to Rome, a minion arrived with a bag full of a mixture of currency. There were US dollars, some sterling and a large number of hundred thousand lira notes. I was now in a real bind. It was illegal to take that amount of cash out of Italy without a permit, and especially illegal to take notes of more than ten thousand lira. There was also a grey area about the legality of taking large amounts of currency into and then out of France, into and then out of the USA and finally into the UK, where hopefully I could pay it into my bank account. However there was nothing I could do other than take a chance and hope for the best. I changed most of the hundred thousand lira notes into lesser denominations at the reception desk, paid my bill, stuffed the large parcel of dough into my flight bag and headed for Fiumicino with Sue. Because she wasn't going on to New York, but was flying back to London from Paris, she suggested that I put the money in her suitcase. That way I wouldn't have to keep carrying it through customs and immigration. I saw the wisdom of that but, after all the trouble I'd had getting it, I decided I'd rather keep it with me and take the risk. A wise decision as it turned out since Sue's baggage went missing between Rome and Paris and we didn't see it again for a couple of months.

I've no idea what *Per Amore* was like—I've never seen it and, for all I know, nobody else has either. Still, it was an interesting experience. Sue had a great time in Italy and, thanks to Uncle Niven's advice, I got paid. After that we shot episode one of *The Emigrants* in England and then returned to Australia to film episodes two and three. I wasn't in episode four so that was that. The only other job I had for the rest of that year was playing Lord Kitchener in a sort of drama-documentary called *Gallipoli*. Not the movie starring Mel Gibson, which came later, but a cut-price production for the ABC. I also had a writing project which greatly interested me.

On one of my many visits to Wentworth Falls to visit Sue's parents, I met the English ex-pat writer Kit Denton, who lived there, near the golf course. His son, Andrew, was still at school at the time and grew up to be one of the best and most talented radio and television performers in Australia. Kit quite liked what he'd seen of my stuff on television and asked my advice about a script he'd written. It was based on his best-selling book, *The Breaker*, which had been published a few years earlier. His script had had no takers but the story of Harry Morant, the eponymous 'Breaker', was a marvellous one and Kit gave me permission to have a go at writing my own version of the script. He gave me all the archival material he had and I spent the end of 1976 and the beginning of 1977 researching and writing.

I sent my first draft to Matt Carroll at the SAFC and he encouraged me to do a second draft. I really enjoyed the job, even though I wasn't getting paid, and turned out what I thought was a really good final script. My own personal assessment was borne out by a number of letters from Matt, which I kept out of interest. He wrote how pleased they were with the work, and in one of them he said that Bruce Beresford, who was coming on board as the director, loved my script.

I was very excited, but then it all went pear-shaped. The Melbourne Theatre Company did a stage play called *Breaker*

Morant based on the court-martial records. It was semi-documentary and of necessity was confined to the courtroom. However, it was a big success and suddenly my script was junked and the SAFC went with the theatrical version written by a chap called Kenneth G Ross. I don't know if Kit Denton ever got a credit, but I certainly didn't. Too bad. There was nothing I could do—the archival and court records were in the public domain and anyone was entitled to write a play or film using them as source material. The fact that the film used many scenes which approximated ones that I had written was irrelevant. The laws of copyright didn't apply and I was screwed. I don't think that anyone deliberately set out to cut me out—I'm sure they didn't—but I *was* somewhat miffed to receive a letter from the SAFC telling me that in the end my script had been judged inferior so they were going with the other. It was especially galling as it was actually Sue who suggested Edward Woodward for Morant—partly because he was a fine and at the time quite 'hot' actor, but mainly because he looked uncannily like Morant.

The film was a big hit and did a lot for the careers of all those associated with it. By coincidence, ten or twelve years later my friend Evan Jones was discussing a possible film subject with Bruce Beresford, who by then had made a Hollywood reputation and was looking for a new project. This new story was based on the wreck of the *Batavia* off the west coast of Australia in the seventeenth century. I had suggested to Evan that he pitch the story to Beresford because at one time in the seventies I had done the voice-over commentary on a documentary which Beresford had made about the wreck. So I knew it would be something he was interested in.

Not surprisingly, Beresford asked Evan how he knew about the story—after all Evan was a Jamaican living in London; not the likeliest person to know or care about that sort of arcane moment in Australian history. Evan mentioned my name and Beresford remembered that I had written the original script of *The Breaker*. With no prompting from Evan, he remarked in passing that it was by far the best script he'd read, and it was a pity it hadn't been the one that was made. Ah well, as Ned Kelly remarked as they slipped the noose round his neck, 'Such is life'. But I'm glad I've kept the letters.

That disappointment was to come some time in the future, and for the moment I had a really enjoyable film to do. I got the lead in *The Irishman*, which was to be made by Tony Buckley and Don Crombie, who had had a great success with *Caddie* a year or two earlier. They were, and still are, first-rate, dedicated film-makers and it was a pleasure to work for them. It was a smashing part—Paddy Doolan was a boozy, loving Irish team-ster who couldn't or wouldn't adapt to the new ways of the twenties, when transport was changing from horse- or bullock-drawn wagons to the new-fangled motor car. I grew the necessary walrus moustache, bought a new pipe, brushed up my Irish accent and in mid-May 1977 drove up to Charters Towers, where we were to make the bulk of the film.

I went up a week or so before shooting was due to start so I could learn something about the harnessing and driving of a team of twenty horses. The team and wagon combined were about as long as a cricket pitch, so you had to be aware of, and under-stand, the logistics of turning or parking. In fact it wasn't as difficult as I feared. The horses belonged to and had been trained by a Queensland farmer called Don. He could make them do anything and, whenever possible, he did the difficult bits of driving from just out of camera shot. However there were times when it had to be me and me alone. The opening shots of the team crossing the river was a case in point. I wasn't too confident, but in the end Don took them across a couple of times in rehearsal and, when the cameras were rolling, I did what he'd done and went along for the ride.

Harnessing the horses on film was a different problem. Most of the horses were eighteen hands, or just a bit less. A long way up to sling the collars and harness, especially when you had to do it twenty times. The harness was quite heavy, with chains and things, and by the time we had the team hitched to the wagon and ready to roll, I was ready for a tea break. I discovered the teamster didn't ride on the wagon but walked alongside it cracking his whip, shouting words of command and encouragement. The hardest bit was getting them to start with the loaded wagon. If they all went forward and hit their straps at the same time, it was fine; sometimes, however, some of them would hang back and then the others would get the hump and stop pulling. Sort of, 'If you think I'm going to do all the work you can bloody well think again'.

I loved it. The art department had transformed the main street of Charters Towers and some of the buildings into 1920s décor, and dressed them with period signs and vehicles. I was told that, after we finished shooting there, the local council left it like that as a tourist attraction. It's probably apocryphal, but an American couple later visited the town and were heard to say, 'We knew Queensland was a bit behind the times, but this is something else'. My son was played by a sixteen-year-old Simon Burke, my wife by Robyn Nevin, and my main rival for the haulage business by Bryan Brown. Other mates came and went as the script dictated and a good time was had by all. Perhaps I should qualify that because we suffered a minor but traumatic tragedy on almost the last day's shooting.

When we finished the shoot in Charters Towers, we moved down to the coast at Cardwell for the last two weeks to shoot in the rainforest and in the backblocks. The scene was Paddy Doolan's death, when his wagon, now reduced to a team of only two horses, runs away and Paddy is thrown to his death over a bridge. We achieved this without too much trouble. The horses crossed the bridge all day without a murmur. 'Okay, Wrap!' We unhitched the horses from the wagon and led them harnessed together back over the bridge for the last time to take them back to base. At that moment they spooked—one of them slipped and its hind legs were over the edge of the bridge. The weight was pulling its team-mate over with him. Farmer Don had to cut it loose and the poor bloody thing fell forty feet into the rocky creek bed, landing on its rump with a noise like a car crash. It scrambled to its feet and struggled down the creek and then collapsed.

Its back was broken and poor Don had to go down and shoot it. I don't know how it could have got to its feet with a broken spine after the initial fall, but it did. We had to leave the body there—it was too big to move—and it was a sad and silent dinner that night.

While I was on location doing *The Irishman* Donald Crombie gave me a script titled *The Battle of Broken Hill*, which had been written by a Turkish lady called Ayten Kulululu. It was dreadful, but the story was an exciting piece of Australian history—about two Turks, living in Broken Hill in 1916, who had declared war on Australia when the town turned on them after the Gallipoli landings. It dealt with racism and prejudice and mob violence, and with how ordinary people can do extraordinary things, both good and bad. I re-wrote the script and for a while it looked like it might get off the ground. Anthony Quinn had shown an interest in playing one of the Turks and several funding bodies had shown interest too. It never happened and the script still sits in my files, one of the best-kept secrets of the Australian film industry. It did keep me busy for a few weeks and I think I got paid some kind of fee.

It was while I was writing this that Sue became pregnant, and suddenly we had to reappraise our lives. I'd been asked to play Prospero in *The Tempest* at the Sydney Opera House for the company that was to become the Sydney Theatre Company, and had committed to doing so—we opened on New Year's Eve 1977 and ran for a couple of months into 1978. We couldn't stay in the Cremorne flat with a new baby and Sue obviously wouldn't be able to work for some time after it was born. So for some reason we decided to go to England for the birth. I think we felt that it might be an advantage to the baby to be born in England— dual nationality and all that—especially as Sue and I weren't married and I therefore had no legal standing as a parent. I contacted my English agent and my brother about the prospects of work back in England, and once again I was very lucky.

Richard had written a television series called *The Foundation*, which had been in production at ATV studios for some time. He contrived to write a character for me to play in eleven episodes if I could be in England in May. Armed with the certainty of at least five months' work and income, we didn't hesitate. We booked our flights, just under the wire in Sue's case as the baby was due in June, and prepared to move back to London.

I enjoyed doing *The Tempest*—it's one of the shortest of Shakespeare's plays—and, even though Prospero is on stage for most of the time, it isn't too tough a part. I always love working at the Sydney Opera House—the Drama Theatre is not what it might be but the ambience almost makes up for it—as it's a special pleasure to rock up to Bennelong Point and admire the view, if nothing else.

I finished the season in late March 1978, and a few days later Sue and I and our embryonic daughter were on our way to England. I'd been in Australia a little over five years and in that time I had done thirty-one television plays. I had also done six movies, two plays, directed another one, and written ten television shows and two movies. I'd been back and forth between Europe and Australia half a dozen times and recorded seventy-six radio productions for the BBC. A remarkable run of employment in this uncertain profession and probably the last time it would ever happen for anyone like me. I was kept very busy for the next ten years in England and Australia, but those five years from February 1973 to April 1978 were truly my glory days.

FOURTEEN

Slow time

We flew to London on April Fool's Day, 1978, and I must confess I did wonder if I was being foolish. I was forty-nine, expecting my third child with a woman to whom I wasn't married, and leaving the relative security of being a biggish fish in a small pond for the uncertainties of being a smallish fish in a big pond. I had the security of part-owning a flat in Sydney and a wonderful relationship with Sue, but I was still legally married to Babs and had ongoing financial commitments to her. I also had the security of a job for five months thanks to Richard, and a place to live in the short term, also thanks to him. We moved into his large and beautiful flat in Green Street, a very grand address in Mayfair, registered Sue with the National Health Service and found her a doctor. We caught up with old friends and Sue finally relaxed a little and waited for parturition.

I re-established relations with Babs and Stephen and MJ at Ormonde Gate, not easy as one of the things I had to do was to start divorce proceedings. It obviously wasn't possible for me to stay married to Babs when I was living with Sue and our child in the same city. Babs was not impressed but there was nothing for her to do other than finally accept that I had left home for good. Stephen was twenty-three by now, and he was showing great promise and talent as an artist. He and I didn't have a problem. As I said, he was nearly eighteen when I'd gone back to Australia to be with Sue in 1973, and understood that these things happened, even in one's own family. We picked up where we'd left off, went to football matches on Saturday afternoons (dedicated Fulham supporters), went to the pub and enjoyed each other's company.

It was a bit trickier with MJ. We'd achieved some sort of rapprochement the previous year when he'd come to Australia for a few weeks' holiday. He'd met Sue and spent some time with me on location in Queensland when I was filming *The Irishman*. He'd learned to drink Bundaberg Rum, and enjoyed himself. But it had been a little touchy sometimes; I'd established a really good relationship with Simon Burke as my fictional son, and suddenly my real son turned up to engage my attentions. They were both the same age, seventeen, and eyed each other with guarded antipathy, or so it seemed to me.

Still, the visit had broken the ice with MJ and he finally seemed to come to terms with my defection when he came to see us in our crappy little flat in Chiswick, which compared pretty unfavourably with the house in Chelsea where he was still living with his mum. He was also in a much happier state of mind generally. He'd finished his schooling at Stowe, which he'd hated, and was launched on a career in journalism. He'd got a place at the London College of Printing, where he did a year's course in journalism. They must have taught him very well because he has never been out of work in twenty-five years and is still hard at it.

I also had to pick up the pieces with my mother and Roland. For some strange reason—mainly pique I'd suggest—they had given Gubbions Hall to the Abbeyfield Trust, which provided accommodation (at a price) to the elderly. The pique had been engendered by both Richard's and my polite and grateful, but categorical, refusal to take over the Hall, which was becoming too big a burden for Ma and Roland to cope with. To my siblings' and my baffled annoyance a very valuable piece of real estate was donated to a commercial enterprise without any consideration for the family. Well, one shouldn't complain, I suppose—it was theirs to do with what they wished—but disin-heritance is never pleasant.

Ma had never really approved of, or liked, Babs, but had main-tained a relationship with her for the sake of the boys and, to be fair, out of a degree of loyalty to me. She was now appalled at my 'irresponsibility' in having another child and refused to allow Sue to visit. So I had to tell her that, if Sue and the baby weren't welcome, then neither was I. She accepted defeat on this matter and she and Sue enjoyed (if that's the word) a superfi-cially cordial relationship until Ma died a few months after her hundredth birthday.

While we were establishing some kind of new life in London and Sue was in the last stages of pregnancy, I was working more or less full-time at ATV Studios in Elstree on Richard's series, *The Foundation*. I played a sort of wizard accountant with an international reputation and an off-beat private life. Tony Buckley and Donald Crombie turned up in London and we spent some time together working on one of the drafts of what became a film called *The Killing of Angel Street*, but which then had the working title of *The Juanita Factor*. Because of the lack of interest in *The Battle of Broken Hill*, we were all looking for something else to do and were interested in this story, which was based on the mysterious disappearance of Juanita Nielsen at Sydney's Kings Cross.

By chance my sister Hilary arrived from New Zealand to touch base with the family. My sister Betty arrived from Canada for the same reason and on 24 June 1978 Jessica Clare arrived from her mother's womb. I was at the birth, somewhat reluctantly I must confess, standing by Sue's head with a cooling sponge, safely removed from the other end where the action was. Mother and baby emerged from the hospital a few days later and that was the end of sleep for the next six months. The combination of a click hip, which necessitated a sort of plaster of Paris nappy to hold her hip joints in place, and a disagreement with mother's milk made Jessica a very fractious child. Once she was weaned and the cast came off, she was angelic; but those first six months were grisly.

The Foundation finished in September and I spent most of October fixing up the new flat we had bought in Chiswick. We had to move as Richard was about to return from America and needed his flat back, but also it was time to really commit to a life in England and have a home of our own.

I was next cast as Bruno Pontecorvo in a drama documentary play called *The Atom Spies*, based on the defection of Burgess and McLean. I have no idea why I was cast as Pontecorvo—I didn't look much like him and I wasn't Italian—but I was in no position to knock back any work, so I was glad to do the deal with Anglia Television and submit to its makeup department. My hair, which was then greying nicely, was dyed an impenetrable black and I think they did something to my nose. The shoot wasn't very memorable until it was over. The makeup department tried to un-dye my hair and it turned pink. My hair that is, not the makeup department, although there were a lot of red faces in the production office. Never mind, they said, we can fix it and they tried again. Sure enough, they got rid of the pink, only to replace it with a coppery green. In the end, after various consultations with chemists and trichologists, it was decided to shampoo me with methylated spirits. This did remove the colour from my hair but it also removed the surface of my scalp, which only recovered after several weeks of real pain.

•

On 12 January 1979 Sue and I got married at Brentford Registry Office. My divorce from Babs had been made final and I managed to persuade Sue that it would be a good thing for us to wed. Both my accountant and solicitor had advised me that marriage was a good idea. Not on any moral grounds—bastardry was nothing to them—but because of tax advantages for me, and immigration and medical benefits for Sue. They weren't very romantic reasons but Sue knew there were plenty of those as well, and finally agreed. On a grey and freezing morning we went through the dreary civil ritual in a dreary Council Office with four friendly witnesses, including Richard. We then went out to lunch in Fulham and back to our Chiswick flat, where we chipped the ice off the inside of the windows for the second time that day and got stuck into the champagne. It was a funny sort of day, but a happy one, and twenty-six years later I haven't regretted it for a second.

Later in January I got the lead in a six-part television series for Granada called *The Danedyke Mystery*, adapted from a book by my old friend Willis Hall. I played a vicar with a Great Dane dog as a surrogate family and I sorted out whatever the mystery was as a part-time detective. It was good fun, even though there was a lot of exterior shooting in woods at night and on a canal barge through one of the coldest winters I can remember.

In March Sue went back to Australia with Jess for some well deserved R and R with her parents in the Blue Mountains. I soldiered on in Manchester as the detective vicar until we finished in early May. I was also working at this time on another draft of *The Juanita Factor*, which I took with me when I joined Sue and Jess in Australia. I caught up with Tony Buckley and Don Crombie again. We had a few meetings and I finished the draft to everyone's muted satisfaction. It was now over to the money boys for further funding and eventual production, or time to forget it and think of something else.

Australia once again proved to be the Lucky Country for me. I was offered a leading part in an eight-part television adaptation of Eleanor Dark's *The Timeless Land* trilogy. Peter Yeldham, a good friend and sometime golfing partner/opponent, had written the scripts. My role was the plum one of Stephen Mannion, the autocratic and ruthless free settler with a beautiful wife, played by Nicola Pagett, and a beautiful convict girl mistress played by Angela Punch McGregor.

Nicola was very hot at the time—she had played the gorgeously up-market Elizabeth Bellamy in the hit English television series *Upstairs and Downstairs*. She followed that up by playing Anna Karenina. Angela Punch (as she was known until she insisted on adding her husband's name to hers, causing some problems with the credits etc.) had made several movies, including one with Michael Caine, and had come to prominence in Phil Noyce's *Newsfront* and Fred Schepisi's *The Chant of Jimmie Blacksmith*. I was only in the first six of the eight episodes as I received my just desserts at the end of the sixth, when I was shot to death by my bastard son, played by Chris Haywood.

Bennelong was played by Charles Yunupingu from Arnhem Land, and he had a wonderful, if dangerous, sense of humour. In one scene he was immersed in a barrel of water while being washed under the eagle eyes of Governor Phillip, aka my old friend Peter Collingwood. Charles submitted to this scrubbing and was supposed to duck his head under the water to rinse off the soap and then emerge from his bath in all his pristine gleaming beauty. He duly ducked his head and disappeared while the cameras rolled and the other actors waited for his reappearance. Nothing happened. The director looked at his continuity person, who checked her watch. The cast and crew shuffled uneasily and at very, very long last—well over two minutes later—Charles bobbed up roaring with laughter as if nothing had happened.

It got hotter and hotter as we worked on into December in a north-facing paddock a few miles from Kellyville, in the outer western suburbs of Sydney. I was costumed in leather breeches and knee boots, a linen shirt, a stock, waistcoat and Harris tweed jacket. The crew sweated and panted in shorts and hats while I dissolved in my finery. In one of the scenes I had a team of eight convicts pulling a plough as my character tried to turn wilderness into arable farmland. According to the script, horses were too valuable to risk pulling a plough so manpower was the alternative. My 'convicts' were tough, healthy, well-fed stunt men but after half a dozen takes they were knackered, even though they were only going through the motions. I couldn't help wondering how the sickly, town-bred pickpockets and pimps who had made up the labour force in 1800 had managed to do it. I suppose the lash was a good incentive but, even so, they must have been a different breed.

We had a two- or three-week break over Christmas and I got a job doing six commercials for the Bank of New Zealand. Apparently *The Foundation* had been a big hit there and my character (the brilliant accountant type) was what they wanted to flog their product. The only problem was that I'd had a moustache in *The Foundation,* so I had to have a matching one made and stuck to my upper lip for the commercials. The money for these six ads was more than I got for the six months on *Timeless Land* so it was worth the discomfort—even the one shot in Singapore when the glue dissolved every five minutes in the humidity, causing a hideous rash to develop on my upper lip.

I shot two of the commercials in Sydney and then went to Auckland to shoot a third. While there I did another New Zealand ad on the side, for insulating material. It was sheer agony as the script ended with the memorable spiel: 'Think thick pink fibreglass batts. That's right, thick pink fibreglass batts.' Peter Piper, eat your heart out!

We carried on with *The Timeless Land* after the Christmas break and on my days off I struggled on with the *The Juanita Factor* filmscript as the money men still couldn't, or wouldn't decide on its viability. Evan Jones turned up on another writing assignment and Buckley and Crombie got him interested in my script, which was in the process of being re-titled *And Not in the Public Interest*. In mid-March I finished my part *The Timeless Land*, and had post-synched what had to be post-synched. On the 26th Sue and Jess and I flew back to London by way of Singapore, where I did the last of the New Zealand Bank commercials. Donald Crombie arrived in the UK soon after us and we spent a lot of time together trying to whip our script into shape. Donald had contacted Julie Christie, and she'd shown an interest in playing the lead, but only if Evan rewrote the script. She'd seen something of his and liked it very much, so why not? In a copy I still have of *And Not in the Public Interest* it is credited as follows: 'Screenplay by Michael Craig & Evan Jones, Additional Material by Cecil Holmes, based on an Original Story by Michael Craig. Copyright July 1980, and owned by Forest Home Films Pty., 141 Penshurst Street, Willoughby, Sydney 2068.'

It was no skin off my nose, and I was anyhow getting more and more disenchanted with the whole project. The more people who became involved, the more it seemed to me that we had to compromise, to satisfy each new point of view. The script seemed to be getting further and further away from what I'd originally written (not necessarily a bad thing) and I was becoming less and less able to add anything much to the project. It was eventually made, *not* with Julie Christie, and was released in 1981 under the title *The Killing of Angel Street*. I saw it in Sydney when I was there doing *Turkey Shoot* and it was okay, but I'm afraid that many of those compromises were only too evident. It wasn't bad, but it could have been better. Still, what writer *didn't* say that about their work?

In June I got a break from writing as I was asked to do an episode in a series called *Shoestring*, a sort of private eye show in which I think I played a baddie. A few days on location in Bristol, a few days in the studio and a few quid into the bank account. My luck had to run out sooner or later and it did—I had no more work for the next two months. But then in late August I had a meeting with some 'suits' at the BBC and was offered a leading role in a new series . . . well, serial, . . . well, sort of soap, really . . . called *Triangle*.

I was to play the Captain of a North Sea ferry plying between Felixstowe, Gothenburg and Antwerp—three legs, hence the triangle. We would shoot everything in situ on the ship or in whichever port we were in. There would be no studio work and we would live and work on the ship while we were filming for ten days at a time. We would start in September and the contract would be for thirteen weeks, in which time we would make twenty-six half-hour episodes. I would be paid £600 an episode. Well that was £15 600 for three months' work, enough to pay for a very merry Christmas, and an offer I couldn't refuse. I'd always loved being at sea and, even though the story-lines were a bit naff, it surely couldn't be that bad, could it? I was wrong; it was.

We were given our scripts for the first four episodes, had wardrobe fittings and were briefly lectured on how we should approach the task of shooting an hour of television drama a week on the *Dana Anglia* without disrupting the normal routine of the ship. As captain, I was in an enviable position—most of my scenes on board would be shot on the bridge or in the captain's quarters, areas which weren't accessible to the travelling public and therefore reasonably protected. Most of the other regular characters were cabin staff, the purser and assistant purser, stewards and stewardesses, cooks and barmen. I felt for them because they would have to play their scenes in the bars and restaurants and public entertainment areas. As anyone who has travelled on an overnight ferry will know, these would be occupied by the seasick and comatose, or the drunken and belligerent, sometimes by both at once. It was not easy for my fellow cast members to play a tender love scene, or even a scene about whose turn it was to do the washing up, while a mob of drunken Scottish football supporters on their way back from Sweden, where their team had been thrashed 3 to 0, offered advice to the lovers and suggestions about where to put the dirty crockery.

We then rehearsed for three days in a rehearsal room, before travelling by bus early one morning to Felixstowe to embark on the *Dana Anglia*. The majority of the cast and the technicians had never been on a ship before, and this was a big ocean-going ferry. The cabins which had been allocated to us weren't too bad, and to the uninitiated it looked like we were onto a pretty good thing. No battling the traffic to get to work—just roll out of bed and saunter down to the makeup cabin half an hour before your call. A cup of coffee and a croissant while you check your lines for the scenes you have to do, and then another leisurely saunter to the set. What no one had mentioned was that September through to December was the time of the equinoctial gales, and the North Sea became a particularly turbulent stretch of water.

On our first night the ship sailed at 6 p.m., stuffed with passengers and motor vehicles. Our lot ate, drank and made assignations as we glided down the estuary and out into a relatively calm North Sea. At about 2 a.m. the wind started to blow and, by the time we were called to work, we were heading into a Force 6 nor'-easter. My call was for 8 a.m., to do some scenes on the bridge, but when I turned up for makeup and wardrobe at 7.30, only one pale-green makeup lady was at work. There was no sign of my fellow actors. Up on the bridge I did my Captain bits while the cameramen and sparks and actors, and even the director, disappeared at odd intervals to get rid of the previous evening's indulgences. Sick bags were being handed out with Quells as we rolled and pitched through the heavy chop on our bumpy way to Sweden. It wasn't a good start, but most of our mob learned a valuable lesson—a night on the booze before leaving port would have its inevitable consequence. What goes down comes up, especially in any sort of conditions above Force 3 on the Beaufort Scale.

Another lesson quickly learned was that it was virtually impossible to shoot any scenes on deck while at sea. The engine noise, plus the wind rush and the crashing of the waves (we'd be travelling at thirty miles per hour—just a bit under fifty kilometres per hour), drowned out any kind of dialogue beyond shouted orders. So, in spite of the scripts being set at sea, we ended up shooting nothing but interiors, which we could have done on a sound stage at White City. To add to the idiocy of it all, the cameras were mounted on stabilising gimbals so there was no sense of the ship's movement apart from the occasional shot of a cast member leaning at an odd angle as he or she struggled to keep their balance while the ship rolled ten or twenty degrees from port to starboard and back again. There was nothing to do but soldier on as best we could for three long months.

Apart from *Triangle* going to air and being roundly panned by everyone, 1981 didn't start off too badly. For once I could only agree with the critics. It was soap of a very low quality, not helped by its vaguely nautical ambience. It was the same clichéd story-lines of love and despair and failure and success and life and death, which have been the staple diet of drama since Euripides. In our case it would probably have been better in Greek. It was actually so awful it became a sort of cult classic of crap television. I don't think it helped what was laughingly known as my career, but I was locked into another series if the BBC decided to carry on. Unhappily they did for another two years. Still, as I've said before, 'think of the money and the pain goes'.

Undeterred by my Old Man of the Sea performance in *Triangle,* Anglia Television gave me a job in their *Tales of the Unexpected* series. I spent the rest of January filming something called *Hijack* for them. Then in February, I started a four-month tour of Noël Coward's *The Marquise*. God knows why anyone wanted to do it—it isn't one of The Master's best. He wrote it in 1926 and, as far as I know, it hasn't been done since. It's a sort of romantic pastiche of derring-do and high comedy set in the eighteenth century, with an on-stage duel scene. It was the first time I'd done a long tour and, apart from having to be away from home, I rather enjoyed it. We opened in Richmond in west London and then played everywhere, from Brighton in the south to Blackpool in the north. Lincoln, however, posed special challenges. The town boasts a beautiful but small theatre with a tiny stage. The ladies in their vast dresses with panniers and trains had to enter and exit sideways and stand very still once on stage to avoid knocking the furniture and their fellow actors into the front row. My duel had to be greatly curtailed in Lincoln—it ended up as a sort of arm wrestle. But, apart from that, the tour was good fun.

In June we flew to Sydney to do a film called *Turkey Shoot,* aka *Escape 2000.* This was a total nightmare from start to finish. The initial premise had seemed mildly interesting—a futuristic society in which criminals were imprisoned in camps where they could be hunted like animals for the enjoyment of the rich and decadent. Most of these prisoners were political revolutionaries challenging the totalitarian government, so they were the goodies and, of course, triumphed in the end. I was cast as the Camp Commandant, a cruel swine, but irresistible to me partly because of the free trip back to Australia, partly because of the money which was moderate, but mainly because the character's name was 'Thatcher'. Every time I administered a particularly cruel piece of punishment, I thought of the then Prime Minister of my fatherland, Attila the Hen, and laid on even harder.

I was told on arrival at the production office in Sydney that the schedule had been cut from eight weeks to five, for financial reasons, and that I should get to Cairns as soon as possible. Cairns was where the camp had been built and was where most of the filming would take place. The co-producer of this epic was David Hemmings, the English actor who had made a name for himself in the 1966 Antonioni film, *Blow Up*. He had also enjoyed a reasonable career for some years afterwards.

The leading lady was an English actress called Olivia Hussey, who had played Juliet in the Zeffirelli film of *Romeo and Juliet* in 1968 and then, as far as I knew, disappeared. She wasn't happy doing *Turkey Shoot*, not so much because of the awfulness of the production, which would have been understandable, but because she had an unreasonable terror of the Australian flora and fauna. Now Cairns isn't exactly Manhattan or Paris, but neither is it a village in the wilds of New Guinea. You are unlikely to be savaged by a feral pig, cassowary, tiger snake or estuarine crocodile at the Northern Heritage Hotel, Trinity Beach, but Olivia wouldn't be reassured. In one scene in the film she had to flee across a small stream, six feet wide and perhaps two feet deep, but refused to do so for fear of lurking crocodiles or sharks. She was finally persuaded after half the crew had splashed about in the water, spoiling the pristine look of the location but proving that there were no man-eaters lying in wait.

One of the other actresses in the film had recently become a vegan and, when required by the script to be seen gutting fish, had to be supplied with synthetic fish made by the prop men, on the grounds that it was against her principles to even *touch* a once-living creature. Yawn, yawn.

The leading man was an American actor called Steve Railsback. He'd had some recent success in an American television adaptation of *From Here to Eternity*, in which he had played the part immortalised by Montgomery Clift. He was very much a Method actor and took himself terribly seriously. In one scene I was extorting information from him by having him confined in a wire mesh cage, barely big enough to contain him. Heavier and heavier weights were being placed on the roof of the cage each time he refused to answer a question. The torture was to hold up all this weight with his arms to avoid being squashed and/or extruded through the wire mesh like hamburger through the mincer. It was a very hot day but Steve was determined to do the right thing, no faking it for him. He insisted on having real weights placed on the roof with the result that all his energy and brainpower were concentrated on avoiding being pulped. Fair enough, but unfortunately it rendered him incapable of remembering his lines, or speaking them even if he had. In the end we had to compromise—the weights were reduced, Steve answered the questions and we moved on to the next set up. Bloody Method!

In the film I finally got my comeuppance by being cut in half by the blade of a bulldozer driven by a maddened prisoner. All the bad guys finished up dead while the good guys triumphed. What a surprise! When *Turkey Shoot* finally hit the cinemas it was ritually slaughtered by the critics and sold off to the video makers, where for over two decades I think it has languished, unwatched and unlamented. Weirdly though, it has recently had some kind of renaissance because Quentin Tarantino said it was one of his favourite films. I've also done an interview to be incorporated into its re-mastered DVD version.

At the end of 1981 I did more episodes for the dreaded *Triangle*. I was getting anxious when I finally got a job in April 1982, after a very slow start to that year. I did a two-handed play called *Duet for One* for a month in Bromley. Not a very enjoyable job as the lady playing the disabled violinist was very tricky. She accused me of constantly up-staging her, which would have been a neat trick to achieve as I was more or less permanently seated at my desk, while she whizzed around the set in her wheelchair. Then I agreed to take over the lead in a play called *Deathtrap*, which was to go on tour after it closed in London. As during the previous year, between September and December we continued making more and more episodes of the seemingly eternal *Triangle*. Towards the end of this purgatory, an old friend from my Rank days, George Baker, joined the cast and helped cheer things up; but we all knew we were flogging the proverbial. *Triangle* was going down with all hands when this third lot of shows finally finished.

In the October Sue was offered a job in Sydney—the first offer she'd had since getting pregnant—and she was very keen to do it. It was a revue called *Four Lady Bowlers in a Golden Holden*, written by John McKellar and to be directed by Richard Wherrett. The Company included many old friends with whom she'd worked before, among them Maggie Dence, Bob Hornery, John Derum and Tony Taylor. It was too good an opportunity to miss so she and Jess flew south while we sailed on and on and on . . .

I flew out to join Sue and Jess in Sydney after Christmas. George Baker turned up—two of his daughters lived in Sydney— and we all went to see Sue do her stuff in *Lady Bowlers*. It was the first time she'd worked in over five years, but the hand hadn't lost its cunning. It was a great evening. By some odd chance she and I were then both cast in a film called *Stanley*, about an eccentric young man (the eponymous Stanley) who rebelled against his even more eccentric millionaire father. That was me. I didn't have a lot to do but it filled in a few weeks in February and March and paid for our trip to Oz and back. I've never seen the film and it doesn't appear in any of my movie and video guides, nor on any website, so perhaps it was a figment of my fevered imagination. Judging by the smell of prohibited substances emanating from the sets while we were filming, it could well have been a pipe dream. Sue does have a photograph of herself in character as Graham Kennedy's wife, Doris Norris, mother of Morris Norris in the film, so I can only conclude it really did happen.

FIFTEEN

About time

We returned to London on 1 April 1983—by coincidence, five years to the day from when we'd come back the first time, in 1978. I started rehearsals for *84 Charing Cross Road* almost immediately. Miriam Karlin was cast as Helen Hanff and me as Frank Dole. It was one of the most enjoyable jobs I ever had, and one of the few in which I take real pride. We were directed by James Roose Evans, the adapter of the book and the play's original director, so we couldn't have been in better hands. We kicked off in Richmond once again, and from the first performance I knew we were a hit. Miriam couldn't have been better cast and, under Jimmy's guidance, I felt secure and comfortable as Frank.

In October I was asked to do Shaw's *Candida* at Guildford with, of all people, Petula Clark as Candida. I don't know why she wanted to do the play or indeed *any* play—she had done a few films as a young woman, nothing very memorable, but I don't think she'd ever appeared on stage in a straight play. She had achieved great success and wealth as a singer and lived in France with a French husband, who was also very well off. She was, I suppose, in her late forties and had absolutely no need to subject herself to the uncertainties and pressures of rehearsals, opening nights and performance. I assume that the Guildford production

was a kind of tryout and, if it and she had gone well, we'd probably have transferred to the West End. But it wasn't to be. As
the parson's wife, Pet was efficient, hard-working, word-perfect
and totally unmemorable. I probably wasn't much better.
However, the customers did come and we did our month or so
to respectable business.

It was a bit of an anti-climax with which to finish the year.
I did a few voice-over jobs but, apart from them, it was a cold
and work-free December and January. I have to say that in those
days, a voice-over job could be immensely lucrative. I didn't get
very many but I remember one for a cat food product called
Catomeat which earned me over £16 000. It took half an hour
of my time in a little studio in Soho and I was paid £200 for
saying, 'Catomeat . . . to show that you really care'. That was
it. Luckily for me, that line was dubbed onto a dozen different
variations on a theme of cat feeding and, under the then existing
contracts, you were paid your recording fee again—that is,
£200—for every six or eight showings of the commercial. Well,
these little thirty-second epics of cat love kept going out on the
telly for nearly a year and the cheques kept coming through
the letterbox.

I was asked to do a production of Shaw's *The Doctor's
Dilemma* at Bromley and Guildford prior to a West End season.
This time I really thought we'd have a good chance of a transfer.
The cast included Emlyn Williams—in his first play for several
years after his huge success with his one-man Dickens shows all
over the world—plus Patrick Cargill, who was a big name on
television, a beautiful American actress called Gayle Hunnicutt,
who'd made a couple of films with some success, and a very young
Colin Firth (now everybody's favourite Mr Darcy, among other
roles). We had good rehearsal time, beautiful sets and costumes
and all should have been well. Unhappily, Emlyn, who was a
friend of many years standing, was unable to learn the part. He
was in his seventies and had lost the knack of working with other
actors. It was clear, as opening night approached, that we were
in big trouble.

My first scene was with him and in it I had to explain my new theory of treatment, involving something called phagocytes. I also had to introduce the play's theme—a doctor's agonising choice between saving an amoral but hugely talented artist, or a worthy but ordinary person (Shaw at his most didactic, but quite a good premise nonetheless). On our opening night at Bromley the audience was full of London managers and agents and celebrities and we were all understandably nervous. But I could see that Emlyn wasn't just nervous—he was out of it.

He made his first entrance, sat down and looked at me with a puzzled smile on his face while I waited for him to speak. When he didn't open his mouth, I had no option but to flounder on, speaking his lines as well as mine. He occasionally roused himself sufficiently to give me a totally inappropriate cue, all of which I had to ignore. Finally, after my eight-minute solo exposition on phagocytes and God knows what else, when I was sitting there shaken, sweating but quietly triumphant at having got through somehow, he asked me the question which he was supposed to have asked me at the top of the scene. The one which provoked the explanation which I'd just painstakingly delivered.

I couldn't believe it. Hadn't he been listening? Did he expect me to go through it all again? I muttered something about having pretty well covered all that, I thought, and to my immense relief Patrick Cargill entered and I was saved for the moment. We limped on without too many other problems as the other actors covered up for Emlyn, but the damage had been done. The audience was even more nervous than we were and couldn't wait to escape. We were dead—no offers from managements, no calls from agents—even the local Bromley paper gave us a bad review. We closed there after our three-week season, then endured another three weeks at Guildford, and that was that.

I used to pick Emlyn up from his flat in Chelsea on my way to Bromley and take him home after the show. Never once did he refer to the hideousness of that opening night, nor in any way seem to take any responsibility for the production's failure. He'd sit in the car on his way home, wittily and maliciously commenting on the various performances of his fellow actors, but never a word about himself. I liked and admired him very much for a great deal of his past work as an actor and writer, but then I was sorely tempted to shove him out of the car and under a passing bus.

In September I went to York to do Sheridan's *The Rivals*. It was the theatre's two hundredth anniversary and they decided to celebrate with a gala production of something from the period of the theatre's foundation. To make the event more memorable they tried to get actors who had worked there in the past. So I was cast as Sir Anthony Absolute and I returned to tread the boards of the old Theatre Royal, thirty-two years after my first engagement there. It was strange being back after all that time. The theatre had been modernised to some extent; the dressing rooms had been greatly improved, but everything else seemed much the same. The Minster still dominated the town, the walls still stood in their Roman solidity and the digs into which I booked myself weren't very different to the ones I'd inhabited when I was twenty-three.

I ran into an elderly man who had worked in the railway yards and moonlighted as call-boy (this was before the days of tannoys in the dressing rooms) and general backstage factotum during my time with the rep. His name was Jimmy and we used to drink together in the pub after the show. Every year he saved up to travel by coach to Wembley and back to York to see the FA Cup Final. Every year he would get so pissed on the coach on his way south that he'd spend his time at Wembley sleeping it off in the coach in the car park while his mates watched Arsenal beat Liverpool or whatever. Every year he'd miss the match and drown his sorrows by getting pissed in the coach on the way back to York. I asked him why he did it and he looked at me as if I was an idiot. 'I'm a fan, Michael. I'm a fooking football fan.' We had a pint for old times' sake and I wondered if he'd ever actually seen a ball kicked in anger in all those years.

The play went well and I enjoyed the challenge of learning and performing the complexities of Restoration Comedy. Sue and Jess came to stay for a few days and, as well as the season at the Theatre Royal, we did four performances in the little town of Richmond, where there was an original eighteenth century theatre. It was tiny and cramped, with the auditorium boxes so close to the stage that you could shake hands with their occupants, but the atmosphere was extraordinary. I thought of Garrick and Peg Woffington, who had played there possibly in one of Sheridan's plays, and for once I was almost seduced by the so-called Romance of the Theatre. The dressing rooms were underneath the stage, and illicitly carved into the beams and banisters were the names of actors who had played there over the preceding centuries. I looked for David Garrick's name but I guess he wasn't into graffitti because it wasn't there.

While still in York doing *The Rivals* I was asked to play Lord Loam in JM Barrie's play, *The Admirable Crichton*, at the Royal Exchange Theatre in Manchester. I was nervous at the prospect—I'd always been wary of playing at the Royal Exchange as it was theatre in the round. I was used to having a proscenium arch between them and us. I wasn't too sure how I'd cope with performing in an arena with the audience surrounding me on all sides. Then I thought, 'That's stupid. Besides it's coming up to Christmas and you need a job.'

I had to learn to play a tune on a concertina and sing a song to my own wheezing accompaniment. It was good fun and, far from finding it intimidating, I enjoyed learning the technique of delivering dialogue in a way that didn't continually present my back to half the audience. I learned to turn this way and that in what I hoped was a realistic way, motivated by the logic of the drama, so I gave everyone a reasonable share of my face. The season was very successful and we played for six weeks until the middle of January 1985.

I got an offer to do an episode in an English television series called *Robin of Sherwood*. This was yet another take on the Robin Hood myth and starred Jason Connery (Sean Connery and Diane Cilento's son) as Robin. George Baker had a sustaining part in it as Maid Marian's father and he suggested me for Robin's dad, the Earl of Huntingdon. It was supposed to be a one-off appearance and should have been a breeze. I didn't have a lot to do except look stern and noble on occasion, and ponce about in doublet and tights while laying down the law to the peasants. Unhappily for me, the director and designer thought it would give the character more class and authority if, while doing all this poncing about, I carried a falcon on my wrist. I should have known better, but I agreed to this act of lunacy and wore the bloody bird like a large ostentatious feathered wristwatch throughout my few days of filming. It was about the size of a small chicken, with beak and talons of lethal quality. It was hooded, of course, and I wore an immense padded gauntlet; but, even so, it was a real problem. Every time I moved, it flapped its wings and uttered muffled shrieks of rage. It was a pain in the arse to me and everyone else. George got a laugh out of it, of course, but falcons have been added to the long list of animals with whom I do not wish to work.

I was asked to do a pre-London tour (ho, ho!) of a play called *Nightcap*. It was a thriller by the same man who had written *Suddenly at Home*. Well, that hadn't been one of my finest moments in the theatre, but *Nightcap* was a good deal worse. Still, I thought, unlike Australian audiences, the British like a good thriller (they even like a bad thriller, as evinced by all those successful Agatha Christie adaptations). The out-of-work actor does a lot of rationalising and I rationalised myself into saying yes. It was a long engagement—five months at least, all over the country—but, unless a miracle occurred and we *did* actually get a London run, I'd be finished by Christmas. Sue was going to Sydney in November to play Amy in Richard Wherrett's production of Stephen Sondheim's *Company*, so I'd be able to join her and Jess for the New Year.

When I did finally extricate myself from *Nightcrap*, as it became known, I found myself in late December scrunched up in my cramped Qantas seat, fighting off boredom and thrombosis as I flew halfway round the world, wondering what the hell I was doing. I was nearing fifty-seven; I'd been back in England for nearly eight years—give or take the time spent in

Australia—and, although I'd done a lot of work and earned a reasonable living, I really couldn't see myself travelling the length and breadth of the British Isles acting in potboilers for the rest of my working life. For one thing, touring was becoming less and less profitable for the theatre managements and, for another, any sort of drawing power that I might still have would soon disappear unless I experienced some kind of successful television or film reincarnation. That didn't seem to be likely, so the future didn't look too promising. I decided to put it all on hold and enjoy myself in Sydney while I could. As it happened, that wasn't difficult—the production of *Company* was a ripper, and Sue was the best thing in it. I was so thrilled and proud of her that I could have watched the show every night I was there.

I went back to London the day after my 58th birthday to start rehearsals for a play called *Mary Mary*, which featured the bankable and popular star Wendy Craig as the Mary of the title; Sue had some weeks of her contract still to run, so I had to leave her and Jess behind. It was a phenomenal success in Guildford but, alas, nowhere else and we closed 'out of town' as they say. The disappointment of the failure was softened by Sue and Jess's return and the prospect of my next job. I was asked to do a couple of episodes of *Doctor Who*. Only four weeks work, at the BBC's lowest rate of pay, but *Doctor Who* had achieved almost mythic status all over the world in its more than twenty years' existence. I was flattered to be asked. A bit like being asked to do *Jackanory* all those years before, it was a 'credit' no English actor should be without. I'd heard the stories, of course—the cheapness of the production, the tackiness of the sets and costumes, the banality of the scripts, and the pathetic special effects in what was rapidly becoming the world of computers and cyberspace. All absolutely true, but so what when set against the glories of the Tardis and the Daleks and the succession of eccentric and extraordinary 'Doctahs'.

My particular Doctor was Colin Baker and I was the commander of a galactic liner, transporting passengers and some naughty vegetable villains called Vervoids from Urk to Blinge, or something like that. I wore the traditional up-market boiler-suit with stripes and padded shoulders and carried a ray gun, which I think had been rescued from a breakfast cereal packet. It was made of pink plastic and it was almost impossible to resist saying 'Pzzzing!' or 'Cheeung!' as I pointed it at the revolting Vervoids and zapped them where they stood. A sort of laser beam was added in post-production, but it was disconcerting to point the bloody gun and wait for the Vervoid to drop without anything happening at the time.

The galactic tornado or meteor storm which my ship had to weather was something else again. Up on the bridge, I and my valiant crew fought heroically to keep the ship on course as it bucked and twisted through this cosmic hell. Actually the ship didn't move at all but we, the crew, had to lurch and stumble and fall as we simulated imminent destruction—always with the proviso that we didn't lurch or stumble or fall into the walls, which were made of cardboard and flimsy to a degree. I suppose there is a weird kind of atavistic charm in such a cheese-paring representation of high-tech engineering. Certainly *Doctor Who* has its dedicated fans, who seem to like it, but to me it was just the jolly old Beeb being its usual miserly self. In all my time in the business I've found it axiomatic that the more successful a television show becomes, the less money the producers want to spend on it. The theory seems to be that the poor bloody public will accept almost anything as long as the show retains its original spirit and ethos. Crap, in my view—but what do I know?

After a wonderful trip to Kenya with Richard and a not-so-wonderful stint in the world premiere of *Barnaby and the Old Boys* at the Clwyd Festival in North Wales (it was an interesting play, dealing with family feuds and sibling rivalries and homosexuality and racial prejudice and anything else you might care to name) I was cast as Lauren Bacall's husband, Lord Peel, in the Agatha Christie thriller *Appointment with Death*. Peter Ustinov played Hercule Poirot, naturally, and, besides him and Ms Bacall, there was a distinguished and expensive cast, including John Gielgud, Piper Laurie, Hayley Mills, Carrie

Fisher, Jenny Seagrove, one or two others and last, and certainly least, there was me.

The director, God help us all, was Michael Winner. What can one write about Mr Winner that hasn't already been written in vitriol and blood? I first met him in the fifties when I was under contract to Rank. He was a very young director then, working on an adjoining sound stage at Pinewood. He had made something of a name and some money with a film called *Around the World with Nothing On*, a documentary nudie, and was now spreading his wings with a film about the pop scene starring Billy Fury and some other currently hot performers. I had been invited onto the set by a friend and in amazement watched Winner speaking to his cast through a loud hailer and looking at them through a viewfinder, as he directed them from a distance of three feet. He was unremittingly rude and deservedly unsuccessful until he teamed up with the actor Charles Bronson in America. Together they made three films called *Death Wish 1*, *2*, and *3*.

Lord Peel was a nothing part. In fact, when I turned up in Jerusalem on the first day, Ms Bacall very grandly asked me why I had been flown out from London to play the role. Surely anyone could have done it—no need to bring an extra all that way. I was floundering as I tried to think of some kind of elegant response; I wanted to tell her where to go when John Gielgud came in and welcomed me warmly. 'Lovely to see you old chap . . . have you got *9 Across*?' he asked, waving a copy of the *Times* at me. He was followed by Peter Ustinov, who was also most affable, and Ms Bacall was forced to look at me in a different light. She was extremely 'old Hollywood', forever talking about 'Bogey' and the Good Old Days and generally being a pain in the arse.

After surviving a night shoot with Winner at his ghastliest, I shook the dust of the Holy Land off my feet and returned to England, home and beauty. As it turned out, beauty, in the shape of Sue and Jess, weren't to be there much longer. Sue had to fly out to Australia to do a play called *Caravan* and I stayed behind for another play called *Sweet William*, about which the less said the better. Nyree Dawn Porter was the leading lady (she'd been extremely popular after the first BBC production of *The Forsyte Saga*) but even her presence in the cast couldn't put the bums on the seats.

These separations are an inevitable part of the jobbing actor's life, particularly if both partners are in the business. I never minded too much, as long as they weren't very long, as it was so great when we all got together again. It was probably hardest on Jess, having to adjust and re-adjust to different schools for a few weeks or months. MJ had had to cope with it when he was small and had survived and thrived, and we were pretty certain Jess would do the same. It may not be an ideal way to conduct a marriage or raise a child, but there is something to say in favour of new experiences and travel broadening the mind—and in any case, the reality was that we had to work to pay the bills and do the jobs we were offered.

Then in January 1988 I got what turned out to be my last job in England—a new production of JB Priestley's *An Inspector Calls*. I started rehearsals in London before going to Northampton for a short season. We packed them in there for a month and then went on the road until the middle of May. Our worst venue was Bournemouth, where we spent the whole of April at the theatre on the end of the pier. Sue and Jess were back from Australia and came down to join me for the Easter holidays.

The weather was abysmal—it blew and rained and stormed the entire time we were there. The journey along the pier to the theatre, which would have been a gentle stroll on a balmy summer evening, became a running of the gauntlet of waves breaking over the boardwalk, with horizontally driven rain and spray. Not surprisingly, the Bournemouth public preferred to stay at home in the warmth and comfort of their living rooms, and there were very few visitors prepared to risk a soaking to watch us perform. Sue and Jess came to a matinee which was attended by thirty-three people sitting in two rows, surrounded by seven hundred and sixty-eight empty seats.

While fulfilling my depressing obligations, I began to have a very serious talk to myself and to Sue. I would be sixty on my next birthday and it seemed to me that I'd run out of luck in England. I couldn't face any more debacles like the one on the end of the pier in Bournemouth. If I stayed in England, it seemed that *that* was all I could look forward to . . . if I was lucky. The housing boom in London had turned our initial £18 000 outlay for the flat in Chiswick into a £140 000's worth of house in Acton, so luck had been with us there. I could sell up, cash in my old insurance annuities and move back to Australia while Jess was still at primary school and wouldn't be too damaged education-ally by such a move.

I didn't know what I'd do in Australia. I was too old to completely start again, but I thought I might be able to buy into a small business—a gas station or a grocery shop perhaps—with somewhere to live. And to work as an actor if and when required. I'd been back and based in England for just over ten years, made a bit of money, mainly out of the property market, but also out of some enjoyable jobs, and watched Jess be born and grow to a ten-year-old. I knew I was going to miss many friends and my family in England. But my two sons and their families were both reasonably well established and successful: Stephen with his painting and teaching, MJ with his journalism and, at thirty-three and twenty-eight respectively, they didn't need Dad to help look after their interests. I'd miss my brother and his family—but, if things went reasonably well for us, I knew that I'd be able to come back and see them from time to time, which is how it has turned out.

On the whole it has worked out pretty well, but there's always that faint feeling that perhaps we should be in England when we're in Australia, and should be in Australia when we're in England. A no win, but also a no lose, situation. Of course, Jess wasn't too thrilled—after all, she'd been born in England and didn't want to live anywhere else. For her Australia was good for holidays, but London was where her friends and heart were. And, although she loves Sydney and has many friends here too, she returned to England as soon as she left school and, after her graduation from Cambridge, has lived there ever since.

SIXTEEN

Operating time

Our return to Australia was a lot less traumatic than it might have been. We had a flat in Neutral Bay to live in, which we'd bought as an investment in 1976 for $27 000. Sue's flat in Cremorne was let and providing her with income, and we had her parents' house in Wentworth Falls to visit when we wanted to get out of the city. We also had the best agent in the world, Bill Shanahan, to look out for us. This he did with his usual mixture of charm and malice. He adored and admired Sue, but was a bit ambivalent about me I always thought. He was brutally frank at times but always honest and I, and all his other clients, were desolate when he died in 1992 at far too young an age.

I have had a number of agents throughout my time in the business, in England and in America, but, with the possible exception of my brother, there was never anyone to compare with Bill. He was irreplaceable and, since his death, the lot of the theatrical agent in Australia has taken several turns for the worse. Casting Consultants, as they call themselves, rule the roost these days and, in spite of what they say, they work for the managements, not for the actors. The inevitable result has been the gradual disempowerment of the agents, who in some cases have become little more than an answering service for their clients without the power to make suggestions or to negotiate. Bill would have fought, and did fight, that trend with all the weight of his experience and the strength of his client list. Perhaps he would have made a considerable difference had he'd survived.

In 1988 Bill was still at his best and told me that I could put my plans to become a shopkeeper or garage owner on hold for a few months if I wanted to. A producer called Jon Nichols planned to bring the English actor Paul Eddington to Australia to direct and star in his successful London productions of Terence Rattigan's double bill of *Harlequinade* and *The Browning Version*. Mr Nichols had offered me the parts of George Chudleigh (a mad old actor) in *Harlequinade*, and Dr Frobisher (a pompous schoolmaster) in *The Browning Version*. We were to rehearse in Melbourne, open at Her Majesty's Theatre in Sydney for four weeks, move to the Comedy Theatre in Melbourne for another four weeks and finish up at His Majesty's Theatre in Perth for a further and final three weeks. All up, it would be about four months' work and the money was okay, if that was of any importance. Bill gazed at me blandly while it took me all of five seconds to make up my mind and say yes.

I was a great admirer of Paul Eddington. I'd seen him in many productions in England and was, of course, a devotee of *The Good Life*, in which he'd first come to major prominence on television, and, subsequently, of the incomparable *Yes Minister* and *Yes, Prime Minister*. I hadn't seen him in the London production of the Rattigan double bill, but I knew both plays quite well. I'd been in a couple of rep productions of *The Browning Version* and had seen the film starring Michael Redgrave back in the fifties, so I had no worries about its quality as a sure-fire piece of drama. However, I was a little dubious about *Harlequinade*, a fairly flimsy farce dealing with the on- and off-stage carryings on of a theatrical couple a little past their use-by date. It depended on an audience's appreciation of the comic possibilities of old-fashioned Shakespearean productions and the megalomania of actor/managers in immediately postwar England. Perhaps not quite the fare for Australia in the late eighties, I suspected. However, I comforted myself with the thought that *The Dresser* had dealt with the same sort of material and, as both a play and a film, had done well enough.

Both Jon Nichols and Paul Eddington were confident and I wasn't really in any position to be choosy. A very good cast was assembled, including Julia Blake, Lewis Fiander, Glenda Linscott and the then doyenne of Australian theatre, Patricia Kennedy. I moved into a small serviced flat in Melbourne for rehearsals, leaving Sue and Jess in Sydney, temporarily in the flat at Neutral Bay while we were in the process of buying a new house at Newport.

Rehearsals in Melbourne went well enough. Paul was a good and amiable director, and the cast was eager and professional. Not all of them were in both plays so there was quite a lot of sitting around waiting for one's turn. Rehearsals were further enlivened by the epic name-dropping and one-upmanship indulged in by some of the cast. I have to admit I dropped the odd name myself (in self-defence, I hasten to add) and there was quite a lot of 'when I was working with Larry' and 'Dame Peggy said to me' and even 'so I told *Sir* Peter Hall to shove it'. All good fun and par for the course as actors do their best to disguise their insecurities in rehearsal and their terror of the approaching opening night. This came soon enough.

It was quite a glamorous occasion at Her Majesty's when the curtain rose on our first night. We'd done a couple of previews to friends and relations and the reaction had been favourable; but previews to friends and relations are notoriously unreliable. It was quite a different matter when it came to the real thing. Paul had a very high profile in Australia, thanks to his television perform-ances, and all the Sydney glitterati turned up to see him in the flesh. Unfortunately, the critics turned up too and either damned us with faint praise or, even worse, praised us with faint damns.

Paul's performance, and Julia's and Lewis's in *The Browning Version,* were widely admired, but *Harlequinade* was universally condemned as dated, self-indulgent and unfunny. Paul had devised a sort of country dance routine for our curtain calls. It was rather longer than it should have been and had to be scrapped after a couple of performances when we danced on and off to the sound of one hand clapping. Fortunately for me, my contributions were largely ignored, except by a few friends and Bill Shanahan, who remarked with his usual honesty that I had been well cast in two undemanding parts. Fair enough.

Business was only moderate and Paul and Jon Nichols started to look a little worried as it became obvious that we weren't reaching our get-out costs. I was a little worried too, but it wasn't my dough in the production and there was no way we wouldn't finish our seasons in Sydney and then Melbourne and Perth, so I just grinned and bore it. Once the hell of opening night was over, we bumbled along peacefully enough to sixty per cent business. I chiefly remember the Sydney season for the pleasure of seeing a large photograph of Sue in her *Gypsy* lack of costume (two ostrich feather fans strategically placed) prominently displayed in the foyer as part of its permanent décor. The original poster, life-size and in colour, was kept in pride of place in the technician's rest room. When the theatre was demolished a few years ago, only twenty-five years after it had been built, I tried to get hold of this poster but it had disappeared. I hope it went to a good home and is happy there.

We served out the rest of our time at Her Majesty's and moved to the Comedy Theatre in Melbourne, where we hoped for better things. They were in fact marginally better, but not sufficient enough to erase the worry lines from Jon's and Paul's faces. Despite Paul's worried look, he never behaved with less than perfect courtesy and gave it his best shot at every performance. What I didn't know was that he was already suffering from a cancer that would eventually kill him a few years later. He had to undergo some sort of radiation therapy every week and after these sessions would arrive at the theatre exhausted with a strange sort of reddish-brown shiny colour, like a recently cooked crayfish. He never mentioned this affliction and he and his wife, who was travelling with him, soldiered on with impeccable charm and good humour. The rest of the company behaved with that bleak acceptance of destiny typical of actors in a semi-flop, and rang their agents in the hope of finding alternative employment when the Perth engagement finished.

We bowed out of the Comedy to scant applause and headed west to His Majesty's in Perth, which had always seemed a slightly weird place to me. It seemed to be full of ex-pat Brits, many of them stuck in a time warp with the attitudes and prejudices of forty years earlier. They automatically assumed that I, as a fellow Brit, would share those prejudices. I had a hard time keeping my cool when some blimpish prat from Dorking, or wherever, would expatiate on the pleasure of being able to walk the streets of Perth without being surrounded by hordes of nig-nogs.

I did have the odd laugh in the West. I was having lunch at one of Perth's top hotels one day and decided on coq au vin. The waiter applauded my choice and asked if I'd like the chicken or the *lamb* coq au vin. I thought perhaps he was joking, but there was no twinkle in his eye and, sure enough, lamb coq au vin *was* featured on the menu. But I had better not go on about the place because that was sixteen years ago and, when I was there with the Bell Shakespeare Company three years ago, I had a terrific time and thoroughly enjoyed myself.

The curtain fell for the last time on the last performance and that was that. We hadn't had much success and poor Jon and Paul probably lost a lot of money but, as far as I was concerned, my life as a shopkeeper had been postponed and I'd made some good friends and some money. Paul made a graceful farewell speech, gave us all autographed copies of *Yes, Prime Minister, Volume II*, and disappeared out of my life. It was enjoyable working with him and I was very sorry to hear of his death a few years later. I have a feeling he was knighted before he died. Although I personally don't much like those sorts of awards, I guess he deserved it as much as anyone else.

A few days after I'd returned to Newport, where we were living by now on Sydney's northern beaches, I was up a ladder painting out the possum pee stains on the ceiling of the living room when the phone rang. Bill Shanahan was on the line asking if I could get my pommy arse up to Gore Hill and do an audition for a new ABC show about doctors.

'Like when?' I asked.

'Like now,' he said, 'if possible.' I groaned. It is over thirty kilometres from Newport to Gore Hill—a fact that was increasingly impressed on me over the next eight years—and I would have to clean the paint out of my hair first.

'It'll take me a couple of hours,' I said.

'Okay,' he said. 'I'll tell them. Ask for the *GP* production office.' He hung up and I retired to the bathroom and the shampoo.

I had actually heard about a show called *GP*, which was in the ABC pipeline, while I was in Perth. Lewis Fiander had been asked to do a screen test for one of the doctors but hadn't been interested. To be honest, I wasn't that interested either and a little miffed at being asked to audition. I had done so many shows for the ABC that I felt they should know what I did and, if they didn't like it, why bother to see me. If they *did* like what I did, why not offer me the part so I could say yes or no. How naive I was. The old order had changed with a vengeance. The good old slap-happy days of boozy lunches at the Seven Two Nine Club (often extended to include a couple of frames of snooker at the expense of rehearsal time) were long gone, and the drama department was a much leaner and meaner machine than in the seventies and early eighties.

Well, if the times had changed, I had to change too. So I put on my suit, collar and tie and, smelling faintly of turpentine, chugged up the Wakehurst Parkway in our old three hundred-dollar Holden Torana. I finally arrived at the ABC studios in Gore Hill, and the production office people were polite but brisk. We did the test scene, which wasn't too demanding. It hadn't taken me long to learn it—a bit of pomposity, a bit of mordant humour, a bit of irritability—and that was that. They thanked me and I set off back to Newport.

It took the best part of an hour from Gore Hill to Newport in the old Torana but, even so, I was surprised to have hardly walked through the front door and taken my tie off before the phone rang and it was Bill again.

'They want you to do it, Michael—a guarantee of thirty episodes, and an option to do another fifteen in the first year. Another option for a second year on the same conditions and so on into infinity.' There was a long pause while I considered. I was quite flattered that the decision had been made so quickly; I must have been pretty good, I thought, as usually these casting decisions drag on for days or weeks. I discovered later that someone had dropped out and I was pretty well last cab off the rank, but at the time I was chuffed.

'What do you think, Bill?'

'Well,' he said, 'they've offered two grand a week, but I can get it up to two five and it's a guarantee of thirty weeks even if you bomb.' I did some quick mental arithmetic—$75 000, less commission, less tax, and I'd be left with about half. But that was still okay—we'd be able to have another very jolly Christmas.

'When do we start?' I asked.

'They want to do some publicity stuff with all the main cast, wardrobe calls and all that crap in late December and shooting starts at the end of January.'

'Terrific!' I said. 'So that's me until the end of August, and maybe longer.'

'Right,' he said. 'And the good thing is, if it's a stinker, no one will see it because it's on the ABC.' For once in his distinguished career he couldn't have been more wrong.

In late December 1988 I presented myself at Gore Hill studios to do the publicity shots, talk about wardrobe, have a chat about the show and its aims and hopes, and meet the rest of the resident cast. We looked at each other with veiled suspicion and hope. I'd met John McTernan, who played my nephew and with whom I shared the house in our fictional practice, a couple of times previously. He'd worked with Sue in a play about Mo McCackie starring Garry McDonald, so we had a nodding acquaintance.

But I'd never met any of the others—Michael O'Neal and Sarah Chadwick as the two other doctors in the practice; Denise Roberts, the receptionist, and her twelve-year-old son played by a fifteen-year-old Brian Rooney who, with voice still unbroken, was performing four shows a week in *Les Miserables* as one of those cute kids on the poster.

Of those original six, Sarah was the first to leave—after a year and a bit, she wanted to try something else. John became one of my dearest friends and I found it hard to forgive him when he was the next to go, leaving after only three years. It was never the same for me after he left, but I did understand his situation— he lived in Melbourne with a wife and a teenaged daughter and, even though he loved *GP*, three years was all he could take of endless hours at Mascot and Tullamarine airports waiting for flights to take him home for a short weekend, and then back on Monday morning. Young Brian left when he could no longer play the cute and rebellious teenager, then Michael went after more than five years, by mutual consent I think. Finally Denise and I left after seven years—or 284 episodes. *GP* went on for another year after we left with new doctors, notably Steve Bisley as the head honcho, but I guess its use-by date had finally arrived. It finished in 1996 after eight years and about 330 programmes.

We started in late January 1989, a few days before my sixtieth birthday, and over the following years the show had its ups and downs. On the whole it was one of the most popular and highest rating programmes the ABC ever made. It has been repeated more than once, in the afternoons and in the wee small hours of the morning, and was sold to some foreign countries but not many. I believe the problem was that some of the story-lines were considered unacceptable for peak viewing times in less tolerant countries than Australia. I expect some of them were—we dealt with some fairly way-out subjects after we hit our straps and stopped doing Illness of the Week stories.

We did an episode about a married chap who developed a syphilitic chancre in his throat from having oral sex with random lovers. *That* got a few phone calls. We did episodes about AIDS

and homosexuality in both sexes; episodes about female circum-
cision, transsexualism, transvestism, the effects of thalidomide
(using a lady who had been affected in her mother's womb by
the drug and had no arms) and my own favourites—episodes
about medical jurisprudence and the wider aspects of medicine
in society. These explored the psychological, physiological and
other social and ethical ramifications of our increasingly self-
absorbed litigious community.

I once did an episode with a young actor called Jamie Croft.
He was about twelve at the time and an extremely nice kid. We
had to do a scene on location which involved Jamie getting some
kind of terrible news and my dealing with him and the situation. It was the first scene of the day, a cool morning in a
suburban street in North Sydney and everything was ready to
roll. Jamie and I knocked at the door of the suburban house,
the actress came out and gave him and me the news that Jamie's
mother had been killed in a car crash (or whatever it was).
Jamie then said his line and started to cry. It was magic, take
one ... a hole in one. I was talking to him later, while they moved
the cameras for the next set up, and I asked him how he achieved
what he'd just done. He looked at me as if I'd asked him how
he walked or talked and said, 'I just imagine I'm the person I'm
supposed to be and then do what I think he'd do.'

Out of the mouths of babes. Drama courses nowadays take
three years and have the equivalent status of a Bachelor of Arts;
absolute crap in my view. It hadn't taken Jamie three years of
expensive tuition to figure that out, but I suppose if all actors
were like him, there would be no jobs for teachers and no
funding for the schools.

For the first, and certainly the last, time in my life I became
that dreadful thing—a celebrity, a household name (well, at least
my alter ego, William Sharp, did). Even now, eight years after I
last pulled on my stethoscope, people in the street still look at
me, do a slight double-take, say 'Hello, Doctor!' and reminisce
about the good old days of *GP*. Such is the power of a successful
television series. I think that if, immediately after I left the show

in 1995, I'd opened 'The William Sharp Clinic' somewhere on the North Shore, staffed of course with real doctors, we could all have made a fortune because the punters would have queued up just to have me greet them in reception and then pass them on to someone who knew what they were doing.

Because of William Sharp and his persona, the inevitable unfairness of show business was demonstrated to me many times. 'Unto he that hath, shall it be given'—and never more so than in the acting game. For some reason a West Australian advertising company ran a survey to find out who the viewers considered the most trustworthy person on television. Well, guess who got the nod? Because of this, I got several lucrative advertising gigs—spieling for housing developments, roads and safety and other slightly up-market products—in Perth. I even got paid a lot of money simply to put my name to a product without having to learn a line of text or appear in front of a camera. Disgraceful really, but it doesn't last very long. Out of sight, out of mind, and there is nothing more passé than the ex-television celeb. Still you might as well make the most of it while it lasts and, as well as enjoying my brief spell of fame and high earning power, I made many good friends and learned a lot.

Like many people, I had always sort of taken doctors for granted. You went to one when you were ill. If he made you better he was a good guy; if he didn't he was a quack. I changed my mind during my spell as William Sharp. I now have the greatest admiration for all doctors and everyone connected with the healing of the sick. I picked up quite a lot of peripheral knowledge and even now am quicker than I should be to diagnose (sometimes correctly) the symptoms of friends and family. I also found out how incredibly tiring performing surgery can be. I did a number of 'operations' over the years, masked and gowned, rubber-booted and rubber-gloved, in which I cut and probed and sewed deep inside a blood-filled cavity provided by the props department, until finally my hands emerged triumphantly holding a lump of calf's liver, which was discreetly screened from the camera before being deposited in a kidney dish and hurried out of sight.

My mock operations would usually be scheduled to take perhaps an hour and a half—shots of me looking stern but relaxed, shots of the patient's comatose body, shots of the anaesthetist and his equipment, shots of scalpels, retractors, forceps and blood. At the end of all this I would be absolutely knackered. The physical strain of standing over the operating table—peering into a cavity, pretending to clamp this and suture that—was enormous. How real surgeons manage three or four operations in a day, some of them lasting up to five hours, is more than I can comprehend. No wonder my old friend Dick Opie was so fit and could hit a golf ball as hard and as well as he did. I learnt how to do simple sutures using an orange as the body part, but I was never much good at it. Our lovely medical adviser, Carol Long, who had been a nurse and knew everything about everything, would usually double my hands for me if the suturing needed to be seen on camera. Carol had fierce battles with some of the directors who tried to play fast and loose with medical reality. She usually won and still does over at Channel 9.

When we started the show we were still using the old-fashioned three-camera technique, cutting between cameras as the scenes played out. This necessitated a great deal of camera rehearsal and, of course, the use of three cameramen for three days. During the two days when we were actually recording, there was also a vision mixer, who sat in a large van switching between the cameras at the director's commands—hopefully getting it right and not including a camera being wheeled out of picture as it moved to its next position. It wasn't the most efficient use of manpower and resources so, after a couple of years, we changed over to the more film-like technique, using two cameras, shooting scene by scene. Rehearse–record it's called, and it dispensed with the need for camera rehearsal days. It also eliminated one cameraman and, of course, the vision mixer because the scenes were now edited electronically at the end of the shoot.

In the first years our week went like this. Saturday morning there would be a read-through of the script, attended by the main cast and guest actors, the writer and script editor, the director, the producer and sometimes by the head cameraman and DOP (director of photography, responsible for the lighting etc.) and maybe a sound technician. The cast would have had their copies of the script for a few days, together with the pink, blue, and buff pages (these were the script amendments, varying from a complete rewrite of a scene to a 'on page 29, sc.17. change *the* catheter, to *a* catheter' amendment. It was always interesting at these readings to note which of the cast had done their home-work and put in the amendments, and which of them hadn't. Usually they'd bluff their way through but occasionally there would be a self-inflicted shot in the foot. I remember a classic case when someone, who shall remain nameless, had clearly not inserted the amendments and hadn't even read the script. This person had the line 'There you are' to start a scene and in this particular context the line should have read 'There you *are*', denoting agreement or the resolution of a discussion. It came out as '*There* you are', denoting surprise at seeing someone. Some-thing like the old chestnut, 'What's that on the road, a head?'

After the read we would disperse to learn our lines or not, as the case might be. On Monday and Tuesday we shot all the location scenes. This was a trial for me as the house where I was supposed to live, and where the surgery was located, was in Peter-sham, an even worse and longer journey than to Gore Hill. It wasn't convenient for anyone really and had the further disad-vantage of being situated under the flight path. Shooting was regularly disrupted in the early morning as jumbo after jumbo jet roared in to land, or screamed skywards in take off.

On Wednesday we would rehearse all the interior scenes with the camera crew, who had been given detailed pages of instruc-tions about where they should be in each scene and which shot they would be asked to get. 'Int. Surgery. MCU [medium close-up] hypodermic syringe. Zoom back to include William pulling on rubber gloves.' Fair enough, but that particular shot might not be made until late on Friday afternoon and it was a bit unre-alistic to expect someone, who might have to remember dozens and dozens of shots and positions, to remember that particular one forty-eight hours later.

On Thursday and Friday we shot all the rest of the scenes, inevitably ending up with John McTernan and me being expected to make up the time we'd lost over the previous days by shooting all our domestic stuff—quarrelling, cooking, cleaning etc.—in the last half hour of the day. It became a bit of a joke, but Johnny and I actually came to quite like it and take pride in our ability to do it. We were supposed to finish at 6 p.m., but that didn't happen very often. Then there would be drinks in the produc-tion office for the cast and crew. The next day, Saturday, the process would begin again.

It was like being back in weekly rep, but better paid and you could go home at night. We also had a lot of fun. There was an on-going poker game in our green room, and all and any were welcome to join in. We didn't play for high stakes but I reck-oned to make my whisky and tobacco money each week out of the players who really believed that poker is a game of bluff. Forget it, sucker—*cards* win hands and money, not bluff.

We also had the good fortune of working with new people every week, and over the years I must have worked with at least two-thirds of the acting profession in New South Wales. Nearly all of them were hard-working, good company and, even more important, pleased to be doing a *GP* episode. It's sad to see how many of those bright, talented, ambitious young performers with whom I worked ten or twelve years ago have dropped out of the business, to be replaced by a new brigade of bright, talented, ambitious performers, most of whom will probably be dropping out in their turn over the next decade. 'Whatever happened to . . . ?' Name any name, and shake your head in dismay. 'Don't give up your day job', as the latest (Throsby) report into the arts was titled.

As well as working with a wide diversity of actors, we worked with many different directors and writers. Some of the best, and now most in-demand, directors cut their teeth and learnt their craft on *GP*. Most of them were easy to work with and as sympathetic to our problems as we were to theirs. One or two took themselves and the whole process rather too seriously and were a pain in the neck. One of these, who has since gone on to a high teaching position (those who can, do; those who can't etc., etc.) was particular painful. He could never keep to the schedule and we often went on and on until late into the evening. He was obsessed with the jargon—the dynamics of the scene, the journey, the arc and, worst of all, the bloody subtext.

I had to do a scene with Johnny Mac in which I was supposed to demonstrate and describe a laser machine, which for some reason my character had introduced into the surgery. The art department mocked up just such a machine—complete with dials and switches and lights and whistles—and installed it on the set. Johnny bet me a slab of beer that I wouldn't get through the scene in one take—it ran about four minutes and included a lot of technological chat about wavelengths and thermo-dynamics, and was indeed quite complicated. I took the bet, the cameras rolled and away I went. Word perfect, every line said, every switch switched at the right moment, every mark hit to a millimetre. I said the last line, nodded at Johnny and walked out the door.

Bingo! I'd got it in one and twenty-four cans of beer were mine for the weekend. I was congratulating myself when the floor manager told me the director wanted to do it again. I was shat-tered and asked him what was wrong with the take. He looked thoughtful and said he thought I'd missed some of the *subtext*. Johnny looked at me and rolled his eyes in sympathy. For crying out loud, there is no subtext in the description of a laser machine, or a vacuum cleaner or any other bloody machine. You either describe it correctly or you don't. No good—we had to do it again. John refused to collect on the bet, which was decent of him but only fair. I did the scene again exactly the same as the first take and the director nodded in a satisfied way and we moved on. I suppose, to be fair to him, he was nervous about having only one take of an important scene, but he could have said he'd like another one for safety rather than hitting me with the subtext rubbish.

Another of my unfavourite directors, who, oddly enough, is also now teaching poor unsuspecting students, was very into Stanislavsky and all things motivational. It was late on a Friday evening and I had the last scene to do at the end of a very long week. We rehearsed and were about to shoot when this chap, wearing his most serious face, asked me where I was coming from. My blood boiled and I heard myself say, 'I am coming from the fucking green room and, if you'll get out of the fucking way, we can shoot this mother and can all go fucking home.'

Generally, however, we all got on pretty well and tried to co-operate and help where we could. I remember doing one scene with Johnny in the kitchen, sitting at the table having a drink. For some reason the director wanted John to move from the table and take up a position near the door. It would make a better picture, he said. This chap is now a very important and successful director and producer for whom I still sometimes work so I will disguise his identity and call him 'Peter'. Johnny argued mildly that he had absolutely no reason to suddenly leave the table and stand by the door while he and I finished our conversation. Peter was insistent and Johnny winked at me and said okay, he'd think of something. We started the scene again and, at the appropriate moment, Johnny suddenly noticed an imaginary fly buzzing round the table and leapt to his feet to swat it. He moved across the set clapping his hands in an effort to catch this non-existent insect and finally caught and killed it on his marks in the doorway. It was brilliant—he'd solved the problem. Unfortunately we couldn't use the take as the camera and sound crews and I were pissing ourselves with laughter and the moment was lost.

So the first three years rolled by, almost effortlessly. The options were exercised each year, we got pay rises, and Bill Shanahan was forced to eat his words as the show became more and more successful and popular. Our ratings were excellent,

244 THE SMALLEST GIANT

Johnny won a Logie for best actor on television and we all went down to Melbourne at the ABC's expense and celebrated.

In the ten-week break we had each year between finishing at Christmas and starting again in early February, there was time for other things. One year I wrote a script for the show—one of three I ultimately wrote—and another year I played a bishop in the mini-series *Brides of Christ*. It wasn't a very big role, only a few scenes, but they were quite important. In one of them I had to deliver an alfresco sermon to a large crowd. We all assembled at a famous girls' school in Sydney's northern suburbs. It was a stinking hot day and my task was made more difficult because I also had to celebrate a mass that hadn't been written correctly in the script I'd been given. Our technical expert, a working priest, kept rewriting what I had to say and directing me through the complexities of the ritual—when to ring a small bell, when to genuflect and make the sign of the cross, when the censer should be swung and so on and so on. To make matters even worse, I was dressed in several layers of ceremonial copes and albs and stoles and knotted cords and God-knows-what-else under my cassock, which was the only part of my costume that was visible. I pointed this out to the wardrobe department but they insisted that I wear the lot—'It has to be authentic, Michael'—so I gritted my teeth, tinkled the bell, swung the censer and muttered away in Latin while the sweat puddled in my priestly brogues under the remorseless sun.

Back on *GP*, when Sarah Chadwick left halfway through the second year she was replaced by the lovely New Zealand actress, Judy Mackintosh. Judy stayed for a couple of years and then went back to New Zealand, where she married a doctor and raised a family. Sue did an episode, as the wife of a character played by Terry Donovan (Jason's father). I was given a Variety Club award and then, in 1990, I too won a Logie. But the Logie happened at a rather strange time in our lives. While Sue was away touring in *Noises Off* at Gosford, I suddenly got very sick. I woke up one night with my right knee swollen and throbbing, burning to the touch and very painful. I went in to work but could hardly hobble so I was sent off to hospital for an examination. The leg was CAT-scanned and diagnosed as being either acute osteomyelitis or cellulitis, and I was in trouble. I finished the day's work at the studio and then checked in to Royal North Shore Hospital, where I was very well known as we often used unoccupied wards for our locations. I was put on an antibiotic drip and there I stayed for five days while the world went on without me.

On the night of the awards a nurse came into my room to tell me that I had won the Silver Logie and was very sweetly excited for me. I'm afraid I didn't respond very well. I've never cared much for the idea of acting awards—it's all far too subjective and political—but, apart from that, all I could think of was the possibility of amputation, which the specialist had warned me was a distinct possibility if the antibiotics didn't work. Fortunately they did, and I still had a leg to stand on when I went back to work the following week. I never found out what caused the infection, but I blame it on the possums in our roof. I had cut my hand while putting up a wire screen to prevent them climbing in and out through the chimney, and I guess some kind of infection had spread from there into the soft tissue in my knee. All grist to the mill; we used the scenario for an episode a few months later.

That year was not a great one for me. Bill Shanahan had become very ill and died in the early autumn. I stayed with his agency for another five years, but it wasn't the same without him so finally I moved to another agent. Sue was away for a lot of the time, doing *Noises Off*, and I was at work more than I was at home. It was very hard on Jess and I think it was this, as much as anything else, which made her want to go to boarding school, which she did the following year. Then in December, in the last episode of the year, Robert Sharp—William Sharp's nephew and partner, my mate John McTernan—breathed his last. For me the best years were over. I still enjoyed doing the show, and in fact continued to do so for another four years, but a lot of the fun had gone.

New cast members joined us, in particular Tony Llewellyn-Jones as a psychiatrist married to Marilynne Paspaley, who had replaced Judy Mackintosh as the resident lady doctor in the practice. Casting Marilynne was a little bizarre. We had tested several actresses—all good and all extremely good-looking; nothing wrong with any of them—and then Marilynne came along: of a certain age, striking but not beautiful and with a great voice. I tested with her and gave her my vote, for what it was worth. She got the job and as far as I was concerned, that was that.

We were all a little surprised when she first turned up for work—driving an expensive car, stylishly dressed and wearing the most beautiful pearls (discreetly, I hasten to add)—and finally the penny dropped. This unknown actress, who was now a member of the *GP* regulars, was a Paspaley of Paspaley Pearls, one of the wealthiest families in Australia. Why she wanted to take on the long hours and hard work of a television series for not a great deal of money is hard to figure, but she did, and never gave it less than a hundred per cent. She had quite a tough row to hoe as the scripts provided her with three teenage children, one of whom had Down's syndrome. The old showbiz adage of never working with children or animals is true up to a point, but Marilynne never complained. She was unfailingly professional and friendly, did her three years and returned to the very different world and life of the Paspaley empire.

During the breaks I wrote another couple of scripts and did the odd commercial job, but on the work front things were becoming a little less agreeable. In the usual way of television production, the more successful *GP* became—and at one time we were out-rating the commercial shows in our time slot, something unheard of at the ABC—the less money they wanted to spend. It was the old BBC *Doctor Who* syndrome all over again. Actors who had appeared in early episodes would now be asked to work for a lower fee. Some did but many wouldn't, which reduced the pool of talent we could call on. Working hours would be extended without permission or overtime if they could get away with it, and the permitted time between finishing work and starting again would be more honoured in the breach than the observance. I personally wouldn't accept a call that breached the agreement—it had taken years of union negotiations to achieve the award and I was damned if I was going to let them unilaterally throw it away—but some of the others weren't as rigid as me. It was especially hard on the women, who had earlier calls for makeup and hairdressing, to resist the production office's blandishments, and of course even harder for guest performers, who didn't want to make waves.

There were good times too, of course. Good scripts, good parties, good friends. On 26 October 1993 I was doing a scene in the studio near knocking-off time and I wasn't too thrilled to be asked to do it again. It had been the usual long hard day—I was tired and, as far as I was concerned, there was nothing wrong with what we'd just done. However there might have been a technical glitch so I climbed the stairs once again and went back to my start mark. I got my cue, descended the stairs, spoke my first two lines and froze. To my horror I saw someone bustling into shot from the back of the set. I wasn't wearing my glasses, so all I could make out was a grey-haired chap in a suit carrying something under his arm. I thought he might have been some extra who'd lost the plot, so I tried to continue with the scene. I ad-libbed a couple of lines before this 'extra' seized me by the arm and uttered those chillingly immortal words: 'Michael Craig, This Is Your Life.'

At first I thought it was a practical joke organised by the crew, but they were all grinning and clapping and people were coming out of the woodwork to join us on the set. I put on my glasses and there he was, Michael Aspel, nodding and smiling and proffering the big red book. On our way to another studio, where *This Is Your Life* (*TIYL*) was to be recorded (this was the English version, of course, not the Australian one, which has fortunately ignored me), I questioned the point of the exercise. I didn't know that many people in Sydney—most of my family and friends were in England or New Zealand or Canada, and there wouldn't be many people to show up and embarrass the hell out of me. Mr Aspel smiled wisely and told me not to worry. I sat on the *TIYL* set and waited.

Sue and Jessica were there of course, although Sue had to leave before long as she was working in the theatre. John McTernan was there, flown up from Melbourne, and one or two other old mates from here and there, but surely not enough to make a show for an audience of several million people. I sat and waited and then they started to arrive. My sister Betty from Canada, my sister Hilary from New Zealand, my brother Richard from Wales, my son Stephen plus his wife Linda and son Jack from London, and my other son Michael John with his new wife Nicola, also from the Old Dart. The whole family was there, and had in fact been in Sydney for several days while Sue and Jess had dutifully kept me in total ignorance. Then the non-family folk turned up—George Baker and Juliet Mills were two who happened to be in Sydney working or seeing friends, and then half a dozen others in pre-recorded video clips. Richard Attenborough, Bryan Forbes, Carmen Silvera, Leslie Phillips, Daniel Massey, Honour Blackman and finally my 94-year-old mother. She looked faintly disapproving, as I'm sure she was, but by the time she showed up I was in a state of shock. It was a surreal evening but, try as I might, I couldn't help being moved and feeling flattered.

After the recording we had a slap-up party courtesy of *TIYL* and another one courtesy of me up at Newport at the weekend. The only sad thing about the whole event was that the family members kept having to leave for home too soon, and of course I hadn't been able to see them or even know they were in the country before we did the recording. I heard that the *TIYL* episode was well received when it went to air in England; it probably startled a few people, who'd assumed that I was dead. We didn't see it in Australia, of course, but I have a copy of it and the big red 'book'. Sadly, Dan and Carmen and my Ma have died in the intervening years, but everyone else is still around, even though I don't see them as often as I'd like.

Sue became a semi regular in my last year with *GP*. She played my lady friend and in the last episode we were married on screen with her mother and Jess making up the numbers. And so Dr and Mrs William Sharp (aka Mr and Mrs Michael Gregson) flew away to Scotland for a honeymoon and retirement, to live happily ever after. Such is the power of television that several of our neighbours couldn't understand why we were still to be seen in the local shops when we were supposedly honeymooning on the banks of Loch Lomond. We got sick of explaining that it was only a *story*, not real life.

The crew and production office gave me a wonderful farewell party and a battery-operated golf buggy when we finished. I was moved and truly sad to say goodbye. It had been a great seven years in spite of the occasional squabbles and I wouldn't have missed a minute of it. Well . . . maybe one or two.

I made some wonderful friends and, at a mundane level, was able to save enough to fund a modest pension. Just as well really, as I haven't worked a hell of a lot since I left the practice at the end of 1995.

SEVENTEEN

Closing time

We had moved to a new house in Lavender Bay by the time we left *GP* Jess had finished school, doing brilliantly in her Higher School Certificate, and was champing at the bit to get back to England. She flew away on New Year's Eve 1995 and, as Sue and I drove back from the airport through the celebrating city, we felt the most overwhelming sense of loss. She was only seventeen and she'd been our focus for every one of those years, and now she had gone. We didn't know then which university she was going to—she'd had offers from Edinburgh, Bristol, Lancaster and Durham—but in the end, and to our great surprise and pleasure, she went to Cambridge.

We sat in the horribly empty house, watching the fireworks on the Harbour Bridge as Sydney saw the New Year in, and the tears ran down my cheeks in a truly pathetic way. I was a mess. Everything seemed to have come to an end in one fell swoop, and I didn't know what I was going to do next. Had I finally retired? Was it to be the gas station and the corner store? I was only sixty-eight but I felt well over a hundred.

Of course life went on much as before; the only difference was a definite lack of Jess. We went to England to see her settle into Cambridge and stayed for a few months. I wrote another script for *GP* while staying in the Wye Valley in my brother's converted barn and caught up with my sons and my grandson Jack, who was now six. It was rather good fun and to my surprise I found that I didn't miss the pressure of work and was glad to be unemployed. It didn't last, of course. When we got back to Sydney I discovered that I hadn't retired after all.

I did a number of offbeat jobs among the more routine ones and managed to tick over fairly well. I went up to Toowoomba for four days to host a concert celebrating the re-opening of their Empire Theatre. We did three sell-out performances in this beautiful building, with Julie Anthony topping the bill, and then another impromptu one in a wine bar where some of us had gathered to have our own little celebration.

Another unexpected gig was playing the poet John Milton in a dramatised reading of *Paradise Lost*. Gordon Honeycombe, who had been a famous and popular newsreader in England, as well as an actor and writer, had moved to Perth, where he organised this production. He had cut and adapted this famously long poem and for some reason wanted me to play Milton. In his adaptation, the poet was the presenter and link between the great set pieces written for Satan, Christ and all the rest of the biblical personnel. It took place in St George's Cathedral with a great cast. Bud Tingwell was the archangel Michael, the gorgeous Sue Lyons was Eve, James Smillie was Satan, Rhys McConnochie was Beelzebub and Bill Kerr—don't laugh—was God. Apart from everything else, it was a meeting of old mates and good fun. Even better, as it was a dramatised reading, we didn't have to learn it. Well, I had to learn the closing verses—not easy—but otherwise it was a breeze.

Another breeze of a job was doing a play called *Love Letters*, which, as the title suggests, is a succession of love letters between a man and a woman over the period of their lives. It was written by an American playwright called AR Gurney and it had wide success all over the world. It was cheap and easy to stage, requiring no set—just two lecterns and two actors who, under Mr Gurney's instructions (bless him), were required to *read* the letters rather than learn and recite them. It was done—dare I say *done to death?*—by practically everyone. Young pairings, middle-aged pairings and, in my case, pairings of the elderly. I did it a few times, with June Salter first, and then with Joan Sidney. Although it was very well written and well received, I always felt slightly ashamed after a performance. It was *too* easy, *too* manipulative, and ultimately not really satisfying.

Another of the more exotic jobs I got was as a presenter for three concerts given by the Sydney Symphony Orchestra at the Opera House. The concerts consisted of music by English composers only, which I guess is why I was asked. Wonderful music by Elgar, Purcell and Britten, amongst others. Nerve-racking for me, as I have a bit of a tin ear, but I was able to read a lot of my introductions so it wasn't too bad. Once again I was amazed by, and filled with admiration for, the insouciance of professional musicians. What confidence in their ability, what pleasure in their own skill, what amazing expertise.

There were also some more conventional assignments, including occasional guest appearances on television—but not many, because the shadow of William Sharp still hung over me and took a long time to disappear. I did a play called *Quartermaine's Terms* at the now defunct Marian Street Theatre in Killara, in which I played a sexually ambivalent old schoolmaster. It wasn't a great success, but at least it got me back into the discipline of working in a play in the theatre after a gap of more than ten years. I also did two plays for the Sydney Theatre Company at the Opera House—*Amy's View* with Sandy Gore, with whom I hadn't worked since the far off days of *Brides of Christ*, followed almost immediately by a very strange and difficult play by Edward Albee called *A Delicate Balance*. I thus renewed my love/hate relationship with the Opera House Drama Theatre, where I had last played in 1978 in *The Tempest*. The love part is the ambience and position of Utzon's marvellous building; the hate part is the sterile ugliness and impracticality of that letterbox stage and auditorium. For both actors and audiences it has all the charm and atmosphere of a lecture hall at a redbrick university.

Between jobs we went to England several times. My son Michael John got married and, after in vitro fertilisation, his wife Nic gave birth to twin boys in July 1997. She'd been unable to conceive naturally but, as so often happens in these cases, gave birth to my first grand-daughter Ellie not much more than a year and a half later without any help from the boffins. My first wife became more and more frail, and died when she was only sixty-nine. Babs had the worst luck with her health all her life. She'd spent two years in a sanatorium with tuberculosis before I met her and had respiratory problems ever after. Between Stephen's birth (ten weeks premature) and Michael John's birth (five weeks premature), she had three miscarriages. She then developed gall-stones and had to have her gall bladder removed; and, if there was any kind of epidemic going round, she'd be sure to get it. She died relatively young, after being more or less bed-ridden with emphysema for the last couple of years. She hadn't helped herself by continuing to smoke a packet of cigarettes a day but, as she said, 'You've got to have something'. She'd had a disappointing life, partly my fault I'm afraid, but she was the best of mothers to Stephen and MJ and a wonderful grandmother to her grandchildren when they arrived.

I was back and forth to England rather more frequently than I wished in the next couple of years. My mother reached the grand age of a hundred in March 1999, and of course we all attended the event in her nursing home in Essex. She wasn't too thrilled about it, or the pathetic *non*-telegram of congratulation she received from Her Majesty. I had to apply for this message at the post office, providing evidence that Ma was actually a hundred, her medical records etc., as if applying for a driving licence, and then the bloody thing wasn't a telegram at all. It was a printed form, without even a facsimile of the Queen's signature on it—just a typewritten 'ELIZABETH R'. A real swiz.

We came back to Sydney after the birthday and then I had to return to England five months later for the funeral. I think that Ma had been anxious to push off for some time. She had explained to Jess that life for her was like being at the airport after you'd been through all the formalities and were sitting in the departure lounge waiting for your flight to be called. When it *was* finally called, I'm sure she was first in the queue with her boarding card in one hand and a nice book for the journey in the other.

The year 2000 started off pretty well. I was engaged to work on the ABC TV series, *Grass Roots*, which boasted a stellar cast and was brilliantly written by Geoffrey Atherden, who created the classic Australian comedy series, *Mother and Son*. I had been originally cast as a member of the local community and was contracted for only two episodes. Then, the day before shooting started, I was asked to take over the part of Gordon Mahon, one of the local councillors, because Max Phipps, who had been their original choice, had to bow out through illness. It was an easy decision to make—an increase from two episodes to eight— and I became Mr Mahon overnight. I never had much to do beyond make up the numbers, but it was a good and happy three months and I'd cheerfully appear as a deaf mute in anything written by Geoffrey Atherden. Sadly Max Phipps died some time later, a lovely man and I'm grateful to him for his inadvertent legacy to me.

It was a very well-organised and jolly sort of production. Everyone was pleased to be working on it and enjoying the brilliance of the writing. I hadn't worked with Chris Haywood for a number of years and it was hard to reconcile the balding, beer-bellied (padding, of course), wheezing old crook with the handsome young blonde bombshell who had played my bastard son and killer in *The Timeless Land* twenty years before.

My favourite character was mad old Harry, the anachronistic socialist caught in a time warp, with his 'Comrades . . . and bizzo . . .' and inability to finish a sentence. It was a wonderful performance by John Clayton, all the more remarkable for the fact that he was ill and in a lot of pain most of the time. He'd done his back in and was strapped into a corset, which became more and more uncomfortable as the weeks went by. He never

complained and kept firing it in with complete sincerity and brilliant comic effect.

There were one or two inevitable mishaps. One concerned
my old friend Vincent Ball, who was cast as a dog-loving local
resident pursuing some feud with the council. He and I had to
meet in the park, exchange a few loaded words, before he was
towed away by his exuberant and powerful collie. The dog
was produced and put through its paces. Everything seemed
okay—it was to sit by Vincent through the dialogue and then,
on a signal from its handler, race away out of shot pulling him
in its wake. When we came to actually shoot the scene, the handler
signalled the dog and nothing happened. It just sat there as though
it were stuffed and Vincent, who was poised to follow it out of
frame at top speed, tripped over it and fell heavily on the concrete
pathway. There was a nasty cracking sound and he went a bit
pale, but he staggered to his feet and we did the scene again.
I could see his right wrist and hand swelling by the second as
he rattled through the scene. This time, mercifully, the dog did
its stuff and all was well. Vince was then despatched to the
hospital, where they discovered that his right wrist was badly
broken with some of the little bones in the back of his hand driven
up into the joint. It took months to mend and goes to show that
it isn't always the spectacular stunts that are the most dangerous.
And one should try to never, ever work with animals! The rest
of us survived, relatively unscathed, and we finished up with high
hopes of a hit show at the end of March.

Sue and I went to England in May for my brother's seventieth birthday which, like mine, was celebrated at Hugo's
restaurant in Soho. It was a fine occasion at which I drank too
much and sang The Wild Colonial Boy with gestures. I also agreed
to accompany Richard on a sea voyage from Le Havre to
Martinique and back on a French container ship, a journey we
undertook the following November.

It was of course Olympics Year in Sydney and, to help celebrate this, the Ensemble Theatre staged a season of Australian
plays. One of these was Travelling North by Australia's most

prolific and successful playwright, David Williamson. It had been first produced several years earlier and also made into a film starring Leo McKern, Julia Blake, Graham Kennedy and Henri Szeps as the doctor. This time I was cast as the doctor and Charles (Bud) Tingwell and Lorraine Bayly were the couple on the northward journey. It was a slightly rocky production. Bud found it hard to remember his lines (if he ever knew them) and poor Lorraine and I, with whom he had most of his scenes, would, more often than was pleasant, be subjected to long pauses while Bud searched for the *mot juste*—or any bloody *mot*—in his script, which he carried with him disguised as a notebook.

He was remarkably laid back about it all, and on one occasion nodded off on stage. In the script he dies in his chair on stage and his death is immediately followed by a brief scene between the wife and the doctor, in which they sum things up and she decides to go on 'travelling north'. Blackout, end of show, curtain calls. When the lights came up and the applause started, Bud was still slumped in his chair in his death pose. Christ, I thought, he really has snuffed it. Not at all—just a quick catnap before his bow and the drive home! Bud is a lovely chap and a very good actor, with whom I worked on a couple of films in England, but there comes a time when even the most stage-struck old ham must realise that if you *can't* do it, don't.

When we did *Travelling North* at a theatre called The Footbridge—which is on the campus of Sydney University, but is frequently used for commercial productions—a rather unsettling incident happened. Some of the University buildings and offices were occupied by various visiting Olympic bodies, so security was supposedly very strict. However, after a matinee one Saturday afternoon I was sitting in the courtyard outside the stage door smoking my pipe, when I noticed a somewhat scruffy, youngish man shambling towards me. I nodded amiably and he pulled a gun from his jacket pocket and pointed it at my crotch. 'Give us your fucking wallet,' he said, and slid the action of the automatic back and forth with a menacing clicking sound. I wasn't totally convinced that it was a real gun, there are a lot of replicas in circulation, but I wasn't game to find out.

He had the slightly varnished look of the habitual boozer and drug addict and was getting more and more agitated as I sat there sucking on my pipe. I was strangely unmoved by it all, and explained as reasonably as I could that I didn't have a wallet, so I was awfully sorry, but I couldn't give it to him. This was true at the time because I was wearing my costume for the play and had left my wallet in the dressing room. There was some more ugly clicking from his gun, which was still pointing at my crotch, and he started to twitch. I pulled some change from my pocket, about four dollars, and offered it to him with my apologies. He looked at it and looked at me and started to cry as well as twitch. 'Fuck it, fuck it, fuck you, fuck everything,' he yelled, and ran off into the gathering twilight without taking the money.

I thought I should report the matter and eventually a couple of policemen arrived and took my statement in a rather grudging and sceptical manner. They then told me I would have to make a statement at Parramatta Police Station the following day and that I'd be told when to report there. I remarked mildly that I'd just given a statement to *them*, so why did I have to give another? I got the old deadpan stare designed to make me feel guilty, which by now I was feeling, and they too disappeared into the dusk. I never heard another word from anyone, which does make me more than a little doubtful about the heroic security measures the Sydney fuzz has instituted to keep us safe from terrorism and the like. Still if one thing doesn't get you, something else will, so what the hell.

I was next engaged by the Bell Shakespeare Company to play the name part in *Julius Caesar* in the January of the New Year. John Bell directed it with great energy and invention and I really enjoyed working with and for him. It ran for just over two hours, played without an interval and people couldn't believe that he hadn't cut great chunks from the text. In fact not more than fifty lines were cut and it was the best and most enjoyable

Shakespearean production I have been in. It was my third time in the play. As a very young actor, I'd had a go at Mark Antony and given a pale imitation of Brando's performance; then, some years after that, I'd been a solid but rather boring Brutus. The part I would really have loved to have played was Cassius, but it never came my way and now I'm too old to do any of them except Caesar. Probably too old for that too, as one of the Sydney critics was at pains to point out.

Apart from him, the notices were very good and so was the business wherever we went. We opened in Sydney and did five weeks at the Opera House Playhouse; then travelled on to Melbourne, Hobart, Canberra and some major New SouthWales and Victorian provincial cities before ending up in Perth, where the show finished. As we were already in the west, Sue and I decided to have a bit of a look round the Margaret River area before returning to Sydney, so we rented a car and headed south. Stunning.

The following year was pretty disappointing and rather reluctantly I found myself retired once again. There were a few scraps to be picked up—an occasional commercial or voice over—and I was busy with the union and with the Actors Benevolent Fund, of which I was chairman. This is a job I take very seriously, as I should, because, unknown to most members of the public, we deal with a lot of people in distress and are responsible for spending serious sums of money. I find it satisfying and irritating in about equal measure. Satisfying because we do give real help to members of the profession who, for a variety of reasons, are down on their luck; and irritating because I can't help feeling that some of those who come to us for help should really have known better. It's hard to bear—once successful and well-paid performers ending up depending on charitable handouts because they never saved and always lived above their means. Makes me want to shake them.

Finally at the beginning of 2002 a new series of *Grass Roots* raised its pretty head, and we made another ten episodes. There were some cast changes, but surprisingly few considering there had been an eighteen-month hiatus (this says something about the state of employment in the acting game). Sophie Heathcote, as the abominable Biddy, was replaced by Jodie Dry and there were a couple of other changes too. I had even less to do the second time around, but again I was delighted to be part of the enterprise and proud of what we achieved.

When we finally pulled the plug, it was very sad for me. Not just because the series had finished, but also because the ABC careers of a number of people with whom I'd been friends for more than thirty years were finished as well. I'd probably never see them again. John Clayton's health had deteriorated, but once again he never let it show. He won the Australian Film Institute (AFI) award for best television actor last year but sadly it was posthumous as he had died some months earlier. Dear John— *Comrade!*—at least you went out on a high.

The rest of the year maintained the odds and ends, bits and pieces scenario. A day as a judge on the film *Fat Pizza* put me firmly in my place. I turned up on location to be met by an assistant director not much older than my eldest grandson, who asked who I was and what part I was there for. I told him my name and that I was the judge. He nodded sternly and remarked, as he bustled away, that he hoped that I'd learned my lines. Ah well.

I played another judge in a sort of dream sequence in an episode of *Always Greener* for Channel 7, where at least they knew my name and didn't question my ability to learn my lines. I also did a dramatised reading of a play called *The Best of Friends* by the English playwright Hugh Whitemore. It consisted of the correspondence between George Bernard Shaw, Dame Laurentia McLachland, a Benedictine nun and abbess, and Sir Sidney Cockerell, who was a senior civil servant and man about town who knew everyone. These letters were written over a period of more than twenty years and dealt with a wide range of topics. Shaw's letters were particularly interesting, and in some ways surprisingly sentimental for a man of his reputation. Betty Lucas was the Dame, Peter Collingwood was Shaw and I was the dilettante Sir Sidney. We did the readings at a number of town halls and little theatres and it was remarkably civilised and pleasant and very well received.

In 2003 I was in a production of Arthur Miller's *Broken Glass* at the Ensemble Theatre. I played an elderly New York tycoon—one of Miller's obligatory gentile characters in American–Jewish society—a small but (so I'm told) important part. And that, as they say, is that.

•

Five years have passed since my seventieth birthday party and that stern lecture from Jess which prompted this rambling discourse. I suppose it is nearing the time for me to head for the airport my mother spoke about. I hope there'll be a long wait after going through customs and immigration, and that my flight will be indefinitely delayed. You never know your luck.

If I had to do it all again, I wouldn't. An actor's life is not to be recommended, even by someone like me who has had more than his full share of good fortune. If I couldn't have stayed at sea, I think I'd like to have been a really good cabinet-maker. I've always enjoyed DIY activities, and have built (inexpertly) cupboards and wardrobes, and found working with wood to be a lasting pleasure. With training I might have made something really beautiful, useful and enduring.

Whether I'd have done things better, I don't know. Maybe, maybe not. Which I suppose is all you can say of anybody's life . . .

Index

Printed in Great Britain
by Amazon